Bertrand Russell

SCEPTICAL ESSAYS

Bertrand Russell

SCEPTICAL ESSAYS

[Edited with Introduction, Author's Information, Complete Text, Select Criticism & Bibliography]

Anshu Mallika Sawhney
M.A. English, Delhi University
M. Phil., Himachal Pradesh University

ANMOL PUBLICATIONS PVT. LTD.
NEW DELHI - 110 002 (INDIA)

ANMOL PUBLICATIONS PVT. LTD.

H.O.: 4374/4B, Ansari Road, Darya Ganj,
New Delhi-110 002 (India)
Ph.: 23278000, 23261597

B.O.: No. 1015, Ist Main Road, BSK IIIrd Stage
IIIrd Phase, IIIrd Block
Bangalore - 560 085 (India)
Visit us at: www.anmolpublications.com

Sceptical Essays

First Published, 2009

PRINTED IN INDIA

Printed at Mehra Offset Press, Delhi.

Contents

Preface vii

1. Introduction 1
2. Russell's Philosophical Work 17
3. Sceptical Essays 36
4. Greek Philosopher, Poet and Lawmaker 202

Bibliography 245

Preface

On 18 May, 1872, Bertrand Russell was born at Trelleck and was brought up by his grandmother, as his parents died at the age of three. He never went to school and was tutored at home by governess. He also attained finest knowledge of German and French. In the year 1890, he obtained a first class with distinction in Philosophy at Trinity College, Cambridge.

He got married to Miss Alys Pearsall in the year 1894. A few of his popular works include German Social Democracy, 1896, Foundations of Geometry, 1897, A Critical Exposition of the Philosophy of Leibniz, 1900, Principles of Mathematics, vol. 1, 1903, Philosophical Essays, 1910, (with Dr. A. N. Whitehead) Principia mathematica, 3 vols, 1910-13, The Problems of Philosophy, 1912, Our Knowledge of the External World as a Field for Scientific Method in Philosophy, 1944

Principles of Social Reconstruction, 1916, Mysticism and Logic and Other Essays, 1918, etc.

Author

Chapter 1

Introduction

BIOGRAPHY

Bertrand Arthur William Russell, 3rd Earl Russell, OM, FRS (18 May 1872- 2 February 1970), was an influential British logician, philosopher, and mathematician, working mostly in the 20th century. A prolific writer, Bertrand Russell was also a populariser of philosophy and a commentator on a large variety of topics, ranging from very serious issues to the mundane. Continuing a family tradition in political affairs, he was a prominent liberal as well as a socialist and anti-war activist for most of his long life. Millions looked up to Russell as a prophet of the creative and rational life; at the same time, his stances on many topics were extremely controversial.

Born at the height of Britain's economic and political ascendancy, he died of influenza nearly a century later when the British Empire had all but vanished; its power dissipated in two victorious, but debilitating world wars. As one of the world's best-known intellectuals, Russell's voice carried enormous moral authority, even into his early 90s. Among his other political activities, Russell was a vigorous proponent of nuclear disarmament and an outspoken critic of the American war in Vietnam.

In 1950, Russell was made a Nobel Laureate in Literature "in recognition of his varied and significant writings in which he champions humanitarian ideals and freedom of thought".

Bertrand Russell was born on 18 May 1872 at Trellech, Monmouthshire, Wales, into an aristocratic English family. His paternal grandfather, John Russell, 1st Earl Russell, had been the British Prime Minister in the 1840s and 1860s, and was the second son of John Russell, 6th Duke of Bedford. The Russells had been prominent for several centuries in Britain, and were one of Britain's leading Whig (Liberal) families. Russell's mother Kate (nee Stanley) was also from an aristocratic family, and was the sister of Rosalind Howard, Countess of Carlisle. Russell's parents were quite radical for their times- Russell's father, Viscount Amberley, was an atheist and consented to his wife's affair with their children's tutor, the biologist Douglas Spalding. Both were early advocates of birth control at a time when this was considered scandalous. John Stuart Mill, the Utilitarian philosopher, was Russell's godfather.

Russell had two siblings: Frank (nearly seven years older than Bertrand), and Rachel (four years older). In June 1875, Russell's mother died of diphtheria, followed shortly by Rachel, and in January 1876 his father died of bronchitis following a long period of depression. Frank and Bertrand were placed in the care of their staunchly Victorian grandparents, who lived at Pembroke Lodge in Richmond Park. The first Earl Russell died in 1878, and his widow the Countess Russell (nee Lady Frances Elliot) was the dominant family figure for the rest of Russell's childhood and youth.

The countess was from a Scottish Presbyterian family, and successfully petitioned a British court to set aside a provision in Amberley's will requiring the children to be raised as agnostics. Despite her religious conservatism, she held progressive views in other areas (accepting Darwinism and supporting Irish Home Rule), and her influence on Bertrand Russell's outlook on social justice and standing up for principle remained with him throughout his life. However, the atmosphere at Pembroke Lodge was one of frequent prayer, emotional repression and formality- Frank reacted to this with open rebellion, but the young Bertrand learned to hide his feelings. Russell's adolescence was very lonely, and he often contemplated suicide. He remarked in his autobiography that his keenest interests were in sex, religion and mathematics, and that only the wish to know more mathematics kept him from suicide. He was educated at home by a series of tutors, and he spent countless hours in his grandfather's library. His brother Frank introduced him to Euclid, which transformed Russell's life. Russell won a scholarship to read mathematics at Trinity College, Cambridge University, and commenced his studies there in 1890. He became acquainted with the younger G.E. Moore and came under the influence of Alfred North Whitehead, who recommended him to the Cambridge Apostles. He quickly distinguished himself in mathematics and philosophy, graduating with a B.A. in the former subject in 1893 and adding a fellowship in the latter in 1895.

Russell first met the American Quaker, Alys Pearsall Smith, when he was seventeen years old. He fell in love with the puritanical, high-minded Alys, who was connected to several educationists and religious activists, and, contrary to his grandmother's wishes, he married her in December 1894. Their marriage began to fall apart in 1902 when Russell realised he no longer loved her; they divorced nineteen years later. During this period, Russell had passionate (and often simultaneous) affairs with, among others, Lady Ottoline Morrell and the actor Lady Constance Malleson. Alys pined for him for these years and continued to love Russell for the rest of her life. Russell began his published work in 1896 with German Social Democracy, a study in politics that was an early indication of a lifelong interest in political and social theory. In 1896 he taught German social democracy at the London School of Economics, where he also lectured on the science of power in the autumn of 1937.

Russell became a fellow of the Royal Society in 1908. The first of three volumes of Principia Mathematica (written with Whitehead) was published in 1910, which (along with the earlier The Principles of Mathematics) soon made Russell world famous in his field. In 1911 he became acquainted with the Austrian engineering student Ludwig Wittgenstein, whose genius he soon recognised (and whom he viewed as a successor who would continue his work on mathematical logic). He spent hours dealing with Wittgenstein's various phobias and his frequent bouts of despair. The latter was often a drain on Russell's energy, but he continued to be fascinated by him and encouraged his academic development, including the publication of Wittgenstein's Tractatus Logico-Philosophicus in 1922.

During the First World War, Russell engaged in pacifist activities, and in 1916, he was dismissed from Trinity College following his conviction under the Defense of the Realm Act. A later conviction resulted in six months' imprisonment in Brixton prison.

In 1920, Russell travelled to Russia as part of an official delegation sent by the British government to investigate the effects of the Russian Revolution. Russell's lover Dora Black also visited Russia independently at the same time- she was enthusiastic about the revolution, but Russell's experiences destroyed his previous tentative support for it.

Russell subsequently lectured in Peking on philosophy for one year, accompanied by Dora. While in China, Russell became gravely ill with pneumonia, and incorrect reports of his death were published in the Japanese press. When the couple visited Japan on their return journey, Dora notified journalists that "Mr Bertrand Russell, having died according to the Japanese press, is unable to give interviews to Japanese journalists".

On the couple's return to England in 1921, Dora was five months pregnant, and Russell arranged a hasty divorce from Alys, marrying Dora six days after the divorce was finalised. Their children were John Conrad Russell, 4th Earl Russell and Katharine Jane Russell (now Lady Katharine Tait). Russell supported himself during this time by writing popular books explaining matters of physics, ethics and education to the layman. Together with Dora, he also founded the experimental Beacon Hill School in 1927. After he left the school in 1932, Dora continued it until 1943.

Upon the death of his elder brother Frank, in 1931, Russell became the 3rd Earl Russell. He once said that his title was primarily useful for securing hotel rooms.

Russell's marriage to Dora grew increasingly tenuous, and it reached a breaking point over her having two children with an American journalist, Griffin Barry. In 1936, he took as his third wife an Oxford undergraduate named Patricia ("Peter") Spence, who had been his children's governess since the summer of 1930. Russell and Peter had one son, Conrad Sebastian Robert Russell, later to become a prominent historian, and one of the leading figures in the Liberal Democrat party.

In the spring of 1939, Russell moved to Santa Barbara to lecture at the University of California, Los Angeles. He was appointed professor at the City College of New York in 1940, but after public outcries, the appointment was annulled by the courts: his radical opinions made him "morally unfit" to teach at the college. The protest was started by the mother of a student who would not have been eligible for his graduate-level course in abstract, mathematical logic. Many intellectuals, led by John Dewey, protested his treatment. Dewey and Horace M. Kallen edited a collection of articles on the CCNY affair in The Bertrand Russell Case. He soon joined the Barnes Foundation, lecturing to a varied audience on the history of philosophy- these lectures formed the basis of A History of Western Philosophy. His relationship with the eccentric Albert C. Barnes soon soured, and he returned to Britain in 1944 to rejoin the faculty of Trinity College.

During the 1940s and 1950s, Russell participated in many broadcasts over the BBC on various topical and philosophical subjects. By this time in his life, Russell was world famous outside of academic circles, frequently the subject or author of magazine and newspaper articles, and was called upon to offer up opinions on a wide variety of subjects, even mundane ones. A History of Western Philosophy (1945) became a best-seller, and provided Russell with a steady income for the remainder of his life. Along with his friend Albert Einstein, Russell had reached superstar status as an intellectual. In 1949, Russell was awarded the Order of Merit, and the following year he received the Nobel Prize in Literature.

In 1952, Russell was divorced by Peter, with whom he had been very unhappy. Conrad, Russell's son by Peter, did not see his father between the time of the divorce and 1968 (at which time his decision to meet his father caused a permanent breach with his mother). Russell married his fourth wife, Edith Finch, soon after the divorce. They had known each other since 1925, and Edith had lectured in English at Bryn Mawr College near Philadelphia, sharing a house for twenty years with Russell's old friend Lucy Donnelly.

Edith remained with him until his death, and, by all accounts, their relationship was close and loving throughout their marriage. Russell's eldest son, John, suffered from serious mental illness, which was the source of ongoing disputes between Russell and John's mother, Russell's former wife, Dora. John's wife Susan was also mentally ill, and eventually Russell and Edith became the legal guardians of their three daughters (two of whom were later diagnosed with schizophrenia). Russell spent the 1950s and 1960s engaged in various political causes, primarily related to nuclear disarmament and opposing the Vietnam War. He wrote a great many letters to world leaders during this period. He also became a hero to many of the youthful members of the New Left. During the 1960s, in particular, Russell became increasingly vocal about his disapproval of the American government's policies. In 1963, he became the inaugural recipient of the Jerusalem Prize, an award for writers concerned with the freedom of the individual in society.

Bertrand Russell published his three-volume autobiography in the late 1960s. While he grew frail, he remained lucid until the end, when, in 1970, he died in his home, Plas Penrhyn, Penrhyndeudraeth, Merioneth, Wales. His ashes, as his will directed, were scattered.

Ancestry

His paternal grandfather, John Russell, 1st Earl Russell, was the second son of John Russell, 6th Duke of Bedford, and had twice been asked by Queen Victoria to form a government, serving her as Prime Minister in the 1840s and 1860s.

The Russells had been prominent in Britain for several centuries before this, coming to power and the peerage with the rise of the Tudor dynasty. They established themselves as one of Britain's leading Whig (Liberal) families, and participated in every great political event from the Dissolution of the Monasteries in 1536-40 to the Glorious Revolution in 1688-8 9 to the Great Reform Act in 1832.

Russell's mother Katherine Louisa (1844 - 1874) was the daughter of Edward Stanley, 2nd Baron Stanley of Alderley, and was the sister of Rosalind Howard, Countess of Carlisle.

Russell's parents were quite radical for their times "Russell's father, Viscount Amberley, was an atheist and consented to his wife's affair with their children's tutor, the biologist Douglas Spalding. Both were early advocates of birth control at a time when this was considered scandalous.

John Stuart Mill, the Utilitarian philosopher, stood as Russell's godfather. Mill died the following year, but his writings had a great effect upon Russell's life.

Childhood and Adolescence

Russell had two siblings: Frank (nearly seven years older than Bertrand), and Rachel (four years older). In June 1874 Russell's mother died of diphtheria, followed shortly by Rachel, and in January 1876 his father also died of bronchitis following a long period of depression. Frank and Bertrand were placed in the care of their staunchly Victorian grandparents, who lived at Pembroke Lodge in Richmond Park. John Russell, 1st Earl Russell, his grandfather, died in 1878, and was remembered by Russell as a kindly old man in a wheelchair. As a result, his widow, the Countess Russell (Lady Frances Elliot), was the dominant family figure for the rest of Russell's childhood and youth.

The countess was from a Scottish Presbyterian family, and successfully petitioned a British court to set aside a provision in Amberley's will requiring the children to be raised as agnostics. Despite her religious conservatism, she held progressive views in other areas (accepting Darwinism and supporting Irish Home Rule), and her influence on Bertrand Russell's outlook on social justice and standing up for principle remained with him throughout his life" her favourite Bible verse, 'Thou shalt not follow a multitude to do evil.' (Exodus 23:2), became his mantra. However, the atmosphere at

Pembroke Lodge was one of frequent prayer, emotional repression and formality; Frank reacted to this with open rebellion, but the young Bertrand learned to hide his feelings.

Russell's adolescence was thus very lonely, and he often contemplated suicide. He remarked in his autobiography that his keenest interests were in sex, religion and mathematics, and that only the wish to know more mathematics kept him from suicide. He was educated at home by a series of tutors, and he spent countless hours in his grandfather's library.

His brother Frank introduced him to the work of Euclid, which transformed Russell's life.

University and First Marriage

Russell won a scholarship to read for the Mathematics Tripos at Trinity College, Cambridge, and commenced his studies there in 1890. He became acquainted with the younger G.E. Moore and came under the influence of Alfred North Whitehead, who recommended him to the Cambridge Apostles. He quickly distinguished himself in mathematics and philosophy, graduating with a B.A. in the former subject in 1893 and adding a fellowship in the latter in 1895.

Russell first met the American Quaker Alys Pearsall Smith when he was seventeen years old. He became a friend of the Pearsall Smith family "they knew him primarily as 'Lord John's grandson' and enjoyed showing him off "and travelled with them to the continent; it was in their company that Bertrand visited the Paris Exhibition of 1889 and was able to climb the Eiffel Tower soon after it was completed.

He soon fell in love with the puritanical, high-minded Alys, who was a graduate of Bryn Mawr College near Philadelphia, and, contrary to his grandmother's wishes, he married her on 13 December 1894. Their marriage began to fall apart in 1901 when it occurred to Russell, while he was out on his bicycle, that he no longer loved her. She asked him if he loved her and he replied that he didn't. Russell also disliked Alys's mother, finding her controlling and cruel. It was to be a hollow shell of a marriage and they finally divorced in 1921, after a lengthy period of separation. During this period, Russell had passionate (and often simultaneous) affairs with a number of women, including Lady Ottoline Morrell and the actress Lady Constance Malleson.

Early Career

Russell began his published work in 1896 with *German Social Democracy*, a study in politics that was an early indication of a lifelong interest in political and social theory. In 1896, he taught German social democracy at the London School of Economics, where he also lectured on the science of power in the autumn of 1937. He was also a member of the Coefficients dining club of social reformers set up in 1902 by the Fabian campaigners Sidney and Beatrice Webb.

Russell became a fellow of the Royal Society in 1908. The first of three volumes of *Principia Mathematica*, written with Whitehead, was published in 1910, which, along with the earlier *The Principles of Mathematics*, soon made Russell world famous in his field. In 1911, he became acquainted with the Austrian engineering student Ludwig Wittgenstein, whom he viewed as a genius and a successor who would continue his work on logic. He spent hours dealing with Wittgenstein's various phobias and his frequent bouts of despair. The latter was often a drain on Russell's energy, but he continued to be fascinated by him and encouraged his academic development, including the publication of Wittgenstein's *Tractatus Logico-Philosophicus* in 1922.

First World War

During the First World War, Russell engaged in pacifist activities, and, in 1916, he was dismissed from Trinity College following his conviction under the Defence of the Realm Act. A later conviction resulted in six months' imprisonment in Brixton prison (see *Activism* below). Russell was released from prison in September 1918.

Between the Wars, and Second Marriage

In August 1920, Russell traveled to Russia as part of an official delegation sent by the British government to investigate the effects of the Russian Revolution. During the course of his visit, he met Lenin and had an hour-long conversation with him. (In his autobiography, he mentions that he found Lenin rather disappointing, and that he sensed an "impish cruelty" in him.) He also cruised down the Volga on a steam-ship. Russell's lover Dora Black also visited Russia independently at the same time â€" she was enthusiastic about the revolution, but Russell's experiences destroyed his previous tentative support for it. Russell subsequently lectured in Beijing on philosophy for one year, accompanied by Dora. While in China, Russell became gravely ill with pneumonia, and incorrect reports of his death were published in the Japanese press. When the couple visited Japan on their return journey, Dora notified the world that "Mr. Bertrand Russell, having died according to the Japanese press, is unable to give interviews to Japanese journalists." The press were not amused and did not appreciate the sarcasm.

On the couple's return to England on 26 August 1921, Dora was six months pregnant, and Russell arranged a hasty divorce from Alys, marrying Dora six days after the divorce was finalised, on 27 September 1921. Their children were John Conrad Russell, 4th Earl Russell, born on 16 November 1921 and Katharine Jane Russell (now Lady Katharine Tait) born on 29 December 1923. Russell supported himself during this time by writing popular books explaining matters of physics, ethics, and education to the layman. Some scholars have suggested that at this point he had an affair with Vivien Eliot, wife of T. S. Eliot.

Together with Dora, he also founded the experimental Beacon Hill School in 1927. After he left the school in 1932, Dora continued it until 1943.

Upon the death of his elder brother Frank, in 1931, Russell became the 3rd Earl Russell. He once said that his title was primarily useful for securing hotel rooms.

Russell's marriage to Dora grew increasingly tenuous, and it reached a breaking point over her having two children with an American journalist, Griffin Barry. They separated in 1932 and finally divorced. On 18 January 1936, Russell married his third wife, an Oxford undergraduate named Patricia ("Peter") Spence, who had been his children's governess since the summer of 1930. Russell and Peter had one son, Conrad Sebastian Robert Russell, later to become a prominent historian and one of the leading figures in the Liberal Democrat party.

Second World War

After the Second World War, Russell taught at the University of Chicago, later moving on to Los Angeles to lecture at the University of California, Los Angeles. He was appointed professor at the City College of New York in 1940, but after a public outcry, the appointment was annulled by a court judgement: his opinions (especially those relating to sexual morality, detailed in *Marriage and Morals* ten years earlier) made him "morally unfit" to teach at the college.

The protest was started by the mother of a student who would not have been eligible for his graduate-level course in mathematical logic. Many intellectuals, led by John Dewey, protested his treatment. Dewey and Horace M. Kallen edited a collection of articles on the CCNY affair in *The Bertrand Russell Case*. He soon joined the Barnes Foundation, lecturing to a varied audience on the history of philosophy; these lectures formed the basis of *A History of Western Philosophy*. His relationship with the eccentric Albert C. Barnes soon soured, and he returned to Britain in 1944 to rejoin the faculty of Trinity College.

LATER LIFE

During the 1940s and 1950s, Russell participated in many broadcasts over the BBC, particularly the Third Programme, on various topical and philosophical subjects. By this time in his life, Russell was world famous outside of academic circles, frequently the subject or author of magazine and newspaper articles, and was called upon to offer up opinions on a wide variety of subjects, even mundane ones. En route to one of his lectures in Trondheim, Russell was one of 24 survivors (among a total of 43 passengers) in a plane crash in Hommelvik October 1948. *A History of Western Philosophy* (1945) became a best-seller, and provided Russell with a steady income for the remainder of his life. In the King's Birthday Honours of June 9, 1949, Russell was awarded the Order of Merit, and the following year he was awarded the Nobel Prize for Literature.

When he was given the Order of Merit, King George VI was affable but slightly embarrassed at decorating a former jailbird, saying that "You have sometimes behaved in a manner that would not do if otherwise adopted." Russell merely smiled, but afterwards claimed that the reply "That's right, just like your brother" immediately came to mind, but he did not say it. In 1952, Russell was divorced by Peter, with whom he had been very unhappy. Conrad, Russell's son by Peter, did not see his father between the time of the divorce and 1968 (at which time his decision to meet his father caused a permanent breach with his mother).

Russell married his fourth wife, Edith Finch, soon after the divorce, on December 15, 1952. They had known each other since 1925, and Edith had taught English at Bryn Mawr College near Philadelphia, Pennsylvania, sharing a house for twenty years with Russell's old friend Lucy Donnelly. Edith remained with him until his death, and, by all accounts, their marriage was a happy, close, and loving one.

Russell's eldest son, John, suffered from serious mental illness, which was the source of ongoing disputes between Russell and John's mother, Russell's former wife, Dora. John's wife Susan was also mentally ill, and eventually Russell and Edith became the legal guardians of their three daughters (two of whom were later diagnosed with schizophrenia).

Political Causes

Russell spent the 1950s and 1960s engaged in various political causes, primarily related to nuclear disarmament and opposing the Vietnam war (see also Russell Vietnam War Crimes Tribunal). The Russell-Einstein Manifesto was a document calling for nuclear disarmament and was signed by 11 of the prominent nuclear physicists and intellectuals of the time. He wrote a great many letters to world leaders during this period. He also became a hero to many of the youthful members of the New Left. During the 1960s, in particular, Russell became increasingly vocal about his disapproval of what he felt to be the American government's near-genocidal policies. In 1963, he became the inaugural recipient of the Jerusalem Prize, an award for writers concerned with the freedom of the individual in society. In October 1965, he tore up his Labour Party card because he feared the party was going to send soldiers to support the Vietnam War.

Final Years and Death

Russell published his three-volume autobiography in 1967, 1968, and 1969. Although he became frail, he remained lucid and clear thinking up to the day of his death. On 23 November 1969 he wrote to the Times newspaper saying that the preparation for show trials in Czechoslovakia was "highly alarming". Also during that month, he appealed to Secretary General U Thant of the United Nations to support an international war crimes commission to investigate alleged "torture and genocide" by the Americans in South Vietnam. Then a month after that, he protested to Alexei Kosygin over the expulsion of Aleksandr Solzhenitsyn from the Writers Union.

On 31 January 1970, Russell issued a statement which condemned Israeli aggression in the Middle East and called for Israeli withdrawal from territory occupied in 1967. The statement said that:

The tragedy of the people of Palestine is that their country was "given" by a foreign power to another people for the creation of a new state. The result was that many hundreds of thousands of innocent people were made permanently homeless. With every new conflict their numbers increased. How much longer is the world willing to endure this spectacle of wanton cruelty? It is abundantly clear that the refugees have every right to the homeland from which they were driven, and the denial of this right is at the heart of the continuing conflict. No people anywhere in the world would accept being expelled en masse from their own country; how can anyone require the people of Palestine to accept a punishment, which nobody else would tolerate? A permanent just settlement of the refugees in their homeland is an essential ingredient of any genuine settlement in the Middle East.

We are frequently told that we must sympathise with Israel because of the suffering of the Jews in Europe at the hands of the Nazis. What Israel is doing today cannot be condoned, and to invoke the horrors of the past to justify those of the present is gross hypocrisy.

This was Russell's final ever political statement or act. It was read out at the International Conference of Parliamentarians in Cairo on 3 February 1970, the day after Russell's death. The next day, 1 February, he spent at his home, Plas Penrhyn, in Penrhyndeudraeth, Merionethshire, Wales quietly. However, on the morning of 2 February Russell said he didn't feel well and remained in bed until just before noon. That evening, whilst reading, he suddenly fell ill. His wife and nurse, after calling his doctor, got him to bed and gave him oxygen, but it was to no avail. Bertrand Russell died of influenza before the doctor arrived.

Upon his death, his peerages descended on his eldest son, John, Viscount Amberley, who thence became the fourth Earl.

Russell was cremated at Colwyn Bay on 5 February 1970. There was no religious ceremony, as Russell had dictated in his will. His ashes were scattered over the Welsh mountains later that year.

Religion and Theology

For most of his adult life Russell maintained that religion is little more than superstition and, despite any positive effects that religion might have, it is largely harmful to people. He believed religion and the religious outlook (he considered communism and other systematic ideologies to be forms of religion) serve to impede knowledge, foster fear and dependency, and are responsible for much of the war, oppression, and misery that have beset the world.

In his 1949 speech, "Am I an Atheist or an Agnostic?", Russell expressed his difficulty over whether to call himself an atheist or an agnostic:

As a philosopher, if I were speaking to a purely philosophic audience I should say that I ought to describe myself as an Agnostic, because I do not think that there is a conclusive argument by which one can prove that there is not a God. On the other hand, if I am to convey the right impression to the ordinary man in the street I think that I ought to say that I am an Atheist, because, when I say that I cannot prove that there is not a God, I ought to add equally that I cannot prove that there are not the Homeric gods.

Though he would later question God's existence, he fully accepted the ontological argument during his undergraduate years:

For two or three years I was a Hegelian. I remember the exact moment during my fourth year [in 1894] when I became one. I had gone out to buy a tin of tobacco, and was going back with it along Trinity Lane, when I suddenly threw it up in the air and exclaimed: "Great God in Boots! — the ontological argument is sound!"

This quote has been used by many theologians over the years, such as by Louis Pojman in his *Philosophy of Religion*, who wish for readers to believe that even a well-known atheist-philosopher supported this particular argument for God's existence. However, elsewhere in his autobiography, Russell also mentions:

About two years later, I became convinced that there is no life after death, but I still believed in God, because the "First Cause" argument appeared to be irrefutable. At the age of eighteen, however, shortly before I went to Cambridge, I read Mill's *Autobiography*, where I found a sentence to the effect that his father taught him the question "Who made me?" cannot be answered, since it immediately suggests the further question "Who made God?" This led me to abandon the "First Cause" argument, and to become an atheist.

Russell made an influential analysis of the omphalos hypothesis enunciated by Philip Henry Gosse "that any argument suggesting that the world was created as if it were already in motion could just as easily make it a few minutes old as a few thousand years:

There is no logical impossibility in the hypothesis that the world sprang into being five minutes ago, exactly as it then was, with a population that "remembered" a wholly unreal past. There is no logically necessary connection between events at different times; therefore nothing that is happening now or will happen in the future can disprove the hypothesis that the world began five minutes ago.

As a young man, Russell had a decidedly religious bent, himself, as is evident in his early Platonism. He longed for eternal truths, as he makes clear in his famous essay, "A Free Man's Worship", widely regarded as a masterpiece of prose, but a work that Russell came to dislike. While he rejected the supernatural, he freely admitted that he yearned for a deeper meaning to life.

Russell's views on religion can be found in his popular book, *Why I Am Not a Christian and Other Essays on Religion and Related Subjects* (ISBN 0-671-20323-1). Its title essay was a talk given on March 6, 1927 at Battersea Town Hall, under the auspices of the South London Branch of the National Secular Society, UK, and published later that year as a pamphlet. The book also contains other essays in which Russell considers a number of logical arguments for the existence of God, including the first cause argument, the natural-law argument, the argument from design, and moral arguments. He also discusses specifics about Christian theology.

His Conclusion:

Religion is based, I think, primarily and mainly upon fear. It is partly the terror of the unknown and partly, as I have said, the wish to feel that you have a kind of elder brother who will stand by you in all your troubles and disputes. A good world needs knowledge, kindliness, and courage; it does not need a regretful hankering after the past or a fettering of the free intelligence by the words uttered long ago by ignorant men.

Chapter 2

Russell's Philosophical Work

Analytic philosophy

Russell is generally recognised as one of the founders of analytic philosophy, indeed, even of its several branches. At the beginning of the 20th century, alongside G. E. Moore, Russell was largely responsible for the British "revolt against Idealism", a philosophy greatly influenced by Georg Hegel and his British apostle, F. H. Bradley. This revolt was echoed 30 years later in Vienna by the logical positivists' "revolt against metaphysics". Russell was particularly appalled by the idealist doctrine of internal relations, which held that in order to know any particular thing, we must know all of its relations. Russell showed that this would make space, time, science and the concept of number unintelligible. Russell's logical work with Whitehead continued this project.

Russell and Moore strove to eliminate what they saw as meaningless and incoherent assertions in philosophy, and they sought clarity and precision in argument by the use of exact language and by breaking down philosophical propositions into their simplest components. Russell, in particular, saw logic and science as the principal tools of the philosopher. Indeed, unlike most philosophers who preceded him and his early contemporaries, Russell did not believe there was a separate method for philosophy.

He believed that the main task of the philosopher was to illuminate the most general propositions about the world and to eliminate confusion. In particular, he wanted to end what he saw as the excesses of metaphysics. Russell adopted William of Ockham's principle against multiplying unnecessary entities, Occam's Razor, as a central part of the method of analysis.

Epistemology

Russell's epistemology went through many phases. Once he shed neo-Hegelianism in his early years, Russell remained a philosophical realist for the remainder of his life, believing that our direct experiences have primacy in the acquisition of knowledge. While some of his views have lost favour, his influence remains strong in the distinction between two ways in which we can be familiar with objects: "knowledge by acquaintance" and "knowledge by description". For a time, Russell thought that we could only be acquainted with our own sense data-momentary perceptions of colours, sounds, and the like- and that everything else, including the physical objects that these were sense data of, could only be inferred, or reasoned to- i.e. known by description-and not known directly. This distinction has gained much wider application, though Russell eventually rejected the idea of an intermediate sense datum. In his later philosophy, Russell subscribed to a kind of neutral monism, maintaining that the distinctions between the material and mental worlds, in the final analysis, were arbitrary, and that both can be reduced to a neutral property- a view similar to one held by the American philosopher, William James, and one that was first formulated by Baruch Spinoza, whom Russell greatly admired. Instead of James' "pure experience", however, Russell characterised the stuff of our initial states of perception as "events", a stance which is curiously akin to his old teacher Whitehead's process philosophy.

Ethics

While Russell wrote a great deal on ethical subject matters, he did not believe that the subject belonged to philosophy or that when he wrote on ethics that he did so in his capacity as a philosopher. In his earlier years, Russell was greatly influenced by G.E. Moore's Principia Ethica. Along with

Moore, he then believed that moral facts were objective, but only known through intuition, and that they were simple properties of objects, not equivalent (e.g., pleasure is good) to the natural objects to which they are often ascribed (see Naturalistic fallacy), and that these simple, undefinable moral properties cannot be analyzed using the non-moral properties with which they are associated. In time, however, he came to agree with his philosophical hero, David Hume, who believed that ethical terms dealt with subjective values that cannot be verified in the same way that matters of fact are.

Coupled with Russell's other doctrines, this influenced the logical positivists, who formulated the theory of emotivism, which states that ethical propositions (along with those of metaphysics) were essentially meaningless and nonsensical or, at best, little more than expressions of attitudes and preferences. Notwithstanding his influence on them, Russell himself did not construe ethical propositions as narrowly as the positivists, for he believed that ethical considerations are not only meaningful, but that they are a vital subject matter for civil discourse. Indeed, though Russell was often characterised as the patron saint of rationality, he agreed with Hume, who said that reason ought to be subordinate to ethical considerations. Russell wrote some books about practical ethical issues such as marriage. His opinions on this field are liberal. He argues that sexual relationships outside of marriages are acceptable. In his book, Human Society in Ethics and Politics (1954), he advocates in favor of the view that we should see moral issues from the point of view of the desires of individuals. Individuals are allowed to do what they desire, as long as there are no conflicting desires among different individuals. Desires are not bad, in and of themselves, but on occasion, their potential or actual consequences are. Russell also writes that punishment is important only in an instrumental sense. Thus we should not punish someone solely for the sake of punishment.

Logical Atomism

Perhaps Russell's most systematic, metaphysical

treatment of philosophical analysis and his empiricist-centric logicism is evident in what he called Logical atomism, which is explicated in a set of lectures, "The Philosophy of Logical Atomism," which he gave in 1918. In these lectures, Russell sets forth his concept of an ideal, isomorphic language, one that would mirror the world, whereby our knowledge can be reduced to terms of atomic propositions and their truth-functional compounds. Logical atomism is a form of radical empiricism, for Russell believed the most important requirement for such an ideal language is that every meaningful proposition must consist of terms referring directly to the objects with which we are acquainted, or that they are defined by other terms referring to objects with which we are acquainted.

Russell excluded certain formal, logical terms such as all, the, is, and so forth, from his isomorphic requirement, but he was never entirely satisfied about our understanding of such terms. One of the central themes of Russell's atomism is that the world consists of logically independent facts, a plurality of facts, and that our knowledge depends on the data of our direct experience of them. In his later life, Russell came to doubt aspects of logical atomism, especially his principle of isomorphism, though he continued to believe that the process of philosophy ought to consist of breaking things down into their simplest components, even though we might not ever fully arrive at an ultimate atomic fact.

Logic and Philosophy of Mathematics

Russell had great influence on modern mathematical logic. The American philosopher and logician Willard Quine said Russell's work represented the greatest influence on his own work.

Russell's first mathematical book, An Essay on the Foundations of Geometry, was published in 1897. This work was heavily influenced by Immanuel Kant. Russell soon realised that the conception it laid out would have made Albert Einstein's schema of space-time impossible, which he understood to be superior to his own system. Thenceforth, he rejected the entire Kantian programme as it related to mathematics and geometry, and he maintained that his own earliest work on the subject was nearly without value.

Interested in the definition of number, Russell studied the work of George Boole, Georg Cantor, and Augustus De Morgan, while materials in the Bertrand Russell Archives at McMaster University include notes of his reading in algebraic logic by Charles S. Peirce and Ernst Schroder. He became convinced that the foundations of mathematics were tied to logic, and following Gottlob Frege took an extensionalist approach in which logic was in turn based upon set theory.

In 1900 he attended the first International Congress of Philosophy in Paris where he became familiar with the work of the Italian mathematician, Giuseppe Peano. He mastered Peano's new symbolism and his set of axioms for arithmetic. Peano was able to define logically all of the terms of these axioms with the exception of 0, number, successor, and the singular term, the. Russell took it upon himself to find logical definitions for each of these.

Between 1897 and 1903 he published several articles applying Peano's notation to the classical Boole-Schroder algebra of relations, among them On the Notion of Order, Sur la logique des relations avec les applications a la theorie des series, and On Cardinal Numbers.

Russell eventually discovered that Gottlob Frege had independently arrived at equivalent definitions for 0, successor, and number, and the definition of number is now usually referred to as the Frege-Russell definition. It was largely Russell who brought Frege to the attention of the English-speaking world. He did this in 1903, when he published The Principles of Mathematics, in which the concept of class is inextricably tied to the definition of number.

The appendix to this work detailed a paradox arising in Frege's application of second- and higher-order functions which took first-order functions as their arguments, and he offered his first effort to resolve what would henceforth come to be known as the Russell Paradox. In writing Principles, Russell came across Cantor's proof that there was no greatest cardinal number, which Russell believed was mistaken. The Cantor Paradox in turn was shown (for example by Crossley) to be a special case of the Russell Paradox. This caused Russell to analyze classes, for it was known that given any number of elements, the number of classes they result in is greater than their number.

In turn, this led to the discovery of a very interesting class, namely, the class of all classes, which consists of two kinds of classes: classes that are members of themselves, and classes that are not members of themselves, which led him to find that the so-called principle of extensionality, taken for granted by logicians of the time, was fatally flawed, and that it resulted in a contradiction, whereby Y is a member of Y, if and only if, Y is not a member of Y.

This has become known as Russell's paradox, the solution to which he outlined in an appendix to Principles, and which he later developed into a complete theory, the Theory of types. Aside from exposing a major inconsistency in naive set theory, Russell's work led directly to the creation of modern axiomatic set theory. It also crippled Frege's project of reducing arithmetic to logic. The Theory of Types and much of Russell's subsequent work have also found practical applications with computer science and information technology.

Russell continued to defend logicism, the view that mathematics is in some important sense reducible to logic, and along with his former teacher, Alfred North Whitehead, wrote the monumental Principia Mathematica, an axiomatic system on which all of mathematics can be built. The first volume of the Principia was published in 1910, which is largely ascribed to Russell.

More than any other single work, it established the specialty of mathematical or symbolic logic. Two more volumes were published, but their original plan to incorporate geometry in a fourth volume was never realised, and Russell never felt up to improving the original works, though he referenced new developments and problems in his preface to the second edition. Upon completing the Principia, three volumes of extraordinarily abstract and complex reasoning,

Russell was exhausted, and he never felt his intellectual faculties fully recovered from the effort. Although the Principia did not fall prey to the paradoxes in Frege's approach, it was later proven by Kurt Godel that neither Principia Mathematica, nor any other consistent system of primitive recursive arithmetic, could, within that system, determine that every proposition that could be formulated within that system was decidable, i.e. could decide whether that proposition or its negation was provable within the system (Godel's incompleteness theorem).

Russell's last significant work in mathematics and logic, Introduction to Mathematical Philosophy, was written by hand while he was in jail for his anti-war activities during World War I. This was largely an explication of his previous work and its philosophical significance.

Philosophy of language

Russell was not the first philosopher to suggest that language had an important bearing on how we understand the world; however, more than anyone before him, Russell made language, or more specifically, how we use language, a central part of philosophy.

Had there been no Russell, it seems unlikely that philosophers such as Ludwig Wittgenstein, Gilbert Ryle, J. L. Austin, and P. F. Strawson, among others, would have embarked upon the same course, for so much of what they did was to amplify or respond, sometimes critically, to what Russell had said before them, using many of the techniques that he originally developed. Russell, along with Moore, shared the idea that clarity of expression is a virtue, a notion that has been a touchstone for philosophers ever since, particularly among those who deal with the philosophy of language.

Perhaps Russell's most significant contribution to philosophy of language is his theory of descriptions, as presented in his seminal essay, "On Denoting", first published in 1905, which the mathematician and philosopher Frank P. Ramsey described as "a paradigm of philosophy." The theory is normally illustrated using the phrase "the present King of

France", as in "The present king of France is bald." What object is this proposition about, given that there is not, at present, a king of France? (Roughly the same problem would arise if there were two kings of France at present: which of them does "the king of France" denote?) Alexius Meinong had suggested that we must posit a realm of "nonexistent entities" that we can suppose we are referring to when we use expressions such as this; but this would be a strange theory, to say the least.

Frege, employing his distinction between sense and reference, suggested that such sentences, although meaningful, were neither true nor false. But some such propositions, such as "If the present king of France is bald, then the present king of France has no hair on his head," seem not only truth-valuable but indeed obviously true.

The problem is general to what are called "definite descriptions." Normally this includes all terms beginning with "the", and sometimes includes names, like "Walter Scott." (This point is quite contentious: Russell sometimes thought that the latter terms shouldn't be called names at all, but only "disguised definite descriptions," but much subsequent work has treated them as altogether different things.) What is the "logical form" of definite descriptions: how, in Frege's terms, could we paraphrase them in order to show how the truth of the whole depends on the truths of the parts? Definite descriptions appear to be like names that by their very nature denote exactly one thing, neither more or less. What, then, are we to say about the proposition as a whole if one of its parts apparently isn't functioning correctly?

Russell's solution was, first of all, to analyze not the term alone but the entire proposition that contained a definite description. "The present king of France is bald," he then suggested, can be reworded to "There is an x such that x is a present king of France, nothing other than x is a present king of France, and x is bald." Russell claimed that each definite description in fact contains a claim of existence and a claim of uniqueness which give this appearance, but these can be broken apart and treated separately from the predication that is the obvious content of the proposition. The proposition as a whole then says three things about some object: the definite description contains two of them, and the rest of the sentence contains the other. If the object does not exist, or if it is not unique, then the whole sentence turns out to be false, not meaningless.

One of the major complaints against Russell's theory, due originally to Strawson, is that definite descriptions do not claim that their object exists, they merely presuppose that it does. Strawson also claims that a denoting phrase that does not, in fact, denote anything could be supposed to follow the role of a "Widgy's inverted truth-value" and expresses the opposite meaning of the intended phrase.

This can be shown using the example of "The present king of France is bald". Taken with the inverted truth-value methodology the meaning of this sentence becomes "It is true that there is no present king of France who is bald" which changes the denotation of 'the present king of France' from a primary denotation to a secondary one.

Wittgenstein, Russell's student, later achieved considerable prominence in the philosophy of language. Russell thought Wittgenstein's elevation of language as the only reality with which philosophy need be concerned was absurd, and he decried his influence and the influence of his followers, especially members of the so-called "Oxford school" of ordinary language philosophy, who he believed were promoting a kind of mysticism. Russell's belief that there is more to philosophy and knowing the world than simply understanding how we use language has regained prominence in philosophy and eclipsed Wittgenstein's language-centric views.

Philosophy of Science

Russell frequently claimed that he was more convinced of his method of doing philosophy, the method of analysis, than of his philosophical conclusions. Science, of course, was one of the principal components of analysis, along with logic and mathematics. While Russell was a believer in the scientific method, knowledge derived from empirical research that is verified through repeated testing, he believed that science reaches only tentative answers, and that scientific progress is piecemeal, and attempts to find organic unities were largely futile.

Indeed, he believed the same was true of philosophy. Another founder of modern philosophy of science, Ernst Mach, placed less reliance on method, per se, for he believed that any method that produced predictable results was satisfactory and that the principal role of the scientist was to make successful predictions. While Russell would doubtless agree with this as a practical matter, he believed that the ultimate objective of both science and philosophy was to understand reality, not simply to make predictions.

The fact that Russell made science a central part of his method and of philosophy was instrumental in making the philosophy of science a full-blooded, separate branch of philosophy and an area in which subsequent philosophers specialised. Much of Russell's thinking about science is exposed in his 1914 book, Our Knowledge of the External World as a Field for Scientific Method in Philosophy. Among the several schools that were influenced by Russell were the logical positivists, particularly Rudolph Carnap, who maintained that the distinguishing feature of scientific propositions was their verifiability. This contrasted with the theory of Karl Popper, also greatly influenced by Russell, who believed that their importance rested in the fact that they were potentially falsifiable.

It is worth noting that outside of his strictly philosophical pursuits, Russell was always fascinated by science, particularly physics, and he even authored several popular science books, The ABC of Atoms (1923) and The ABC of Relativity (1925).

Religion and Theology

Russell's ethical outlook and his personal courage in facing controversies were certainly informed by his religious upbringing, principally by his paternal grandmother, who instructed him with the Biblical injunction, "Thou shalt not follow a multitude to do evil" (Exodus 23:2), something he said influenced him throughout his life. For most of his adult life, however, Russell thought it very unlikely that there was a god, and he maintained that religion is little more than superstition and, despite any positive effects that religion might have, it is largely harmful to people. He believed religion and the religious outlook (he considered communism and other systematic ideologies to be species of religion) serve to impede knowledge, foster fear and dependency, and are responsible for much of the war, oppression, and misery that have beset the world.

In his 1949 speech, "Am I an Atheist or an Agnostic?", Russell expressed his difficulty over whether to call himself an atheist or an agnostic:

"As a philosopher, if I were speaking to a purely philosophic audience I should say that I ought to describe myself as an Agnostic, because I do not think that there is a conclusive argument by which one prove that there is not a God. On the other hand, if I am to convey the right impression to the ordinary man in the street I think that I ought to say that I am an Atheist, because, when I say that I cannot prove that there is not a God, I ought to add equally that I cannot prove that there are not the Homeric gods."

Russell also made an influential analysis of the omphalos hypothesis enunciated by Philip Henry Gosse-that any argument suggesting that the world was created as if it were already in motion could just as easily make it a few minutes old as a few thousand years:

"There is no logical impossibility in the hypothesis that the world sprang into being five minutes ago, exactly as it then was, with a population that "remembered" a wholly unreal past. There is no logically necessary connection between events at different times; therefore nothing that is happening now or will happen in the future can disprove the hypothesis that the world began five minutes ago."

- Bertrand Russell, The Analysis of Mind, 1921, pp. 159 "60; cf. Philosophy, Norton, 1927, p. 7, where Russell acknowledges Gosse's paternity of this anti-evolutionary argument.

As a young man, Russell had a decidedly religious bent, himself, as is evident in his early Platonism. He longed for eternal truths, as he makes clear in his famous essay, "A Free Man's Worship", widely regarded as a masterpiece in prose, but one that Russell came to dislike. While he rejected the supernatural, he freely admitted that he yearned for a deeper meaning to life.

Russell's views on religion can be found in his popular book, Why I Am Not a Christian and Other Essays on Religion and Related Subjects, whose title essay was a talk given March 6, 1927 at Battersea Town Hall, under the auspices of the South London Branch of the National Secular Society, UK. The speech was published later that year as a pamphlet, which, along with other essays, was eventually published as a book. In the book, Russell considers a number of logical arguments for the existence of God, including the first cause argument, the natural-law argument, the argument from design, and moral arguments. He also goes into specifics about Christian theology.

Influence on Philosophy

It would be difficult to overstate Russell's influence on modern philosophy, especially in the English-speaking world. While others were also influential, notably, Frege, Moore, and Wittgenstein, more than any other person, Russell made analysis the dominant approach to philosophy. Moreover, he is the founder or, at the very least, the prime mover of its major branches and themes, including several versions of the philosophy of language, formal logical analysis, and the philosophy of science. The various analytic movements throughout the last century all owe something to Russell's earlier works.

Russell's influence on individual philosophers is singular, and perhaps most notably in the case of Ludwig Wittgenstein, who was his student between 1911 and 1914. It should also be observed that Wittgenstein exerted considerable influence on Russell, especially in leading him to conclude, much to his regret, that mathematical truths were trivial, tautological truths. Evidence of Russell's influence on Wittgenstein can be seen throughout the Tractatus, which Russell was responsible for having published. Russell also helped to secure Wittgenstein's doctorate and a faculty position at Cambridge, along with several fellowships along the way.

However, as previously stated, he came to disagree with Wittgenstein's later linguistic and analytic approach to philosophy, while Wittgenstein came to think of Russell as "superficial and glib," particularly in his popular writings. Russell's influence is also evident in the work of A. J. Ayer, Rudolph Carnap, Kurt Godel, Karl Popper, W. V. Quine, and a number of other philosophers and logicians.

Some see Russell's influence as mostly negative, primarily those who have been critical of Russell's emphasis on science and logic, the consequent diminishment of metaphysics, and of his insistence that ethics lies outside of philosophy. Russell's admirers and detractors are often more acquainted with his pronouncements on social and political matters, or what some (e.g., Ray Monk) have called his "journalism," than they are with his technical, philosophical work. Among non-philosophers, there is a marked tendency to conflate these matters, and to judge Russell the philosopher on what he himself would certainly consider to be his non-philosophical opinions. Russell often cautioned people to make this distinction.

Russell left a large assortment of writing. Since adolescence, Russell wrote about 3,000 words a day, in long hand, with relatively few corrections; his first draft nearly always was his last draft, even on the most complex, technical matters. His previously unpublished work is an immense treasure trove, and scholars are continuing to gain new insights into Russell's thought.

Russell's Activism

Political and social activism occupied much of Russell's time for most of his long life, which makes his prodigious and seminal writing on a wide range of technical and non-technical subjects all the more remarkable.

Russell remained politically active to the end, writing and exhorting world leaders and lending his name to various causes. Some maintain that during his last few years he gave his youthful followers too much license and that they used his name for some outlandish purposes that a more attentive Russell would not have approved. There is evidence to show that he became aware of this when he fired his private secretary, Ralph Schoenman, then a young firebrand of the radical left.

Pacifism, War and Nuclear Weapons

While never a complete pacifist (in 'The Ethics of War', an article published in 1915, Russell stated that colonial wars were legitimate where the side with the stronger culture could put the land to better use), Russell opposed British participation in World War I. As a result, he was first fined, then lost his professorship at Trinity College, Cambridge, and was later imprisoned for six months. In 1943 Russell called his stance "relative political pacifism"- he held that war was always a great evil, but in some particularly extreme circumstances (such as when Adolf Hitler threatened to take over Europe) it might be a lesser of multiple evils. In the years leading to World War II, he supported the policy of appeasement; but by 1940, he acknowledged that in order to preserve democracy, Hitler had to be defeated.

Russell was a prominent opponent of nuclear weapons. On November 20, 1948, in a public speech at Westminster School, addressing a gathering arranged by the New Commonwealth, Russell shocked some observers by suggesting that a preemptive nuclear strike on the Soviet Union was justified. Russell argued that the threat of war between the United States and the Soviet Union would enable the United States to force the Soviet Union to accept the Baruch Plan for international atomic energy control. (Earlier in the year he had written in the same vein to Walter W. Marseille.) Russell felt this plan "had very great merits and showed considerable generosity, when it is remembered that America still had an unbroken nuclear monopoly." (Has Man a Future?, 1961).

Russell later relented from this stance, instead arguing for mutual disarmament by the nuclear powers, possibly linked to some form of world government.

In 1955, Russell released the Russell-Einstein Manifesto, co-signed by Albert Einstein and nine other leading scientists and intellectuals, which led to the first of the Pugwash Conferences on Science and World Affairs in 1957. In 1958, Russell became the first president of the Campaign for Nuclear Disarmament. He resigned two years later when the CND would not support civil disobedience, and formed the Committee of 100. In 1961, when he was in his late eighties, he was imprisoned for a week for inciting civil disobedience, in connection with protests at the Ministry of Defense and Hyde Park.

The Bertrand Russell Peace Foundation began work in 1963, in order to carry forward Russell's work for peace, human rights and social justice. He opposed the Vietnam War and, along with Jean-Paul Sartre, he organised a tribunal intended to expose U.S. war crimes; this came to be known as the Russell Tribunal.

Russell was an early critic of the official story in the John F. Kennedy assassination; his "16 Questions on the Assassination" from 1964 is still considered a good summary of the apparent inconsistencies in that case.

Communism and Socialism

Russell visited the Soviet Union and met Lenin in 1920, and on his return wrote a critical tract, The Practice and Theory of Bolshevism. He was unimpressed with the result of the communist revolution, and said he was "infinitely unhappy in this atmosphere-stifled by its utilitarianism, its indifference to love and beauty and the life of impulse." He believed Lenin to be similar to a religious zealot, cold and possessed of "no love of liberty."

Politically, Russell envisioned a kind of benevolent, democratic socialism, not unlike the conception promoted by the Fabian Society. He was extremely critical of the totalitarianism exhibited by Stalin's regime, and of Marxism and communism generally. Russell was an enthusiast for world government, and advocated the establishment of an international or world government in some of the essays collected in "In Praise of Idleness" (1935), and also in Has Man a Future? (1961).

"One who believes as I do, that free intellect is the chief engine of human progress, cannot but be fundamentally opposed to Bolshevism as much as to the Church of Rome. The hopes which inspire communism are, in the main, as admirable as those instilled by the Sermon on the Mount, but they are held as fanatically and are as likely to do as much harm."- Bertrand Russell, The Practice and Theory of Bolshevism, 1920

"For my part, while I am as convinced a Socialist as the most ardent Marxian, I do not regard Socialism as a gospel of proletarian revenge, nor even, primarily, as a means of securing economic justice. I regard it primarily as an adjustment to machine production demanded by considerations of common sense, and calculated to increase the happiness, not only of proletarians, but of all except a tiny minority of the human race."

Bertrand Russell, "The Case for Socialism" (In Praise of Idleness, 1935)

"Modern methods of production have given us the possibility of ease and security for all; we have chosen, instead, to have overwork for some and starvation for the others. Hitherto we have continued to be as energetic as we were before there were machines; in this we have been foolish, but there is no reason to go on being foolish for ever."

-Bertrand Russell, In Praise of Idleness, 1935

Women's Suffrage

As a young man, Russell was a member of the Liberal Party and wrote in favor of free trade and women's suffrage. In his 1910 pamphlet, Anti-Suffragist Anxieties, Russell wrote that some men opposed suffrage because they "fear that their liberty to act in ways that are injurious to women will be curtailed." In 1907 he was nominated by the National Union of Suffrage Societies to run for Parliament in a by-election, which he lost by a wide margin.

Sexuality

Russell wrote against Victorian notions of morality. Marriage and Morals (1929) expressed his opinion that sex between a man and woman who are not married to each other is not necessarily immoral if they truly love one another, and advocated "trial marriages" or "companionate marriage". Formalised relationships whereby young people could legitimately have sexual intercourse without being expected to remain married in the long term or to have children (an idea first proposed by Judge Ben Lindsey).

This might not seem extreme by today's standards, but it was enough to raise vigorous protests and denunciations against him during his visit to the United States shortly after the book's publication. Russell was also ahead of his time in advocating open sex education and widespread access to contraception. He also advocated easy divorce, but only if the marriage had produced no children - Russell's view was that parents should remain married but tolerant of each other's sexual infidelity, if they had children. This reflected his life at the time- his second wife Dora was openly having an affair, and would soon become pregnant by another man, but Russell was keen for their children John and Kate to have a "normal" family life.

Russell's private life was even more unconventional and freewheeling than his published writings revealed, but that was not well known at the time. For example, philosopher Sidney Hook reports that Russell often spoke of his sexual prowess and of his various conquests.

Eugenics and Race

Some critics of Russell have pointed out racist passages in his early writings, as well as his initial praise for the then-fashionable idea of eugenics. For example, in a letter to Alys Pearsall he wrote: "Thee might observe incidentally that if the

State paid for child-bearing it might and ought to require a medical certificate that the parents were such as to give a reasonable result of a healthy child- this would afford a very good inducement to some sort of care for the race, and gradually as public opinion became educated by the law, it might react on the law and make that more stringent, until one got to some state of things in which there would be a little genuine care for the race, instead of the present haphazard higgledy-piggledy ways."

- Bertrand Russell, on eugenics to Alys Pearsall Smith, 2 October 1894.(Selected Letters, vol. 1, p. 128)

And early editions of his book Marriage and Morals (1929) asserted:

"In extreme cases there can be little doubt of the superiority of one race to another.... It seems on the whole fair to regard negroes as on the average inferior to white men, although for work in the tropics they are indispensable, so that their extermination (apart from questions of humanity) would be highly undesirable."

Bertrand Russell, Marriage and Morals (1929)

Although Russell changed "It seems on the whole fair to..." to "There is no reason to..." in much later editions of the book, he did not change the sentence "women are on the average stupider than men".

Later in his life, Russell criticized eugenic programs for their impracticality (chiefly their vulnerability to corruption), and by 1932 he was to condemn the "unwarranted assumption" that "Negroes are congenitally inferior to white men" (Education and the Social Order, Chap. 3). Racism rapidly declined in acceptance throughout the second half of the 20th century. In fact, Russell seems to have been one of the leaders of change in this sphere. He wrote a chapter on "Racial Antagonism" in New Hopes for a Changing World (1951):

"It is sometimes maintained that racial mixture is biologically undesirable. There is no evidence whatever for this view. Nor is there, apparently, any reason to think that

Negroes are congenitally less intelligent than white people, but as to that it will be difficult to judge until they have equal scope and equally good social conditions."

- Bertrand Russell, New Hopes for a Changing World (London: Allen & Unwin, 1951, p. 108)

There is a much later condemnation-in-passing of racism in Russell's "16 Questions on the Assassination" (1964), in which he mentions "Senator Russell of Georgia and Congressman Boggs of Louisiana... whose racist views have brought shame on the United States".

Russell Summing up his life

Admitting to failure in helping the world to conquer war and in winning his perpetual intellectual battle for eternal truths, Russell wrote this in "Reflections on My Eightieth Birthday", which also served as the last entry in the last volume of his autobiography, published in his 98th year:

"I have lived in the pursuit of a vision, both personal and social. Personal: to care for what is noble, for what is beautiful, for what is gentle; to allow moments of insight to give wisdom at more mundane times. Social: to see in imagination the society that is to be created, where individuals grow freely, and where hate and greed and envy die because there is nothing to nourish them. These things I believe, and the world, for all its horrors, has left me unshaken."

Chapter 3

Sceptical Essays

The time has come to review my life as a whole, and to ask whether it has served any useful purpose or has been wholly concerned in futility. Unfortunately, no answer is possible for anyone who does not know the future. Modern weapons make it practically certain that the next serious war will exterminate the human race. This is admitted by all competent authorities, and I shall not waste time in proving it. Any man who cares what the future may have in store therefore has to choose between nothingness and conciliation, not once, but throughout future ages until the sun grows cold.

Unfortunately, our politicians are not accustomed to such a choice. However hard they try, their minds inevitably slide back to the courtroom and the criminal world. If, out of kindness, the last man foresees the murder of the last man but one, the whole law-enforcement campaign imagines all the apparatus of police, Scotland Yard, judges and wigs ready to catch and punish him. But this is not how the scene will be. There will be first the death of nearly all the inhabitants of New York or London or Peking or Tokyo, then a gradual extension of deaths to the country, then famine due to failure of trade, and at last gasping, horrifying lonely death in the mountains, and then eternal silence. If the Great Powers continue their present policies, some such end as this is inevitable. When two or more Powers disagree, what can they do? A can yield to B, or B can yield to A, or they can reach a compromise, or they can fight. If either yields, it is thought pusillanimous: either it loses caste, or, next time, it must fight; or it must secure an ally. Since the number of States is finite, this process must soon come to an end. We have seen all the steps in this development since the end of the Second War. Consider what happened in the Cuba crisis. Both sides were willing to fight, but at the last possible moment Khrushchev's nerve failed and he allowed the world to live till the next crisis. But it turned out that Russia would have preferred death, and Khrushchev fell.

Can we Count on this Always Happening? What is the Present System

When there is a quarrel, a conference is summoned, each side debates, they reach two compromises, one favoured by one side, the other by the other. If each contains disarmament clauses, each is aware that they may be infringed. Each considers the tiniest chance of infringement a greater misfortune than the end of the human race. And so nothing is done. The powers must learn that *peace is the paramount interest of everybody*. To cause this to be realized by governments should be the supreme aim.

What has been Achieved Towards this end, and what have I Personally Contributed

Publicly, in the relations between states, very little, but still something. Russia has expressed willingness to transform NATO by joining it; but China is a new threat. The Vietnam war seems likely to end in negotiation. Generally, the powers (except the U.S.) show a reluctance to go to war. France is uncertain, but leaves room for hope. At any rate, the stark opposition of Communist and non-Communist is breaking down. If peace can be preserved for the next 10 years, it will be possible to hope.

What Can Private Persons do Meanwhile

They can agitate, by pointing out the effects of modern war and the danger of the extinction of Man. They can teach men not to hate peoples other than their own, or to cause themselves to be hated. They can value, and cause others to value, what Man has achieved in art and science. They can emphasize the superiority of co-operation to competition. Finally, have I done anything to further such ends? Something perhaps, but sadly little in view of the magnitude of the evil. Some few people in England and the U.S.A. I have encouraged in the expression of liberal views, or have terrified with the knowledge of what modern weapons can do. It is not much, but if everybody did as much this Earth would soon be a paradise.

Consider for a moment what our planet is and what it might be. At present, for most, there is toil and hunger, constant danger, more hatred than love.

There could be a happy world, where co-operation was more in evidence than competition, and monotonous work is done by machines, where what is lovely in nature is not destroyed to make room for hideous machines whose sole business is to kill, and where to promote joy is more respected than to produce mountains of corpses.

Do not say this is impossible: it is not. It waits only for men to desire it more than the infliction of torture. There is an artist imprisoned in each one of us. Let him loose to spread joy everywhere.

Am I An Atheist Or An Agnostic

A Plea For Tolerance In The Face Of New Dogmas

I speak as one who was intended by my father to be brought up as a Rationalist.

He was quite as much of a Rationalist as I am, but he died when I was three years old, and the Court of Chancery decided that I was to have the benefits of a Christian education. I think perhaps the Court of Chancery might have regretted that since. It does not seem to have done as much good as they hoped. Perhaps you may say that it would be rather a pity if Christian education were to cease, because you would then get no more Rationalists.

They arise chiefly out of reaction to a system of education which considers it quite right that a father should decree that his son should be brought up as a Muggletonian, we will say, or brought up on any other kind of nonsense, but he must on no account be brought up to think rationally. When I was young that was considered to be illegal.

Sin And The Bishops

Since I became a Rationalist I have found that there is still considerable scope in the world for the practical importance of a rationalist outlook, not only in matters of geology, but in all sorts of practical matters, such as divorce and birth control, and a question which has come up quite recently, artificial insemination, where bishops tell us that something is gravely sinful, but it is only gravely sinful because there is some text in the Bible about it. It is not gravely sinful because it does anybody harm, and that is not the argument. As long as you can say, and as long as you can persuade Parliament to go on saying that a thing must not be done solely because there is some text in the Bible about it, so long obviously there is great need of Rationalism in practice. As you may know, I got into great trouble in the United States solely because, on some practical issues, I considered that the ethical advice given in the Bible was not conclusive, and that on some points one should act differently from what the Bible says. On this ground it was decreed by a Law Court that I was not a fit person to teach in any university in the United States, so that I have some practical ground for preferring Rationalism to other outlooks.

Don't Be Too Certain

The question of how to define Rationalism is not altogether an easy one. I do not think that you could define it by rejection of this or that Christian dogma. It would be perfectly possible to be a complete and absolute Rationalist in the true sense of the term and yet accept this or that dogma. The question is how to arrive at your opinions and not what your opinions are. The thing in which we believe is the supremacy of reason. If reason should lead you to orthodox conclusions, well and good; you are still a Rationalist. To my mind the essential thing is that one should base one's arguments upon the kind of grounds that are accepted in science, and one should not regard anything that one accepts as quite certain, but only as probable in a greater or a less degree. Not to be absolutely certain is, I think, one of the essential things in rationality.

Proof of God

Here there comes a practical question, which has often troubled me. Whenever I go into a foreign country or a prison or any similar place they always ask me what is my religion.

I never know whether I should say "Agnostic" or whether I should say "Atheist". It is a very difficult question and I daresay that some of you have been troubled by it. As a philosopher, if I were speaking to a purely philosophic audience I should say that I ought to describe myself as an Agnostic, because I do not think that there is a conclusive argument by which one prove that there is not a God. On the other hand, if I am to convey the right impression to the ordinary man in the street I think I ought to say that I am an Atheist, because when I say that I cannot prove that there is not a God, I ought to add equally that I cannot prove that there are not the Homeric gods. None of us would seriously consider the possibility that all the gods of homer really exist, and yet if you were to set to work to give a logical demonstration that Zeus, Hera, Poseidon, and the rest of them did not exist you would find it an awful job. You could not get such proof.

Therefore, in regard to the Olympic gods, speaking to a purely philosophical audience, I would say that I am an Agnostic. But speaking popularly, I think that all of us would say in regard to those gods that we were Atheists. In regard to the Christian God, I should, I think, take exactly the same line.

Skepticism

There is exactly the same degree of possibility and likelihood of the existence of the Christian God as there is of the existence of the Homeric God. I cannot prove that either the Christian God or the Homeric gods do not exist, but I do not think that their existence is an alternative that is sufficiently probable to be worth serious consideration. Therefore, I suppose that that on these documents that they submit to me on these occasions I ought to say "Atheist", although it has been a very difficult problem, and sometimes I have said one and sometimes the other without any clear principle by which to go. When one admits that nothing is certain one must, I think, also admit that some things are much more nearly certain than others. It is much more nearly certain that we are assembled here tonight than it is that this or that political party is in the right. Certainly, there are degrees of certainty, and one should be very careful to emphasize that fact, because otherwise one is landed in an utter skepticism, and complete skepticism would, of course, be totally barren and completely useless.

Persecution

On must remember that some things are very much more probable than others and may be so probable that it is not worth while to remember in practice that they are not wholly certain, except when it comes to questions of persecution.

If it comes to burning somebody at the stake for not believing it, then it is worthwhile to remember that after all he may be right, and it is not worth while to persecute him.

In general, if a man says, for instance, that the earth is flat, I am quite willing that he should propagate his opinion as hard as he likes. He may, of course, be right but I do not think he is. In practice you will, I think, do better to assume that the earth is round, although, of course, you may be mistaken. Therefore, I do not think we should go in for complete skepticism, but for a doctrine of degrees of probability. I think that, on the whole, that is the kind of doctrine that the world needs. The world has become very full of new dogmas. he old dogmas have perhaps decayed, but new dogmas have arisen and, on the whole, I think that a dogma is harmful in proportion to its novelty. New dogmas are much worse that old ones.

Bertrand Russell's Best - Psychology

Vanity is a motive of immense potency. Anyone who has much to do with children knows how they are constantly performing some antic, and saying: "Look at me." "Look at me" is one of the fundamental desires of human heart. It can take innumerable forms, from buffoonery to the pursuit of posthumous fame.

There was a Renaissance Italian princeling who was asked by a priest on his death-bed if he had anything to repent of. "Yes," he said, "there is one thing. On one occasion I had a visit from Emperor and the Pope simultaneously. I took them to the top of my tower to see the view, and I neglected the opportunity to throw them both down, which would have given me immortal fame." History does not relate whether the priest gave him absolution.

I once befriended two little girls from Estonia, who had narrowly escaped death from starvation in a famine. They lived in my family, and of course had plenty to eat. But they spent all their leisure visiting neighbouring farms and staling potatoes, which they hoarded. Rockefeller, who in his infancy had experienced great poverty, spent his adult life in a similar manner.

Human beings show their superiority to the brutes by their capacity for boredom, though I have sometimes thought in examining the apes at the zoo, that they, perhaps, have the rudiments of this tiresome emotion. However that may be, experience shows that escape from boredom is one of the really powerful desires of almost all human beings. When white men first effect contact with some unspoiled race of savages, they offer them all kinds of benefits, from the light of the gospel to pumpkin pie.

These, however, much as we may regret it, most savages receive with indifference. What they really value among the gifts that we bring to them is intoxicating liquor, which enables them to have the illusion, for a few brief moments, that it is better to be alive than dead.

What vanity needs for its satisfaction is glory, and it's easy to have glory without power. The people who enjoy the greatest glory in the United States are film stars, but they can be put in their place by the committee for Un-American Activities, which enjoys no glory whatever.

The desire for excitement is very deep-seated in human beings, especially in males. I suppose that in the hunting stage it was more easily gratified than it has been since. The chase was exciting, war was exciting, courtship was exciting. A savage would manage to commit adultery with a woman while her husband is asleep beside her. This situation, I imagine, is not boring. But with the coming of agriculture life began to grow dull, except, of course, for the aristocrats, who remained, and still remain, in the hunting stage.

The completely untraveled person will view all foreigners as the savage regards the members of another herd. But the man who has traveled, or who has studied international politics, will have discovered that, if he had to prosper, it must, to some degree, become amalgamated with other herds. If you are English and someone says to you: "The French are your brothers," your instinctive feeling will be "Nonsense, they shrug their shoulders, and talk French. And I am even told that they eat frogs.

If he explains to you that one may have to fight the Russians, that, if so, it will be desirable to defend the line of the Rhine, and that, if the line of the Rhine is to be defended, the help of the French is essential, you will begin to see what he means when he says that French are our brothers. But if some fellow-traveler were to go on and say that the Russians are also your brothers, he would be unable to persuade you, unless he could show that we are in danger from the Martians. We love those who hate our enemies, and if we had no enemies, there would be very few people whom we should love.

Civilized life has altogether grown too tame, and, if it is to be stable, it must provide a harmless outlets for the impulses which our remote ancestors satisfied in hunting. In Australia, where people are few, and rabbits are many, I watched the whole populace satisfying the primitive impulse in the primitive manner by the skillful slaughter of many thousands of rabbits. But, in London or New York, where people are many and rabbits are few, some other means must be found to gratify primitive impulse. I think every big town should contain artificial waterfalls that people can descend in very fragile canoes, and they should contain bathing pools full of mechanical sharks. Any person found advocating a preventive war should be condemned to two hours a day with these ingenious creatures.

Every isolated passion, is, in isolation, insane; sanity may be defined as synthesis of insanities. Every dominant passion generates a dominant fear, the fear of its non-fulfillment. Every dominant fear generates a nightmare, sometimes in form of explicit and conscious fanaticism, sometimes in paralyzing timidity, sometimes in an unconscious or subconscious terror which finds expression only in dreams. The man who wishes to preserve sanity in a dangerous world should summon in his own mind a parliament of fears, in which each in turn is voted absurd by all the others.

The frequency with which a man experiences lust depends upon his own physical condition, whereas the occasion which rouse such feelings in him depend upon the social conventions to which he is accustomed. To an early Victorian man a woman's ankles were sufficient stimulus, whereas the modern man remains untouched by anything up to the thigh.

This is merely a question of fashion in clothing. If nakedness were the fashion, it would cease to excite us, and women would be forced, as they are in certain savage tribes, to adopt clothing as means of making themselves sexually attractive. Exactly similar considerations apply to the literature and pictures: what was exciting in the Victorian Age, would leave a man of franker epoch quite unmoved. The more prudes restrict the permissible degree of sexual appeal, the less is required to make such an appeal effective. Nine-tents of thew appeal of pornography is due to indecent feelings which moralists inculcate in the young; the other tents is psychological, and will occur in one way of another, whatever the state of the law may be. On these grounds, although I fear that few will agree with me, I am firmly persuaded that there ought to be no law whatsoever on the subject of obscene publications.

Men who allow their love of power to give them a

distorted view of the world are to be found in every asylum: one man will think that he is the Governor of the Bank of England, another will think he is the King, and yet another will think he is God. Highly similar delusions, if expressed by educated men in obscure language, lead to professorships in philosophy; and if expressed by emotional men in eloquent language, lead to dictatorships.

Anthropologist have described how Papuan head hunters, deprived by white authority of their habitual sport, lose all their zest, and are no longer able to be interested by anything. I do not wish to infer that they should have been allowed to go on hunting heads, but I do mean that it would have been worth while if psychologists had taken some trouble to find some innocent substitute activity.

Civilized Man everywhere is, to some degree, in the position of the Papuan victims of virtue. We have all kinds of aggressive impulses, and also creative impulses, which society forbids us to indulge, and the alternatives it supplies in the shape of football matches and all-in wrestling are hardly adequate. Anyone who hopes in time it may be possible to abolish wart should give serious thought to the problem of satisfying harmlessly the instincts which we inherit from log generations of savage. For my part, I find a sufficient outlet in detective stories, where I alternately identify myself with the murderer and the huntsman-detective, but I know there are those to which this vicarious outlet is too mild, and for them something stronger should be provided.

In Lisbon, where heretics were publicly burned, it sometimes happened that one of them, by particularly edifying recantation, would be granted a boon of being strangled before being put to into the flames. This would make the spectators so furious, that he authorities had a great difficulty preventing them from lynching the penitent and burning him on their own account.

The spectacle of writhing torments of the victims was, in fact, one of the principal pleasures to which the populace looked forward to enliven a somewhat drab existence. I cannot doubt that pleasure greatly contributed to the general belief that burning of heretics was a righteous act. The same sort of thing applies to war. People who are vigorous and brutal often find war enjoyable, provided that it is a victorious war, and that there is not too much interference with rape and plunder. This is a great help in persuading people that wars are righteous.

In order to be happy we require all kinds of supports to our self-esteem. We are human beings, therefore human beings are the purpose of gods creation. We are Americans, therefore America is God's own country. We are White, and therefore God cursed Ham and his descendants who were black. We are Protestant or Catholic, as the case may be, therefore Catholics or Protestants as the case may be, are an abomination. We are male, therefore women are unreasonable; we are women, therefore men are brute.

We are Easterners, therefore West is wild and wooly; or Westerners and therefore East is effete. We work with our brains, and therefore it is the educated classes that are important; or we work with our hands, and therefore manual labour alone gives dignity. Finally, and above all, we each have one merit which is entirely unique: we are Ourself. With these comforting reflections we go out to do battle with the world; without them, our courage might fail. Without them, as things are, we should feel inferior, because we have not learned the sentiment of equality. If we would feel genuinely that we are equals of our neighbours, neither their betters nor their inferiors, perhaps life would become less a battle and we should need less in the way of intoxicating myth to give us Dutch courage.

There was, until the end of the eighteenth century, a theory that insanity is due to a possession by devils. It was inferred that any pain suffered by the patient is also suffered by the devils, so that the best cure for is to make the patient suffer so much that the devils will decide to abandon him. The insane, in accordance with this theory, were savagely beaten.

This treatment was tried on king George III when he was mad, but without success. It is a curious and painful fact that almost all the completely futile treatments that have been believed in during the long history of medical folly have been such as caused acute suffering to the patient. When anesthetics were discovered pious people considered them an attempt to evade a will of God.

It was pointed out, however, that when God extracted Adam's rib he put him into a deep sleep. This provided that anesthetics were all right for men; women, however, ought to suffer because of the curse of Eve. In the West votes for women proved this doctrine mistaken, but in Japan, to this day, women at childbirth are not allowed any alleviation through anesthetics. As the Japanese do no believe in Genesis, this piece of sadism must have some other justification.

By self-interest, Man has become gregarious, but in instinct he has remained to a great extent solitary; hence the need of religion and morality to reinforce self-interest. But the habit of foregoing present satisfactions for the sake of the future advantages is irksome, and when passions are roused and prudent restraints of social behaviour become difficult to endure.

Those who, at such times, throw them off, acquire a new energy and sense of power from cessation of inner conflict, and, though they may come to disaster in the end, enjoy meanwhile a sense of God-like exaltation which, though known to the great mystics, can never be experienced by a merely pedestrian virtue. The solitary part of their nature reasserts itself, but if the intellect survives the reassertion must clothe itself in a myth.

The mystic becomes one with God, and in the contemplation of the infinite he feels himself absolved from the duty to his neighbour. The anarchic rebel does even better, he feels himself not one one with God, but God. Truth and duty, which represent our subjection to matter and to our neighbours, exist no longer for the man who has become God; for others, truth is what he posits, duty what he commands. If we could all live solitary and without labour, we could all enjoy this ecstasy of independence; since we cannot, its delights are only available to madmen and dictators.

Happiness is promoted by association of persons who

share similar tastes and similar opinions. Social intercourse may be expected to develop more and more along these lines, and it may be hoped that by these means the loneliness that now afflict so many unconventional people will be gradually diminished almost to vanishing point. This will undoubtedly increase their happiness, but it will of course diminish the sadistic pleasure which the conventional at present derive from having the unconventional at their mercy. I do not think, however, that this is a pleasure which we need to be greatly concerned to preserve.

Our mental make-up is suited to a life of very severe physical labour. I used, when I was younger, to take my holidays walking. I would cover 25 miles a day, and when the evening came I had no need of anything to keep me from boredom, since the delight of sitting amply suffice.

But modern life cannot be constructed on these physically strenuous principles. A great deal of work is sedentary, and most manual work exercises only a few specialized muscles. When crowd assemble at Trafalgar Square to cheer to the echo of an announcement that the government has decided to have them killed, they would not do so if they had all walked 25 miles that day.

This cure for bellicosity is, however, impracticable, and if human race is to survive - a thing which is perhaps, undesirable - other means must be found for securing the innocent outlet for the unused physical energy that produces love of excitement. This is a matter which has been too little consider, both by moralists and by social reformers. The social reformers are of the opinion that they have more serious things to consider. The moralists, on the other hand, are immensely impressed with the seriousness of all permitted outlet of the love of excitement; the seriousness; however, in their minds, is that of Sin. Dance halls, cinemas, this age of jazz, are all, if we may believe our ears, gateways to Hell, and we should be better employed sitting at home contemplating our sins. I find myself unable to be in entire agreement with the grave men who utter these warnings.

The devil has many forms, some designed to deceive the

young, and some designed to deceive the old and serious. If it is the devil that tempts the young to enjoy themselves, is it not, perhaps, the same personage that persuades the old to condemn their enjoyment? And is it not, perhaps, a drug which- like opium- has to be taken in continually stronger doses to produce the desired effect? Is it not to be feared that, beginning with the wickedness of the cinema, we should be led step by step to condemn the opposite political party, dagoes, wops, Asiatics, and, in short, everybody except the fellow members of our club? And it is from just such condemnations, when widespread, that wars proceed. I have never heard of a war that proceeded from dance halls.

There is no greater reason for children to honor parents than for parents to honor children except, that while the children are young, the parents are stronger that children. The same thing, of course, happened in the relations of men and women. It was the duty of wives to submit to husbands, not of husbands to submit to wives. The only basis for this view was that if wives could be induced to accept it, it saved trouble for their husbands. "The man is not of the woman, but the woman of the man; neither was the man created for the woman, but the woman for a man.". I defy anyone to find any basis for this view, except that men have stronger muscles then women.

A large proportion of the human race, it is true, is obliged to work so hard in obtaining the necessaries that little energy is left over for the other purposes; but those whose livelihood is assured do not, on that account, cease to be active. Xerxes had no lack of food or raiment or wives at the time he embarked upon the Athenian expedition. Newton was certain of material comfort from the moment he became a Fellow of Trinity, but it was after this that he wrote the Principia. St. Francis and Ignatius Loyola had no need to found Orders to escape form want.

These were eminent men, but the same characteristic, in varying degrees, is to be found in all but a small exceptionally sluggish minority. Mrs. A, who is quite sure of her husband's success in business, and has no fear of the workhouse, likes to be better dressed than Mrs. B, although she could escape the danger of pneumonia at much less expense.

Some astronomers try to cheer us up in the moments of depression by assuring us that one fine day the sun will explode, and in the twinkling of an eye we shall all be turned into gas. I do not know whether this is going to happen, nor when it will happen if it does happen, but I think it's safe to say that if it does it will be a matter outside human control, and that even the best astronomers would be unable to prevent it. This is an extreme example and one, which is useless to think about, because there is no way in which human behaviour can be adopted to it.

It does, however, serve one purpose, which is to remind us that we are not gods. You may exclaim indignantly, "but I never thought we were!" No doubt, dear reader, you are not one of those who suffer from the most extreme follies of our age, for if you were, you would not be one of my readers. But if you consider the Politbureau or the American technocrats you will see that there are those who escape atheism by impiously imagining themselves on the throve of Almighty.

Mass hysteria is a phenomenon not confined to human beings; it may be seen in any gregarious species. I once saw a photograph of a large herd of wild elephants in Central Africa Seeing an airplane for the first time, and all in a state of wild collective terror.

The elephant, at most times, is calm and sagacious beast, but this unprecedented phenomenon of a noisy, unknown animal in the sky, had thrown the whole herd completely off its balance. Each separate animal was terrifies, and its terror communicated itself to the others, creating a vast multiplication of panic. As, however, there were no journalists among them, the terror died down when the airplane was out of sight.

The criminal law has, from the point of view of thwarted virtue, the merit of allowing an outlet for those impulses of aggression which cowardice, disguised as morality, restrains in their more spontaneous forms. War has the same merit. You must not kill you neighbour, whom perhaps you genuinely hate, but by a little propaganda this hate can be transferred to some foreign nation, against whom all your murderous impulses become patriotic heroism

If you ask a modern anti-Semite why he dislikes Jews, he will tell you that they are unscrupulous and sharp in business and merciless to their debtors; he will tell you that they are always on the make, always intriguing, always supporting each other against gentile competitors. If you say you have sometimes found similar characteristics among Christians, the anti-Semite will say: "Oh, of course I don't deny there are ruffians who are not Jews. And I have some very good friends among Jews. But I am speaking of the average." If you question him when he is off his guard, you will find that whenever a Jew engages in a bit of share practice he says, "how like a Jew," but when a Gentile does likewise he says "and, you know, the astonishing thing is that he is not a Jew." This is not a scientific method of arriving at averages.

Young men and young women meet each other with much less difficulty than was formerly the case, and every housemaid expects at least once a week as much excitement as would have lasted a Jane Austen heroine throughout a whole novel.

Everybody has had at some time nightmares of falling, which seem to suggest an origin in the lives of our arboreal ancestors, though this perhaps is fanciful. Hymns and myths tend to speak of refuges from storm and of images of water in parched land. Moses striking the rock makes a universal appeal, even to those who have never been very thirsty. Hymns represent heaven as a refuge from the storms of life, not as a place where one escapes the dangers of being run over by a motor-bus, although the latter danger is much more frequent experience in modern life.

Now, apart from the arguments as to the proved fallibility of memory, there is one awkward consideration, which the skeptic may urge. Remembering, which occurs now, cannot possibly- he may say- prove that what is remember occur at some other time, because the world might have sprung into being five minutes ago, exactly as it then was, full of acts of remembering which were entirely misleading. Opponents of Darwin, such as Edmund Gosse's father, urged a very similar argument against evolution. the world, they said, was created in 4004 B.C., complete with fossils, which were inserted to try our faith. The world was created suddenly, but was made such as it would have been if it had evolved. there is no logical impossibility about this view. And similarly there is no logical impossibility in the view that the world was created five minutes ago, complete with memories and records. They may seem and improbable hypothesis, but it is not logically refutable.

If I wish to travel by plane to New York, the reason tells me that it is better to take a plane which is going to New York, than one which is going to Constantinople. I suppose that ones who think me unduly rational, consider that I ought to become so agitated at the airport as to jump into the first plane that I see, and when it lands me at Constantinople I ought to curse the people among whom I find myself for being Turks and not American. This would be fine, full-blooded way of behaving, and would, I suppose, meet with the commendation of my critics.

My first advice (on how not to grow old) would be to choose you ancestors carefully. although both my parents died young, I have done well in this respect as regards my other ancestors. My maternal grandfather, it is true, was cut off in the flower of his youth, at the age of sixty-seven, but my other three grandparents all lived to be over eighty. Of remoter ancestors I can only discover one who did not live to a great age, and he died of a disease which is now rare, namely, having his head cut off.

The difference between mind and brain is not a difference of quality, but a difference of arrangement. It is like the difference between arranging people in geographical order or in alphabetical order, both of which are done in the post office directory.

The same people are arranged in both cases, but in different contexts. In like manner, the context of visual sensation for physics is physical, and outside the brain. Going backwards, it takes you to the eye, and thence to a photon and thence to a quantum transition in some distant object. The context of visual sensation for psychology is quite different. Suppose, for example, the visual sensation is tat of a telegram saying that you are ruined. A number of events will take place in your mind in accordance with the laws of physical causation, and it may be quite a long time before there is any purely physical effect, such as tearing your hair or exclaiming "Woe is me!"

BERTRAND RUSSELL'S BEST - RELIGION

I observe that a very large portion of the human race does not believe in God and suffers no visible punishment in consequence. And if there were a God, I think it very unlikely that he would have such an uneasy vanity as to be offended by those who doubt his existence.

Although we are taught the Copernican astronomy in our textbooks, it has not yet penetrated to our religion or our morals, and has not even succeeded in destroying belief in astrology. People still think that the Divine Plan has special reference to human beings, and that a special Providence not only looks after the good, but also punishes the wicked. I am sometimes shocked by the blasphemies of those who think themselves pious-for instance, the nuns who never take a bath without wearing a bathrobe all the time. When asked why, since no man can see them, they reply: 'Oh, but you forget the good God.' Apparently, they conceive of the Deity as a Peeping Tom, whose omnipotence enables Him to see through bathroom walls, but who is foiled by bathrobes. This view strikes me as curious.

Christians hold that their faith does good, but other faiths do harm. At any rate, they hold this about the Communist faith. What I wish to maintain is that all faiths do harm. We may define 'faith' as a firm belief in something for which there is no evidence. When there is evidence, no one speaks of 'faith.' We do not speak of faith that two and two are four or that the earth is round. We only speak of faith when we wish to substitute emotion for evidence.

The Church attacked the habit of the bath on the ground that everything which makes the body more attractive tends towards sin Dirt was praised and the odor of sanctity became more and more penetrating. 'The purity of the body and its garments,' said St. Paula, 'means the impurity of the soul.' (Havelock Ellis, Studies in the Psychology of Sex, Vol. IV, p. 31.) Lice were called the pearls of God, and to be covered with them was an indispensable mark of a holy man.

Since evolution became fashionable, the glorification of Man has taken a new form. We are told that evolution has been guided by one great Purpose: through the millions of years when there were only slime, or trilobites, throughout the ages of dinosaurs and giant ferns, of bees and wild flowers, God was preparing the Great Climax. At last, in the fullness of time, He produced Man, including such specimens as Nero and Caligula, Hitler and Mussolini, whose transcendent glory justified the long painful process. For my part, I find even eternal damnation less incredible, certainly less ridiculous, than this lame and impotent conclusion which we are asked to admire as the supreme effort of Omnipotence.

Mankind... are a mistake. The universe would be sweeter and fresher without them. When the morning dew sparkles like diamonds in the rising sun of a September morning, there is beauty and exquisite purity in each blade of grass, and it is dreadful to think of this beauty being beheld by sinful eyes, which smirch its loveliness with their sordid and cruel ambitions. I cannot understand how God, who sees this loveliness, can have tolerated so long the baseness of those who boast blasphemously that they have been made in His image. Perhaps... it may yet fall to my lot to be the more thoroughgoing instrument of the Divine Purpose, which was carried out half-heartedly in the days of Noah.

It is not by prayer and humility that you cause things to go as you wish, but by acquiring a knowledge of natural laws. The power you acquire in this way is much greater and more reliable than that formerly supposed to be acquired by prayer, because you never could tell whether your prayer would be favorably heard in Heaven. The power of prayer, moreover, had recognized limits; it would have been impious to ask too much. But the power of science has no known limits. We were told that faith could remove mountains, but no one believed it; we are now told that the atomic bomb can remove mountains, and everyone believes it.

According to St. Thomas, the soul is not transmitted with the semen, but is created afresh with each man. There is, it is true, a difficulty: when a man is born out of wedlock, this seems to make God an accomplice in adultery. This objection, however, is only specious.

There is a grave objection which troubled St. Augustine, and that is as to the transmission of original sin. It is the soul that sins, and if the soul is not transmitted, but created afresh, how can it inherit the sin of Adam? This is not discussed by St. Thomas.

I am constantly asked: What can you, with your cold rationalism, offer to the seeker after salvation that is comparable to the cozy homelike comfort of a fenced dogmatic creed? To this the answer is many-sided. In the first place, I do not say that I can offer as much happiness as is to be obtained by the abdication of reason. I do not say that I can offer as much happiness as is to be obtained from drink or drugs or amassing great wealth by swindling widows and orphans. It is not the happiness of the individual convert that concerns me; it is the happiness of mankind. If you genuinely desire the happiness of mankind, certain forms of ignoble personal happiness are not open to you.

If your child is ill, and you are a conscientious parent, you accept medical diagnosis, however doubtful and discouraging; if you accept the cheerful opinion of a quack and your child consequently dies, you are not excused by the pleasantness of belief in the quack while it lasted. If everything must have a cause, then God must have a cause.

If there can be anything without a cause, it may just as well be the world as God, so that there cannot be any validity in that argument. It is exactly of the same nature as the Indian's view, that the world rested upon an elephant and the elephant rested upon a tortoise; and when they said, 'How about the tortoise?' the Indian said, 'Suppose we change the subject.' The argument is really no better than that.

The agnostic is not quite so certain as some Christians are as to what is good and what is evil. He does not hold, as most Christians in the past held, that people who disagree with the Government on abstruse points of theology ought to suffer a painful death. He is against persecution, and rather chary of moral condemnation. As for 'sin,' he thinks it not a useful notion. He admits, of course, that some kinds of conduct are desirable and some undesirable, but he holds that the punishment of undesirable kinds is only to be commended when it is deterrent or reformatory, not when it is inflicted because it is thought a good thing on its own account that the wicked should suffer. It was this belief in vindictive punishment that made men accept hell. This is part of the harm done by the notion of 'sin.'

It was geology, Darwin, and the doctrine of evolution, that first upset the faith of British men of science. If man was evolved by insensible gradations from lower forms of life, a number of things became very difficult to understand. At what moment in evolution did our ancestors acquire free will? At what stage in the long journey from the ameba did they begin to have immortal souls? When did they first become capable of the kinds of wickedness that would justify a benevolent Creator in sending them into eternal torment? Most people felt that such punishment would be hard on monkeys, in spite of their propensity for throwing coconuts at the heads of Europeans. But how about Pithecanthropus Erectus? Was it really he who ate the apple? Or was it Homo Pekiniensis?

There is something feeble and a little contemptible about a man who cannot face the perils of life without the help of comfortable myths. Almost inevitably some part of him is aware that they are myths and that he believes them only because they are comforting. But he dare not face this thought! Moreover, since he is aware, however dimly, that his opinions are not rational, he becomes furious when they are disputed.

What Galileo and Newton had done for astronomy Darwin did for biology. The adaptations of animals and plants to their environments were a favorite theme of pious naturalists in the eighteenth and early nineteenth centuries. These adaptations were explained by the Divine Purpose. It is we that the explanation was sometimes a little odd. If rabbits were theologians, they might think the exquisite adaptation of weasels to the killing of rabbits hardly a matter for thankfulness. And there was a conspiracy of silence about the tapeworm.

I do not understand where the 'beauty' and 'harmony' of nature are supposed to be found. Throughout the animal kingdom, animals ruthlessly prey upon each other. Most of them are either cruelly killed by other animals or slowly die of hunger. For my part, I am unable to see any very great beauty or harmony in the tapeworm. Let it not be said that this creature is sent as a punishment for our sins, for it is more prevalent among animals than among humans. I suppose what is meant by this 'beauty' and 'harmony' are such things as the beauty of the starry heavens. But one should remember that the stars every now and again explode and reduce everything in their neighbourhood to a vague mist.

One of the last questions discussed by St. Thomas in book four is the resurrection of the body. Here, as elsewhere, Aquinas states very fairly the arguments that have been brought against orthodox position. One of these, at first sight, offers great difficulties. What is to happen, asks the Saint, to a man who never, throughout his life, ate anything but human flesh, and whose parents did likewise? It would seem unfair to his victims that they should be deprived of their bodies at the last day as a consequence of his greed; yet, if not, what will be left to make up his body? I am happy to say that this difficulty which might at first sight seem insuperable, is triumphantly met.

The identity of the body, St. Thomas points out, is not dependent on the persistence of the same material particles; during life, by the processes of eating and digesting, the matter composing the body undergoes perpetual change. The cannibal may, therefore, receive the same body at the resurrection, even if it is not composed of the same matter as was in his body when he died. With this comforting thought we may. end our abstract of the Summa contra Gentiles.

There is little of the true philosophic spirit in Aquinas. He does not, like the Platonic Socrates, set out to follow wherever the argument may lead. He is not engaged in an inquiry, the result of which it is impossible to know m advance. Before he begins to philosophize, he already knows the truth; it is declared in the Catholic faith. If he can find apparently rational arguments for some parts of the faith, so much the better; if he cannot, he need only fall back on revelation. The finding of arguments for a conclusion given I in advance is not philosophy, but special pleading.

The raw fruits of the earth were made for human sustenance. Even the white tails of rabbits, according to some theologians, have a purpose, namely to make it easier for sportsmen to shoot them. There are, it is I true, some inconveniences: lions and tigers are too l fierce, the summer is too hot, and the winter too cold. But these things only began after Adam ate the apple; I before that, all animals were vegetarians, and the season was always spring. If only Adam had been content with peaches and nectarines, grapes and pears and pineapples, these blessings would still be ours.

According to St. Thomas, astrology is to be rejected, for the usual reasons. In answer to the question 'Is there such a thing as fate?' Aquinas replies that we might give the name 'fate' to the order impressed by Providence, but it is wiser not to do so, as 'fate' is a pagan word. This leads to an argument that prayer is useful although Providence is unchangeable (I have failed to follow this argument), God sometimes works miracles, but no one else can. Magic, however, is possible with the help of demons; this is not properly miraculous, and is not by the help of the stars.

How far has the American outlook on life and the world influenced Europe, and how far is it likely to do so? And first of all: What is the distinctively American outlook? And what, in comparison, is the distinctively European outlook? Traditionally, the European outlook may be said to be derived from astronomy.

When Abraham watched his flocks by night, he observed the stars in their courses: they moved with a majestic regularity utterly remote from human control. When the Lord answered Job out of the whirlwind, He said: 'Canst thou bind the sweet influences of Pleiades, or loose the bands of Orion?' The reply was in the negative. Even more relevant is the question: 'Knowest thou the ordinances of heaven? Canst thou set the dominion thereof in the earth?' To which Job answered: 'Behold, I am vile; what shall I answer thee? I will lay my hand upon my mouth.' The conclusion is that man is a feeble creature, to whom only submission and worship are becoming. Pride is insolence, and belief in human power is impiety.

Nature, it is true, still sees to it that we are mortal, but with the progress in medicine it will become more and more common for people to live until they have had their fill of life. We are supposed to wish to live forever and to look forward to the unending joys of heaven, of which, by miracle, the monotony will never grow stale. But in fact, if you question any candid person who is no longer young, he is very likely to tell you that, having tasted life in this world, he has no wish to begin again as a 'new boy' in another.

We read in the Old Testament that it was a religious duty to exterminate conquered races completely, and that to spare even their cattle and sheep was an impiety. Dark terrors and misfortunes in the life to come oppressed the Egyptians and Etruscans, but never reached their full development until the victory of Christianity.

Gloomy saints who abstained from all pleasures of sense, who lived in solitude in the desert, denying themselves meat and wine and the society of women, were, nevertheless, not obliged to abstain from all pleasures. The pleasures of the mind were considered to be superior to those of the body, and a high place among the pleasures of the mind was assigned to the contemplation of the eternal tortures to which the pagans and heretics would hereafter be subjected.

The standpoint of modern liberal theologians is well set forth by Dr. Tennant in his book The Concept of Sin. to him sin consists in acts of will that are in conscious opposition to a known law, the moral law being known by Revelation as God's will. It follows that a man destitute of religion cannot sin.

One occasion for theological intervention to prevent the mitigation of human suffering was the discovery of anesthetics. Simpson, in 1847, recommended their use in childbirth, and was immediately reminded by the clergy that God said to Eve: 'In sorrow shalt thou bring forth children' (Gen. id. 16). And how could she sorrow if she was under the influence of chloroform? Simpson succeeded in proving that there was no harm in giving anesthetics to men, because God put Adam into a deep sleep when He extracted his rib. But male ecclesiastics remained unconvinced as regards the sufferings of women, at any rate in childbirth.

The conception of purpose is a natural one to apply to a human artificer A man who desires a house cannot, except in the Arabian Nights, have it rise before him as a result of his mere wish; time and labour must be expended before his wish can be gratified. But Omnipotence is subject to no such limitations.

If God really thinks well of the human race-an unplausible hypothesis, as it seems to me-why not proceed, as in Genesis, to create man at once? What was the point of the ichthyosaurs, dinosaurs, diplodochi, mastodons, and so on? Dr. Barnes himself confesses, somewhere, that the purpose of the tapeworm is a mystery What useful purpose is served by rabies and hydro phobia? It is no answer to say that the laws of nature inevitably produce evil as well as good, for God decreed the laws of nature.

The evil which is due to sin may be explained as the result of our free will, but the problem of evil in the pre-human world remains. I hardly think Dr. Barnes will accept the solution offered by William Gillespie, that the bodies of beasts of prey were inhabited by devils, whose first sins antedated the brute creation; yet it is difficult to see what other logically satisfying answer can be suggested. The difficulty is old, but none the less real. An omnipotent Being who created a world containing evil not due to sin must Himself be at least partially evil.

The Greek Church is blamed for denying the double

procession of the Holy Ghost and the supremacy of the Pope. We are warned that, although Christ was conceived of the Holy Ghost, we must not suppose that He was the son of the Holy Ghost according to the flesh.

Belief in God and a future life makes it possible to go through life with less of stoic courage than is needed by skeptics. A great many young people lose faith in these dogmas at an age at which despair is easy, and thus have to face a much more intense unhappiness than that which falls to the lot of those who have never had a religious upbringing. Christianity offers reasons for not fearing death or the universe, and in so doing it fails to teach adequately the virtue of courage.

The craving for religious faith being largely an outcome of fear, the advocates of faith tend to think that certain kinds of fear are not to be deprecated. In this, to my mind, they are gravely mistaken. To allow oneself to entertain pleasant beliefs as a means of avoiding fear is not to live in the best way. In so far as religion makes its appeal to fear, it is lowering to human dignity.

The whole conception of God is a conception derived from the ancient Oriental despotisms. It is a conception quite unworthy of free men. When you hear people in church debasing themselves and saying that they are miserable sinners, and all the rest of it, it seems contemptible and not worthy of self-respecting human beings. We ought to stand up and look the world frankly in the face.

We ought to make the best we can of the world, and if it is not so good as we wish, after all it will still be better than what these others have made of it in all these ages. A good world needs knowledge, kindliness, and courage; it does not need a regretful hankering after the past, or a fettering of the free intelligence by the words uttered long ago by ignorant men.

Religion is based, I think, primarily and mainly upon fear. It is partly the terror of the unknown, and partly the wish to feel that you have a kind of elder brother who will stand by you in all your troubles and disputes. Fear is the basis of the whole thing- fear of the mysterious, fear of defeat, fear of death.... Science can help us to get over this craven fear in which mankind has lived for so many generations. Science can teach us, and I think our own hearts can teach us, no longer to look round for imaginary supports, no longer to invent allies in the sky, but rather to look to our own efforts here below to make this world a fit place to live in, instead of the sort of place that the Churches in all these centuries have made it.

Owing to their miraculous powers, priests (in the eleventh century) could determine whether a man should spend eternity in heaven or in hell. If he died while excommunicated, he went to hell; if he died after priests had performed all the proper ceremonies, he would ultimately go to heaven provided he had duly repented and confessed. Before going to heaven, how ever, he would have to spend some time- perhaps a very long time- suffering the pains of purgatory. Priests could shorten this time by saying masses for his soul, which they were willing to do for a suitable money payment.

Sir James Jeans considers it very doubtful whether, at the present time, there is life anywhere else. Before the Copernican revolution, it was natural to suppose that God's purposes were especially concerned with the earth, but now this has become an unplausible hypothesis. If it is the purpose of the Cosmos to evolve mind, we must regard it as rather incompetent in having produced so little in such a long time.... If we accept the rather curious view that the Cosmic Purpose is specially concerned with our little planet, we still find that there is reason to doubt whether it intends quite what the theologians say it does. The earth (unless we use enough poison gas to destroy all life) is likely to remain habitable for some considerable time, but not for ever. Perhaps our atmosphere will gradually fly off into space; perhaps the tides will cause the earth to turn always the same face to the sun, so that one hemisphere will be too hot and the other too cold; perhaps (as in a moral tale by J. B. S. Haldane) the moon will tumble into the earth. If none of these things happen first, we shall in any case be all destroyed when the sun explodes and becomes a cold white dwarf, which, we are told by Jeans, is to happen in about a million years, though the exact date is still somewhat uncertain. A million years gives us some time to prepare for the end, and we may hope that in the meantime both astronomy and gunnery will have made considerable progress. The astronomers may have discovered another star with habitable planets, and the gunners may be able to fire us off off it with a speed approaching that of light, in which case, if the passengers were all young to begin with, some might arrive before dying of old age. It is perhaps a slender hope, but let us make the best of it.

I do not believe that a decay of dogmatic belief can do anything but good. I admit at once that new systems of dogma, such as those of the Nazis and the Communists, are even worse than the old systems, but they could never have acquired a hold over men's minds if orthodox dogmatic habits had not been instilled in youth.

Stalin's language is full of reminiscences of the theological seminary in which he received his training. What the world needs is not dogma, but an attitude of scientific inquiry, combined with a belief that the torture of millions is not desirable, whether inflicted by Stalin or by a Deity imagined in the likeness of the believer.

For four and a half months in 1918, I was in prison for pacifist propaganda; but, by the intervention of Arthur Balfour, I was placed in the first division, so that while in prison I was able to read and write as much as I liked, provided I did no pacifist propaganda. I found prison in many ways quite agreeable. I had no engagements, no difficult decisions to make, no fear of callers, no interruptions to my work. I read enormously; I wrote a book, Introduction to Mathematical Philosophy, and began the work for Analysis of Mind. I was rather interested in my fellow prisoners, who seemed to me in no way morally inferior to the rest of the population, though they were on the whole slightly below the usual level of intelligence, as was shown by their having been caught. For anybody not in the first division, especially for a person accustomed to reading and writing, prison is a severe and terrible punishment; but for me, thanks to Arthur Balfour, this was not so.

I was much cheered on my arrival by the warder at the gate, who had to take particulars about me. He asked my religion, and I replied 'agnostic.' He asked how to spell it, and remarked with a sigh: 'Well, there are many religions, but I suppose they all worship the same God.' This remark kept me cheerful for about a week.

The most influential school of philosophy in Britain at the present day maintains a certain linguistic doctrine to which I am unable to subscribe. I do not wish to misrepresent this school, but I suppose any opponent of any doctrine is thought to misrepresent it by those who hold it. The doctrine, as I understand it, consists in maintaining that the language of daily life, with words used in their ordinary meanings, suffices for philosophy, which has no need of technical terms or of changes in the signification of common terms.

I find myself totally unable to accept this view...Orthodox Christianity asserts that we survive death. What does it mean by this assertion? And in what sense, if any, is the assertion true? The philosophers with whom I am concerned will consider the first of these questions, but will say that the second is none of their business.

I agree entirely that, in this case, a discussion as to what is meant is important and highly necessary as a preliminary to a consideration of the substantial question, but if nothing can be said on the substantial question, it seems a waste of time to discuss what it means. These philosophers remind me of the shopkeeper of whom I once asked the shortest way to Winchester. He called to a man in the back premises:

"Gentleman wants to know the shortest way to Winchester."

"Winchester?" an unseen voice replied.

"Aye."

"Way to Winchester?"

"Aye."

"Shortest way?"

"Aye."

"Dunno."

He wanted to get the nature of the question clear, but took no interest in answering it. This is exactly what modern

philosophy does for the earnest seeker after truth. Is it surprising that young people turn to other studies?

Bertrand Russell's Best - Sex And Marriage

It is odd that neither the Church nor modern public opinion condemns petting, provided it stops short at a certain point. At what point sin begins is a matter as to which casuists differ. One eminently orthodox Catholic divine laid it down that a confessor may fondle a nun's breasts, provided he does it without evil intent. But I doubt whether modern authorities would agree with him on this point.

The phrase 'in the sight of God' puzzles me. One would suppose that God sees everything, but apparently, this is a mistake. He does not see Reno, for you cannot be divorced in the sight of God. Register offices are a doubtful point. I notic that respectable people, who would not call on anybody wh lives in open sin, are quite willing to call on people who ha had only a civil marriage; so apparently God does see regis offices.

Tolstoy and Mahatma Gandhi, in their old age, la down that all sexual intercourse is wicked, even in mar and with a view to offspring. The Manicheans tho likewise, relying upon men's native sinfulness to suppl with a continually fresh crop of disciples. This do however, is heretical, though it is equally heretical to m that marriage is as praiseworthy as celibacy. Tolsto tobacco almost as bad as sex; in one of his novels, a is contemplating murder smokes a cigarette first in generate the necessary homicidal fury. Tobacco, h not prohibited in the Scriptures, though, as Sam points out, St. Paul would no doubt have denour had known of it.

[According to St. Thomas] Divine Law dire God; also, in a lesser degree, our neighbou fornication, because the father should stay wi while the children are being reared. It forbids b being against nature; it does not, however, forbid life-long celibacy. Matrimony should

because the father is needed in the education of the children, both as more rational than the mother, and as having more physical strength when punishment is required.

Not all carnal intercourse is sinful, since it is natural; but to think the married state as good as continence is to fall into the heresy of Jovinian. There must be strict monogamy; polygamy is unfair to women, and polyandry makes paternity uncertain. Incest is to be forbidden because it would complicate family life. Against brother-sister incest there is a very curious argument: that if the love of husband and wife were combined with that of brother and sister, mutual attraction would be so strong as to cause unduly frequent intercourse.

St. Paul's views were emphasized and exaggerated by the early Church; celibacy was considered holy and men retired into the desert to wrestle with Satan while he filled their imaginations with lustful visions.

If the old morality is to be re-established, certain things are essential; some of them are already done, but experience shows that these alone are not effective. The first essential is that the education of girls should be such as to make them stupid and superstitious and ignorant; this requisite is already fulfilled in schools over which the churches have any control. The next requisite is a very severe censorship upon all books giving information on sex subjects; this condition also is oming to be fulfilled in England and in America, since the ensorship, without change in the law, is being tightened up y the increasing zeal of the police. These conditions, however, nce they exist already, are clearly insufficient.

The only thing that will suffice is to remove from young omen all opportunity of being alone with men: girls must forbidden to earn their living by work outside the home; y must never be allowed an outing unless accompanied by ir mother or an aunt; the regrettable practice of going to ces without a chaperon must be sternly stamped out. It t be illegal for an unmarried woman under fifty to possess otor-car, and perhaps it would be wise to subject all arried women once a month to medical examination by doctors, and to send to a penitentiary all such as were

found to be not virgins. The use of contraceptives must, of course, be eradicated, and it must be illegal in conversation with unmarried women to throw doubt upon the dogma of eternal damnation.

These measures, if carried out vigorously for a hundred years or more, may perhaps do something to stem the rising tide of immorality. I think, however, that in order to avoid the risk of certain abuses, it would be necessary that all policemen and all medical men should be castrated. Perhaps it would be wise to carry this policy a step further, in view of the inherent depravity of the male character.

I am inclined to think that moralists would be well advised to advocate that all men should be castrated, with the exception of ministers of religion since reading Elmer Gantry, I have begun to feel that even this exception is perhaps not quite wise.

Christianity, and more particularly St. Paul, introduced an entirely novel view of marriage, that it existed not primarily for the procreation of children, but to prevent the sin of fornication.... (I Cor. vii. 1-9.) St. Paul makes no mention whatever of children; the biological purpose of marriage appears to him wholly unimportant. This is quite natural, since he imagined that the Second Coming was imminent and that the world would soon come to an end. At the Second Coming men were to be divided into sheep and goats, and the only thing of real importance was to find oneself among the sheep on that occasion. St. Paul holds that sexual intercourse, even in marriage, is something of a handicap in the attempt to win salvation (I Cor. vii. 32-4). Nevertheless it is possible for married people to be saved, but fornication is deadly sin, and the unrepentant fornicator is sure to find himself among the goats.

I remember once being advised by a doctor to abandon the practice of smoking, and he said that I should find it easier if, whenever the desire came upon me, I proceeded to suck an acid drop. It is in this spirit that St. Paul recommends marriage. He does not suggest that it is quite as pleasant as fornication, but he thinks it may enable the weaker brethren to withstand temptation; he does not suggest for a moment that there may be any positive good in marriage, or that affection between husband and wife may be a beautiful and desirable thing, nor does he take the slightest interest in the family; fornication holds the center of the stage in his thoughts, and the whole of his sexual ethics is arranged with reference to it. It is just as if one where to maintain that the sole reason for baking bread is to prevent people from stealing cake.

The Puritans, in their determination to avoid the pleasures of sex, became somewhat more conscious than people had been before of the pleasures of the table. As a seventeenth-century critic of Puritanism says: "Would you enjoy gay nights and pleasant dinners? Then must you board with saints and bed with sinners." It would seem, therefore, that the Puritans did not succeed in subduing the purely corporeal part of our human nature, since what they took away from sex they added to gluttony. Gluttony is regarded by the Catholic Church as one of the seven deadly sins, and those who practice it are placed by Dante in one of the deeper circles of hell, but it is a somewhat vague sin, since it is hard to say where a legitimate interest in food ceases, and guilt begins to be incurred. Is it wicked to eat anything that is not nourishing? If so, with every salted almond we risk damnation.

Men have from time immemorial been allowed in practice, if not in theory, to indulge in illicit sexual relations. It has not been expected of a man that he should be a virgin on entering marriage, and even after marriage, infidelities are not viewed very gravely if they never come to the knowledge of a man's wife and neighbours.

The possibility of this system has depended upon prostitution. This institution, however, is one which it is difficult for a modern to defend, and few will suggest that women should acquire the same rights as men through the establishment of a class of male prostitutes for the satisfaction of women who wish, like their husbands, to seem virtuous without being so.... Every conventional moralist who takes the trouble to think it out will see that he is committed in practice to what is called the double standard, that is to say, the view that sexual virtue is more essential in a woman than in a man.

It is all very well to argue that his theoretical ethic demands continence of men also. To this there is the obvious retort that the demand cannot be enforced on the men since it is easy for them to sin secretly. The conventional moralist is thus committed against his will not only to an inequality as between men and women, but also to the view that it is better for a young man to have intercourse with prostitutes than with girls of his own class, in spite of the fact that with the latter, though not with the former, his relations are not mercenary and may be affectionate and altogether delightful.

Moralists, of course, do not think out the consequences of advocating a morality which they know will not be obeyed; they think that so long as they do not advocate prostitution they are not responsible for the fact that prostitution is the inevitable outcome of their teaching. This, however, is only another illustration of the well-known fact that the professional moralist in our day is a man of less than average intelligence.

The Catholic Church has not remained so unbiological as St. Paul and the hermits of the baid. From St. Paul one gathers that marriage is to be regarded solely as a more or less legitimate outlet for lust. One would not gather from his words that he would have any objection to birth control: on the contrary, one would be led to suppose that he would regard as dangerous the periods of continence involved in pregnancy and childbirth. The Church has taken a different view.

Marriage in the orthodox Christian doctrine has two purposes: one. that recognized by St. Paul, the other, the procreation of children. The consequence has been to make sexual morality even more difficult than it was made by St. Paul. Not only is sexual intercourse only legitimate within marriage, but even between husband and wife it becomes a sin unless it is hoped that it will lead to pregnancy. The desire for legitimate offspring is, in fact, according to the Catholic Church, the only motive which can justify sexual intercourse. But this motive always justifies it, no matter what cruelty may accompany it.

If the wife hates sexual intercourse, if she is likely to die of another pregnancy, if the child is likely to be diseased or insane, if there is not enough money to prevent the utmost extreme of misery, that does not prevent the man from being justified in insisting on his conjugal rights, provided only that he hopes to beget a child. The view of the orthodox moralist (this includes the police and the magistrates, but hardly any modern educators) on the question of sex knowledge may, I fancy, be fairly stated as follows.... There is no doubt that sexual misconduct is promoted by sexual thoughts, and that the best road to virtue is to keep the young occupied in mind and body with matters wholly unconnected with sex. They must, therefore, be told nothing whatever about sex; they must as far as possible be prevented from talking about it with each other, and grownups must pretend that there is no such topic. It is possible by these means to keep a girl in ignorance until the night of her marriage, when it is to be expected that the facts will so shock her as to produce exactly that attitude towards sex which every sound moralist considers desirable in women. Catholic teaching... has a two-fold basis; it rests, on the one hand, upon the asceticism which we already find in St. Paul, on the other, upon the view that it is good to bring into the world as many souls as possible, since every soul is capable of salvation. For some reason which I do not understand, the fact that souls are equally capable of damnation is not taken into account, and yet it seems quite as relevant.

Catholics, for example, use their political influence to prevent Protestants from practicing birth control, and yet they must hold that the great majority of Protestant children whom their political action causes to exist will endure eternal torment in the next world. This makes their action seem somewhat unkind, but doubtless these are mysteries which the profane cannot hope to understand. Within the monogamic family there are many varieties. Marriages may be decided by the parties themselves or by their parents. In some countries the bride is purchased; in others, e.g. France, the bridegroom.

Then there may be all kinds of differences as regards divorce, from the Catholic extreme, which permits no divorce, to the law of old China, which permitted a man to divorce his wife for being a chatterbox. Constancy or quasi-constancy in sex relations arises among animals, as well as among human beings, where, for the preservation of the species, the participation of the male is necessary for the rearing of the young. Birds, for example, have to sit upon their eggs continuously to keep them warm, and also have to spend a good many hours of the day getting food. To do both is, among many species, impossible for one bird, and therefore male co-operation is essential.

The consequence is that most birds are models of virtue. Among human beings the co-operation of the father is a great biological advantage to the offspring, especially in unsettled times and among turbulent populations; but with the growth of modern civilization the role of the father is being increasingly taken over by the State, and there is reason to think that a father may cease before long to be biologically advantageous, at any rate in the wage-earning class. If this should occur, we must expect a complete breakdown of traditional morality, since there will no longer be any reason why a mother should wish the paternity of her child to be indubitable. Plato would have us go a step further, and put the State not only in place of the father but in that of the mother also. I am not myself sufficiently an admirer of the State, or sufficiently impressed with the delights of orphan asylums, to be enthusiastic in favor of this scheme.

Malinowski found it quite impossible, in spite of his best argumentative efforts, to persuade his friends on the islands that there is such a thing as paternity. They regarded this as a silly story invented by the missionaries. Christianity is a patriarchal religion, and cannot be made emotionally or intellectually intelligible to people who do not recognize fatherhood. Instead of 'God the Father' it would be necessary to speak of 'God the Maternal Uncle,' but this does not give quite the right shade of meaning, since fatherhood implies both power and love, whereas in Melanesia the maternal uncle has the power and the father has the love.

The idea that men are God's children is one, which cannot be conveyed to the Trobriand Islanders, since they do not think that anybody is the child of any male. Consequently, missionaries are compelled to tackle first the facts of physiology before they can go on to preach their religion. One gathers from Malinowksi that they have had no success in this initial task, and have, therefore, been quite unable to proceed to the teaching of the Gospel.

Cruelty is in theory a perfectly adequate ground for divorce, but it may be interpreted so as to become absurd. When the most eminent of all film stars was divorced by his wife for cruelty, one of the counts in the proof of cruelty was that he used to bring home friends who talked about Kant. I can hardly suppose that it was the intention of the California legislators to enable any woman to divorce her husband on the ground that he was sometimes guilty of intelligent conversation in her presence.

The need for prostitution arises from the fact that many men are either unmarried or away from their wives on journeys, that such men are not content to remain continent, and that in a conventionally virtuous community they do not find respectable women available. Society therefore sets apart a certain class of women for the satisfaction of those masculine needs which it is ashamed to acknowledge yet afraid to leave wholly unsatisfied.

The prostitute has the advantage, not only that she is available at a moment's notice, but that, having no life outside her profession, she can remain hidden without difficulty, and the man who has been with her can return to his wife, his family, and his church with unimpaired dignity. She, however, poor woman, in spite of the undoubted service she performs, in spite of the fact that she safeguards the virtues of wives and daughters and the apparent virtue of church-wardens, is universally despised, thought to be an outcast, and not allowed to associate with ordinary people except in the way of business. This blazing injustice began with the victory of the Christian religion; and has been continued ever since.

Missionaries may argue that the superiority of the Christian code is known by revelation. The philosopher however, must observe that other religions make the same claim... the Manicheans thought it wicked to eat any animal food except fish, but many sects have considered this exception an abomination. The Dukhobors refused military service, but held it proper to dance naked all together round a camp fire; being persecuted for the former tenet in Russia, they emigrated to Canada, where they were persecuted for the latter. The Mormons had a divine revelation in favor of polygamy, but under pressure from the United States Government they discovered that the revelation was not binding.

The recognition of children as one of the purposes of marriage is very partial in Catholic doctrine. It exhausts itself in drawing the inference that intercourse not intended to lead to children is sin. It has never gone so far as to permit the dissolution of a marriage on the ground of sterility. However ardently a man may desire children, if it happens that his wife is barren, he has no remedy in Christian ethics. The fact is that the positive purpose of marriage, namely procreation, plays a very subordinate part, and its main purpose remains, as with St. Paul, the prevention of sin. Fornication still holds the center of the stage, and marriage is still regarded essentially as a somewhat less regrettable alternative.

It is permissible with certain precautions to speak in print of coitus, but it is not permissible to employ the monosyllabic synonym for this word. This has recently been decided in the case of Sleeveless Errand Sometimes this prohibition of simple language has grave consequences; for example, Mr.s. Sanger's pamphlet on birth control, which is addressed to working women, was declared obscene on the ground that working women could understand it.

Dr. Marie Stopes's books, on the other hand, are not illegal, because their language can only be understood by persons with a certain amount of education. The consequence is that, while it is permissible to teach birth control to the well-to do, it is criminate to teach it to wage-earners and their wives. I commend this fact to the notice of the Eugenic Society, which is perpetually bewailing the fact that wage-earners breed faster than middle-class people, while carefully abstaining from any attempt to change the state of the law which is the cause of this fact. The commonest objection to birth control is that it is against 'nature.' (For some reason we are not allowed to say that celibacy is against nature; the only reason I can think of is that it is not new.) Malthus saw only three ways of keeping down the population: moral restraint, vice, and misery. Moral restraint, he admitted, was not likely to be practiced on a large scale. 'Vice,' i.e., birth control, he, as a clergyman, viewed with abhorrence. There remained misery. In his comfortable parsonage, he contemplated the misery of the great majority of mankind with equanimity, and pointed out the fallacies of the reformers who hoped to alleviate it.

Very few men or women who have had a conventional upbringing have learnt to feel decently about sex and marriage. Their education has taught them that deceitfulness and lying are considered virtues by parents and teachers; that sexual relations, even within marriage, are more or less disgusting, and that in propagating the species men are yielding to their animal nature while women are submitting to a painful duty. This attitude has made marriage unsatisfying both to men and to women, and the lack of instinctive satisfaction has turned to cruelty masquerading as morality.

A boy should be taught that in no circumstances is conversation on sexual subjects permissible, not even in marriage. This increases the likelihood that when he marries he will give his wife a disgust of sex and thus preserve her from the risk of adultery.

Sex outside marriage is sin; sex within marriage is not sin, since it is necessary to the propagation of the human species, but is a disagreeable duty imposed on man as a punishment for the Fall, and to be undertaken in the same spirit in which one submits to a surgical operation. Unfortunately, unless great pains are taken, the sexual act tends to be associated with pleasure, but by sufficient moral care this can be prevented, at any rate in the female. It is illegal in England to state in print that a wife can and should derive sexual pleasure from intercourse. (I have myself heard a pamphlet condemned as obscene in a court of law on this among other grounds.) It is on the above outlook in regard to sex that the attitude of the law, the Church, and the old-fashioned educators of the young is based.

Sex relations as a dignified, rational, wholehearted activity in which the complete personality co-operates, do not often, I think, occur in America outside marriage. To this extent the moralists have been successful. They have not prevented fornication; on the contrary, if anything, their opposition, by making it spicy, has made it more common. But they have succeeded in making it almost as undesirable as they say it is, just as they have succeeded in making much of the alcohol consumed as poisonous as they assert all alcohol to be.

They have compelled young people to take sex neat, divorced from daily companionship, from a common work, and from all psychological intimacy. The more timid of the young do not go so far as complete sexual relations, but content themselves with producing prolonged states of sexual excitement without satisfaction, which are nervously debilitating, and calculated to make the full enjoyment of sex at a later date difficult or impossible.

Most men and women, given suitable conditions, will feel passionate love at some period of their lives. For the inexperienced, however, it is very difficult to distinguish passionate love from mere sex hunger; especially is this the case with well-brought-up girls, who have been taught that they could not possibly like to kiss a man unless they loved him.

If a girl is expected to be a virgin when she marries, it will very often happen that she is trapped by a transient and trivial sex attraction, which a woman with sexual experience could easily distinguish from love. This has undoubtedly been a frequent cause of unhappy marriages. Even where mutual love exists, it may be poisoned by the belief of one or both that it is sinful. This belief may, of course, be well founded. Parnell, for example, undoubtedly sinned in committing adultery, since he thereby postponed the fulfillment of the hopes of Ireland for many years.

Peasant children early become accustomed to what are called the facts of life, which they can observe not only among human beings but among animals. They are thus saved from both ignorance and fastidiousness. The carefully educated children of the well-to-do, on the contrary, are shielded from all practical knowledge of sexual matters, and even the most modern parents, who teach children out of books, do not give them that sense of practical familiarity which the peasant child early acquires. The triumph of Christian teaching is when a man and woman marry without either having had previous sexual experience.

Bertrand Russell's Best - Education

Man, it would seem, has descended from arboreal apes. They lived a happy life in tropical forests, eating coconuts when they were hungry, and throwing them at each other when they were not. They were perpetually occupied in gymnastics, and acquired an agility, which to us is truly astonishing. But after some millions of years of this arboreal paradise, their numbers increased to the point where the supply of coconuts was no longer adequate. The population problem set in, and was dealt with in two different ways: those who lived in the middle of the forest learned to throw coconuts with such accuracy as to disable adversaries, whose consequent death relieved the pressure of population, but those who lived on the edge of the forest found another method: they looked out over the fields and discovered that they yielded delicious fruits of venous kinds quite as pleasant as coconuts, and gradually they came down from the trees and spent more and more time in the open on the ground... they soon discovered that if you live on the ground it is easy to pick up stones, which are more effective missiles than coconuts.

I am not myself in any degree ashamed of having changed my opinions. What physicist who was already active in 1900 would dream of boasting that his opinions had not changed during the last half century? In science men change their opinions when new knowledge becomes available, but philosophy in the minds of many is assimilated rather to theology than to science. A theologian proclaims eternal truths. The creeds remain unchanged since the Council of Nicaea.

Where nobody knows anything, there is no point in changing your mind.

Owing to the identification of religion with virtue, together with the fact that the most religious men are not the most intelligent, a religious education gives courage to the stupid to resist the authority of educated men, as has happened, for example, where the teaching of evolution has been made illegal. So far as I can remember, there is not one word in the Gospels in praise of intelligence; and in this respect ministers of religion follow gospel authority more closely than in some others.

If you think that your belief is based upon reason, you will support it by argument, rather than by persecution, and will abandon it if the argument goes against you. But if your belief is based on faith, you will realize that argument is useless, and will therefore resort to force either in the form of persecution or by stunting and distorting the minds of the young in what is called 'education.' This last is peculiarly dastardly since it takes advantage of the defenselessness of immature minds. Unfortunately it is practiced in a greater or less degree in the schools of every civilized country.

Punctuality is a quality the need of which is bound up with social co-operation. It has nothing to do with the relation of the soul to God, or with mystic insight, or with any of the matters with which the more elevated and spiritual moralists are concerned. One would be surprised to find a saint getting drunk, but one would not be surprised to find him late for an engagement And yet in the ordinary business of life punctuality is absolutely necessary.

To modern educated people, it seems obvious that matters of fact are to be ascertained by observation, not by consulting ancient authorities. But this is an entirely modern conception, which hardly existed before the seventeenth century. Aristotle maintained that women have fewer teeth than men; although he was twice married, it never occurred to him to verify this statement by examining his wives' mouths. He said also that children would be healthier if conceived when the wind is in the north.

One gathers that the two Mr.s. Aristotles both had to run out and look at the weathercock every evening before going to bed. He states that a man bitten by a mad dog will not go mad, but any other animal will; that the bite of the shrewmouse is dangerous to horses, especially if the mouse is pregnant; that elephants suffering from insomnia can be cured by rubbing their shoulders with salt, olive oil, and warm water and so on and so on. Nevertheless, classical dons, who have never observed any animal except the cat and the dog, continue to praise Aristotle for his fidelity to observation.

It is not altogether true that persuasion is one thing and force is another. Many forms of persuasion, even many of which everybody approves, are really a kind of force. Consider what we do to our children. We do not say to them: 'Some people think the earth is round, and others think it flat; when you grow up, you can, if you like, examine the evidence and form your own conclusion.' Instead of this we say: 'The earth is round.' By the time our children are old enough to examine the evidence, our propaganda has closed their minds, and the most persuasive arguments of the Flat Earth Society make no impression. The same applies to the moral precepts that we consider really important, such as 'don't pick your nose' or 'don't eat peas with a knife., There may, for ought I know, be admirable reasons for eating peas with a knife, but the hypnotic effect of early persuasion has made me completely incapable of appreciating them.

In universities, mathematics is taught mainly to men who are going to teach mathematics to men who are going to teach mathematics to.... Sometimes, it is true, there is an escape from this treadmill. Archimedes used mathematics to kill Romans, Galileo to improve 3 the Grand Duke of Tuscany's artillery, modern physicists (grown more ambitious) to exterminate the human race. It is usually on this account that the study of mathematics is commended to the general public as worthy of State support.

Until the time of Galileo, astronomers, following Aristotle, believed that everything in the heavens, from the moon upwards, is unchanging and incorruptible Since Laplace, no reputable astronomer has held this view. Nebulae, stars, and planets, we now believe, have all developed gradually. Some stars, for instance the companion of Sirius, are 'dead'; they have at some time undergone a cataclysm which has enormously diminished the amount of light and heat radiating from them. Our own planet, in which philosophers are apt to take a parochial and excessive interest, was once too hot to support life, and will in time be too cold. After ages during which the earth produced harmless trilobites and butterflies, evolution progressed to the point at which it generated Neros, Genghis Khans, and Hitters. This, however, is a passing nightmare; in time the earth will become again incapable of supporting life, and peace will return.

Generalizing, we may say that Dr. Dewey, like everyone else, divides beliefs into two classes, of which one is good and the other bad. He holds, however, that a belief may be good at one time and bad at another. A belief about some event in the past is to be classified as 'good' or 'bad,' not according to whether the event really took place, but according to the future effects of the belief.

The results are curious. Suppose somebody says to me: 'Did you have coffee with your breakfast this morning?' If I am an ordinary person, I shall try to remember. But if I am a disciple of Dr. Dewey I shall say: 'Wait a while; I must try two experiments before I can tell you.' I shall, then, first make myself believe that I had coffee, and observe the consequences, if any; I shall then make myself believe that I did not have coffee, and again observe the consequences, if any. I shall then compare the two sets of consequences, to see which I found the more satisfactory.

If there is a balance on one side I shall decide for that answer. If there is not, I shall have to confess that I cannot answer the question. But this is not the end of our trouble. How am I to know the consequences of believing that I had coffee for breakfast? If I say 'the consequences are such-and such,' this in turn will have to be tested by its consequences before I can know whether what I have said was a 'good' or a 'bad' statement. And even if this difficulty were overcome, how am I to judge which set of consequences is the more satisfactory? One decision as to whether I had coffee may fill me with contentment, the other with determination to further the war effort. Each of these may be considered good, but until I have decided which is better I cannot tell whether I had coffee for breakfast.

The date of the creation of the world (according to the orthodox view) can be inferred from the genealogies in Genesis, which tell how old each patriarch was when his oldest son was born. Some margin of controversy was permissible, owing to certain ambiguities and to differences between the Septuagint and the Hebrew text; but in the end Protestant Christendom generally accepted the date 4004 B.C., fixed by Archbishop Usher.

Dr. Lightfoot, Vice-Chancellor of the University of Cambridge, who accepted this date for the Creation, thought that a careful study of Genesis made even greater precision possible; the creation of man, according to him, took place at 9.00 A.M. on October 23rd. This, however, has never been an article of faith; you might believe, without risk of heresy, that Adam and Eve came into existence on October 16th or October 30th, provided your reasons were derived from Genesis. The day of the week was, of course, known to have been Friday, since God rested on the Saturday.

The first German to take notice of Hume was Immanuel Kant, who had been content, up to the age of about forty-five, with the dogmatic tradition derived from Leibniz. Then, as he says himself, Hume 'awakened him from his dogmatic slumbers.' After meditating for twelve years, he produced his great work, the Critique of Pure Reason; seven years later, at the age of sixty-four, he produced the Critique of Practical Reason, in which he resumed his dogmatic slumbers after nearly twenty years of uncomfortable wakefulness.

Children are made to learn bits of Shakespeare by heart, with the result that ever after they associate him with pedantic boredom. If they could meet him in the flesh, full of jollity and ale, they would be astonished, and if they had never heard of him before they might be led by his jollity to see what he had written. But if at school they had been inoculated against him, they will never be able to enjoy him. The same sort of thing applies to music lessons.

Human beings have certain capacities for spontaneous enjoyment, but moralists and pedants possess themselves of the apparatus of these enjoyments, and having extracted what they consider the poison of pleasure they leave them dreary and dismal and devoid of everything that gives them value. Shakespeare did not write with a view to boring school-children; he wrote with a view to delighting his audiences. If he does not give you delight, you had better ignore him.

Fichte laid it down that education should aim at de-, straying free will, so that, after pupils have left school, they shall be incapable, throughout the rest of their lives, of thinking or acting otherwise than as their schoolmasters would have wished. But in his day this was an unattainable ideal. What he regarded as the best system in existence produced Karl Marx. In future such failures are not likely to occur where there is dictatorship. Diet, injections, and injunctions will combine, from a very early age, to produce the sort of character and the sort of beliefs that the authorities consider desirable, and any serious criticism of the powers that be will become psychologically impossible. Even if all are miserable, all will believe themselves happy, because the government will tell them that they are so.

Boys and young men acquire readily the moral sentiments of their social milieu, whatever these sentiments may be. The boy who has been taught at home that it is wicked to swear, easily loses this belief when he finds that the schoolfellows whom he most admires are addicted to blasphemy.

Dread of disaster makes everybody act in the very way that increases the disaster. Psychologically the situation is analogous to that of people trampled to death when there is a panic in a theatre caused by a cry of 'Fire!' In the situation that existed in the great depression, things could only be set right by causing the idle plant to work again.

But everybody felt that to do so was to risk almost certain loss. Within the framework of classical economics there was no solution. Roosevelt saved the situation by bold and heretical action. He spent billions of public money and created a huge public debt, but by so doing he revived production and brought his country out of the depression. Businessmen, who in spite of such a sharp lesson continued to believe in old-fashioned economics, were infinitely shocked, and although Roosevelt saved them from ruin, they continued to curse him and to speak of him as 'the madman in the White House.' Except for Fabre's investigation of the behaviour of insects, I do not know any equally striking example of inability to learn from experience. You may, if you are an old-fashioned schoolmaster, wish to consider yourself full of universal benevolence, and at the same time derive great pleasure from caning boys. In order to reconcile these two desires you have to persuade yourself that caning has a reformatory influence. If a psychiatrist tells you that it has no such influence on some peculiarly irritating class of young sinners, you will fly into a rage and accuse him of being coldly intellectual. There is a splendid example of this pattern in the furious diatribe of the great Dr. Arnold of Rugby against those who thought ill of flogging. Until very recently, it was universally believed that men are congenitally more intelligent than women; even so enlightened a man as Spinoza decides against votes for women on this ground. Among white men, it is held that white men are by nature superior to men of other colours, and especially to black men; in Japan, on the contrary, it is thought that yellow is the best colour. In Haiti, when they make statues of Christ and Satan, they make Christ black and Satan white. Aristotle and Plato considered Greeks so innately superior to barbarians that slavery is justified so long as the master is Greek and the slave barbarian.

Male superiority in former days was easily demonstrated, because if a woman questioned her husband's he could beat her. From superiority in this respect others were thought to follow. Men were more reasonable than women, more inventive, less swayed by their emotions, and so on. Anatomists, until the women had the vote, developed a number of ingenious arguments from the study of the brain to show that men's intellectual capacities must be greater than women's. Each of these arguments in turn was proved to be fallacious, but it always gave place to another from which the same conclusion would follow.

It used to be held that the male fetus acquires a soul after six weeks, but the female only after three months. This opinion also has been abandoned since women have had the vote. Thomas Aquinas states parenthetically, as something entirely obvious, that men are more rational than women. For my part, I see no evidence of this.

Some 'advanced Thinkers' are of opinion that anyone who differs from the conventional opinion must be in the right. This is a delusion; if it were not, truth would be easier to come by than it is. There are infinite possibilities of error, and more cranks take up unfashionable errors than unfashionable truths. I met once an electrical engineer whose first words to me were: 'How do you do? There are two methods of faith-healing, the one practiced by Christ and the one practiced by most Christian Scientists. I practice the method practiced by Christ.' Shortly afterwards, he was sent to prison for making out fraudulent balance sheets. The law does not look kindly on the intrusion of faith into this region.

I knew an eminent lunacy doctor who took to philosophy, and taught a new logic, which, as he frankly confessed, he had learned from his lunatics. When he died he left a will founding a professorship for the teaching of his new scientific methods, but unfortunately, he left no assets. Arithmetic proved recalcitrant to lunatic logic. On one occasion, a man came to ask me to recommend some of my books, as he was interested in philosophy. I did so, but he returned next day saying that he had been reading one of them, and had found only one statement he could understand, and that one seemed to him false. I asked him what it was, and he said it was the statement that Julius Caesar is dead. When I asked him why he did not agree, he drew himself up and said: 'Because I am Julius Caesar.'

The demand for certainty is one which is natural to man, but is nevertheless an intellectual vice. If you take your children for a picnic on a doubtful day, they will demand a dogmatic answer as to whether it will be fine or wet, and be disappointed in you when you cannot be sure. The same sort of assurance is demanded, in later life, of those who undertake to lead populations into the Promised Land. 'Liquidate the capitalists and the survivors will enjoy eternal bliss.' 'Exterminate the Jews and everyone will be virtuous.' 'Kill the Croats and let the Serbs reign.' 'Kill the Serbs and let the Croats reign.' These are samples of the slogans that have won wide popular acceptance in our time. Even a modicum of philosophy would make it impossible to accept such bloodthirsty nonsense.

But so long as men are not trained to withhold judgment in the absence of evidence, they will be led astray by cocksure prophets, and it is likely that their leaders will be either ignorant fanatics or dishonest charlatans. To endure uncertainty is difficult, but so are most of the other virtues. For the learning of every virtue there is an appropriate discipline, and for the learning of suspended judgment the best discipline is philosophy.

Those who have a passion for quick returns and for an exact balance sheet of effort and reward may feel impatient of a study which cannot, in the present state of our knowledge, arrive at certainties, and which encourages what may be thought the time-wasting occupation of inconclusive meditation on insoluble problems. To this view I cannot in any degree subscribe.

Some kind of philosophy is a necessity to all but the most thoughtless, and in the absence of knowledge it is almost sure to be a silly philosophy. The result of this is that the human race becomes divided into rival groups of fanatics, each group firmly persuaded that its own brand of nonsense is sacred truth, while the other side's is damnable heresy. Arians and Catholics, Crusaders and Moslems, Protestants and adherents of the Pope, Communists, and Fascists, have filled large parts of the last 1,600 years with futile strife, when a little philosophy would have shown both sides in all these disputes that neither had any good reason to believe itself in the right.

When the journey from means to end is not too long, the means themselves are enjoyed if the end is ardently desired. A boy will toil uphill with a toboggan for the sake of the few brief moments of bliss during the descent; no one has to urge him to be industrious, and however he may puff and pant he is still happy. But if instead of the immediate reward you promised him an old-age pension at seventy, his energy would very quickly flag.

Herd pressure is to be judged by two things: first, its intensity, and second, its direction. If it is very intense, it produces adults who are timid and conventional, except in a few rare instances. This is regrettable, however excellent may be the moral standards by which the herd is actuated. In Tom Brown's Schooldays, there is a boy who is kicked for saying his prayers. This book had a great effect, and among my contemporaries, I knew one who had been kicked at school for not saying his prayers. I regret to say that he remained through life a prominent atheist.

Dr. Arnold, the hero of Tom Brown's Schooldays, and the admired reformer of public schools, came across some cranks who thought it a mistake to flog boys. Anyone reading his outburst of furious indignation against this opinion will be forced to the conclusion that he enjoyed inflicting floggings, and did not wish to be deprived of this pleasure.

Men of science are being increasingly compelled to pursue the ends of governments rather than those proper to science.... The scientist who discovers how to injure others is therefore at least as much honored as the one who shows us how to benefit ourselves. The pursuit of knowledge for its own sake, which was once the purpose of science, is lost sight of; there are even philosophers who tell us that there is no such thing. A physicist who wishes to study uranium can have access to any amount of public money, but if he wished to devote equal skill and equal labour to the study of (say) carbon, he would have to persuade his government that he was on the track of a method of inventing robots.

In the welter of conflicting fanaticisms, one of the few unifying forces is scientific truthfulness, by which I mean the habit of basing our beliefs upon observations and inferences as impersonal, and as much divested of local and temperamental bias as is possible For human beings. To have insisted upon the introduction of this virtue into philosophy, and to have invented a powerful method by which it can be rendered Fruitful, are the chief merits of the philosophical school of which I am a member. The habit of careful veracity acquired in the practice of this philosophical method can be extended to the whole sphere of human activity, producing, wherever it exists, a lessening of fanaticism with an increasing capacity of sympathy and mutual understanding.

I was a solitary, shy, priggish youth. I had no experience of the social pleasures of boyhood and did not miss them. But I liked mathematics, and mathematics was suspect because it has no ethical content. I came also to disagree with the theological opinions of my family, and as I grew up I became increasingly interested in philosophy, of which they profoundly disapproved. Every time the subject came up they repeated with unfailing regularity, 'What is mind? No matter. What is matter? Never mind.' After some fifty or sixty repetitions, this remark ceased to amuse me.

I think the first thing that led me toward philosophy (though at that time the word 'philosophy' was still unknown to me) occurred at the age of eleven. My childhood was mainly solitary as my only brother was seven years older than I was. No doubt as a result of much solitude I became rather solemn, with a great deal of time for thinking but not much knowledge for my thoughtfulness to exercise itself upon. I had, though I was not yet aware of it, the pleasure in demonstrations, which is typical of the mathematical mind. After I grew up I found others who felt as I did on this matter.

My friend G. H. Hardy, who was professor of pure mathematics, enjoyed this pleasure in a very high degree. He told me once that if he could find a proof that I was going to die in five minutes he would of course be sorry to lose me, but this sorrow would be quite outweighed by pleasure in the proof. I entirely sympathized with him and was not at all offended. Before I began the study of geometry somebody had told me that it proved things and this caused me to feel delight when my brother said he would teach it to me. Geometry in those days was still 'Euclid.' My brother began at the beginning with the definitions.

These I accepted readily enough. But he came next to the axioms. 'These,' he said, 'can't be proved, but they have to be assumed before the rest can be proved.' At these words my hopes crumbled. I had thought it would be wonderful to find something that one could prove, and then it turned out that this could only be done by means of assumptions of which there was no proof. I looked at my brother with a sort of indignation and said: 'But why should I admit these things if they can't be proved?' He replied, 'Well, if you won't, we can't go on.'

There are some simple maxims which I think might be commended to writers of expository prose. First: never use a long word if a short word will do. So, if you want to make a statement with a great many qualifications, put some of the qualifications in separate sentences. Third: do not let the beginning of your sentence lead the reader to an expectation which is contradicted by the end.

Take, say, such a sentence as the following, which might occur in a work on sociology: 'Human beings are completely exempt from undesirable behaviour patterns only when certain prerequisites, not satisfied except in a small percentage of actual cases, have, through some fortuitous concourse of favorable circumstances, whether congenital or environmental, chanced to combine in producing an individual in whom many factors deviate from the norm in a socially advantageous manner.' Let us see if we can translate this sentence into English.

I suggest the following: 'All men are scoundrels, or at any rate almost all. The men who are not must have had unusual luck, both in their birth and in their upbringing.' This is shorter and more intelligible, and says just the same thing. But I am afraid any professor who used the second sentence instead of the first would get the sack. This suggests a word of advice to such of my readers as may happen to be professors. I am allowed to use plain English because everybody knows that I could use mathematical logic if I chose. Take the statement: 'Some people marry their deceased wives' sisters.' I can express this in language which only becomes intelligible after years of study, and this gives me freedom.

I suggest to young professors that their first work should be written in a jargon only to be understood by the erudite few. With that behind them, they can ever after say what they have to say in a language 'understand of the people.' In these days, when our very lives are at the mercy of the professors, I cannot but think that they would deserve our gratitude if they adopted my advice prevented from pursuing his work largely because he Oppenheimer is disgraced and doubted the practicability of the hydrogen bomb at a time when the doubt was entirely rational. The F.B.I., which had only the level of educating policemen, considers itself competent to withhold visas from the most learned men in Europe on grounds which every person capable of understanding the matters at issue knows to be absurd. This evil has reached such a point that international conferences of learned men in the United States have become impossible.

Those who advocate common usage in philosophy sometimes speak in a manner that suggests the mystique of the 'common man.' They may admit that in organic chemistry there is need of long words, and that quantum physics requires formulas that are difficult to translate into ordinary English, but philosophy (they think) is different.

It is not the function of philosophy - so they maintain- to teach something that uneducated people do not know; on the contrary, its function is to teach superior persons that they are not as superior as they thought they were, and that those who are really superior can show their skill by making sense of common sense.

No one wants to alter the language of common sense, any more than we wish to give up talking of the sun rising and setting. But astronomers find a different language better, and I contend that a different language is better in philosophy. Let us take an example, that of perception. There is here an admixture of philosophical and scientific questions, but this admixture is inevitable in many questions, or, if not inevitable, can only be avoided by confining ourselves to comparatively unimportant aspects of the matter in hand. Here is a series of questions and answers.

Q. When I see a table, will what I see be still there if I shut my eyes?

Ans. That depends upon the sense in which you use the word 'see.'

Q. What is still there when I shut my eyes?

Ans. This is an empirical question. Don't bother me with it, but ask the physicists.

Q. What exists when my eyes are open, but not when they are shut?

Ans. This again is empirical, but in deference to previous philosophers I will answer you: coloured surfaces.

Q. May I infer that there are two senses of 'see'? In the first, when I 'see' a table, I 'see' something conjectural about which physics has vague notions that are probably wrong. In the second, I 'see' coloured surfaces, which cease to exist when I shut my eyes.

Ans. That is correct if you want to think clearly, but our philosophy makes clear thinking unnecessary. By oscillating between the two meanings, we avoid paradox and shock, which is more than most philosophers do.

Bertrand Russell's Best - Politics

I am persuaded that there is absolutely no limit in the absurdities that can, by government action, come to be generally believed. Give me an adequate army, with power to provide it with more pay and better food than falls to the lot of the average man, and I will undertake, within thirty years, to make the majority of the population believe that two and two are three, that water freezes when it gets hot and boils when it gets cold, or any other nonsense that might seem to serve the interest of the State.

Of course, even when these beliefs had been generated, people would not put the kettle in the refrigerator when they wanted it to boil. That cold makes water boil would be a Sunday truth, sacred and mystical, to be professed in awed tones, but not to be acted on in daily life. What would happen would be that any verbal denial of the mystic doctrine would be made illegal, and obstinate heretics would be 'frozen' at the stake. No person who did not enthusiastically accept the official doctrine would be allowed to teach or to have any position of power. Only the very highest officials, in their cups, would whisper to each other what rubbish it all is; then they would laugh and drink again.

There are some desires which, though very powerful, have not, as a rule, any great political importance. Most men at some period of their lives desire to marry, but as a rule they can satisfy this desire without having to take any political action. There are, of course, exceptions; the rape of the Sabine women is a case in point.

When the British Government very unwisely allowed the Kaiser to be present at a naval review at Spithead, the thought which arose in his mind was not the one which we had intended. What he thought was: 'I must have a navy as good as Grand mama's. And from this thought have sprung all our subsequent troubles. The world would be a happier place if acquisitiveness were always stronger than rivalry. But in fact, a great many men will cheerfully face impoverishment if they can thereby secure complete ruin for their rivals Hence the present level of the income tax.

If politics is to become scientific, and if the event is not to be constantly surprising, it is imperative that our political thinking should penetrate more deeply into the springs of human action. What is the influence of hunger upon slogans? How does their effectiveness fluctuate with the number of calories in your diet? If one man offers you democracy and another offers you a bag of grain, at what stage of starvation will you prefer the grain to the vote?

One of the troubles about vanity is that it grows with what it feeds on. The more you are talked about, the more you will wish to be talked about. The condemned murderer, I am told- I have had no personal experience- who is allowed to see the account of his trial in the Press is indignant if he finds a newspaper which has reported it inadequately. And the more he finds about himself in other newspapers, the more indignant he will be with the one whose reports are meager. Politicians and literary men are in the same case. And the more famous they become, the more, difficult the press cutting agency finds it to satisfy them.

It is scarcely possible to exaggerate the influence of vanity throughout the range of human life from the child of three to the potentate at whose frown the world trembles. Mankind have even committed the impiety of attributing similar desires to the Deity, whom they imagine avid for continual praise.

Most political leaders acquire their position by causing large numbers of people to believe that these leaders are actuated by altruistic desires. It is well understood that such a belief is more readily accepted under the influence of excitement. Brass bands, mob oratory, lynching, and war are stages in the development of the excitement I suppose the advocates of unreason think that there is a better chance of profitably deceiving the populace if they keep it in a state of effervescence. Perhaps it is my dislike of this sort of process, which leads people to say that I am unduly rational.

The increase of organization has brought into existence new positions of power. Every body has to have executive officials, in whom, at any moment, its power is concentrated. It is true that officials are usually subject to control, but the control may be slow and distant. From the young lady who sells stamps in a post office all the way up to the Prime Minister, every official is invested, for the time being, with some part of the power of the State.

You can complain of the young lady if her manners are bad, and you can vote against the Prime Minister at the next election if you disapprove of his policy. But both the young lady and the Prime Minister can have a very considerable run for their money before (if ever) your discontent has any effect. This increase in the power of officials is a constant source of irritation to everybody else. In most countries they are much less polite than in England; the police, especially in America for instance, seem to think you must be a rare exception if you are not a criminal. This tyranny of officials is one of the worst results of increasing organization, and one against which it is of the utmost importance to find safeguards if a scientific society is not to be intolerable to all but an insolent aristocracy of Jacks-in-office.

Politics is largely governed by sententious platitudes which are devoid of truth. One of the most widespread popular maxims is, 'Human nature cannot be changed.' No one can say whether this is true or not without first defining 'human nature.' But as used it is certainly false. When Mr.. A utters the maxim, with an air of portentous and conclusive wisdom, what he means is that all men everywhere will always continue to behave as they do in his own home town. A little anthropology will d - dispel this belief.

Among the Tibetans, one wife has many husbands, because men are too poor to support a whole wife; yet family life, according to travelers, is no more unhappy than elsewhere. The practice of lending one's wife to a guest is very common among uncivilized tribes. The Australian aborigines, at puberty, undergo a very painful operation which, throughout the rest of their lives, greatly diminishes sexual potency. Infanticide, which might seem contrary to human nature, was almost universal before the rise of Christianity, and is recommended by Plato to prevent over-population. Private property is not recognized among some savage tribes. Even among highly civilized people, economic considerations will override what is called 'human nature.'

The conscientious Radical is faced with great difficulties. He knows that he can increase his popularity by being false to his creed, and appealing to hatreds that have nothing to do with the reforms in which he believes. For example: a community that suffers from Japanese competition can easily be made indignant about bad labour conditions in Japan, and the unfair price-cutting that they render possible. But if the speaker goes on to say that it is Japanese employers who should be opposed, not Japanese employees, he will lose a large part of the sympathy of his audience.

The Radical's only ultimate protection against demagogic appeals to misguided hatreds lies in education: he must convince intellectually a sufficient number of people to form the nucleus of a propagandist army This is undoubtedly a difficult task, while the whole force of the State and the plutocracy is devoted to the fostering of unreason. But it is perhaps not so hopeless a task as many are now inclined to believe and in any case it cannot be shirked, since the appeal to unreasoning emotion can always be better done by charlatans.

I cannot be content with a brief moment of riotous living followed by destitution, and however clever the scientists may be, there are some things that they cannot be expected to achieve. When they have used up all the easily available sources of energy that nature has scattered carelessly over the surface of our planet, they will have to resort to more labourious processes, and these will involve a gradual lowering of the standard of living.

Modern industrialists are like men who have come for the first time upon fertile virgin land, and can live for a little while in great comfort with only a modicum of labour. It would be irrational to hope that the present heyday of industrialism will not develop far beyond its present level, but sooner or later, owing to the exhaustion of raw material, its capacity to supply human needs will diminish, not suddenly, but gradually. This could, of course, be prevented if men exercised any restraint or foresight in their present frenzied exploitation. Perhaps before it is too late they will learn to do so.

How long will it be before the accessible oil in the world is exhausted? Will all the arable land be turned into dustbowls as it has been in large parts of the United States? Will the population increase to the point where men again, like their remote ancestors, have no leisure to think of anything but the food supply? Such questions are not to be decided by general philosophical reflections. Communists think that there will be plenty of oil; if there are no capitalists. Some religicus people think that there will be plenty of food if we trust in Providence. Such ideas are superficial, even when they are called scientific, as they are by the Communists. We all know that the price of food goes up, but most of us attribute this to the wickedness of the Government. If we live under a progressive Government, it makes us reactionary; if we live under a reactionary Government, it turns us into Socialists. Both these reactions are superficial and frivolous. All Governments, whatever their political complexion, are at present willy-nilly in the grip of natural forces which can only be dealt with by a degree of intelligence of which mankind hitherto has shown little evidence.

I do not think any reasonable person can doubt that in India, China and Japan, if the knowledge of birth control existed, the birth-rate would fall very rapidly. In Africa the process might take longer, but there also it could be fairly easily achieved if Negro doctors, trained in the West, were given the funds to establish medical clinics in which every kind of medical information would be given. I do not suppose that America would contribute to this beneficent work, because if either party favored it, that party would lose the Catholic vote in New York State, and therefore the Presidency. This obviously would be a greater disaster than the extermination of the human race by atomic war.

Some opponents of Communism are attempting to produce an ideology for the Atlantic Powers, and for this purpose they have invented what they call 'Western Values.' These are supposed to consist of toleration, respect for individual liberty, and brotherly love. I am afraid this view is grossly unhistorical. If we compare Europe with other continents, it is marked out as the persecuting continent. Persecution only ceased after long and bitter experience of its futility; it continued as long as either Protestants or Catholics had any hope of exterminating the opposite party. The European record in this respect is far blacker than that of the Mohammedans, the Indians or the Chinese. No, if the West can claim superiority in anything, it is not in moral values but in science and scientific technique.

Everything done by European administrators to improve the lot of Africans is, at present, totally and utterly futile because of the growth of population. The Africans, not unnaturally, though now mistakenly, attribute their destitution to their exploitation by the white man. If they achieve freedom suddenly before they have men trained in administration and a habit of responsibility, such civilization as white men have brought to Africa will quickly disappear. It is no use for doctrinaire liberals to deny this; there is a standing proof in the island of Haiti.

If two hitherto rival football teams, under the influence of brotherly love, decided to co-operate in placing the football first beyond one goal and then beyond the other, no one's happiness would be increased. There is no reason why the zest derived from competition should be confined to athletics. Emulation between teams or localities or organizations can be a useful incentive. But if competition is not to become ruthless and harmful, the penalty for failure must not be disaster, as in war, or starvation, as in unregulated economic competition, but only loss of glory. Football would not be a desirable sport if defeated teams were put to death or left to starve.

In a shipwreck the crew obey orders without the need of reasoning with themselves, because they have a common purpose which is not remote, and the means to its realization are not difficult to understand. But if the Captain were obliged, like the Government, to explain the principles of currency in order to prove his commands wise, the ship would sink before his lecture was finished.

The savage, in spite of his membership of a small community, lived a life in which his initiative was not too much hampered by the community. The things that he wanted to do, usually hunting and war, were also the things that his neighbours wanted to do, and if he felt an inclination to become a medicine man he only had to ingratiate himself with some individual already eminent in that profession, and so, in due course, to succeed to his powers of magic. If he was a man of exceptional talent, he might invent some improvement in weapons, or a new skill in hunting. These would not put him into any opposition to the community, but, on the contrary, would be welcomed. The modern man lives a very different life. If he sings in the street he will be thought to be drunk and if he dances a policeman will reprove him for impeding the traffic.

Two great religions- Buddhism and Christianity- have sought to extend to the whole human race the cooperative feeling that is spontaneous towards fellow tribesmen. They have preached the brotherhood of man, showing by the use of the word 'brotherhood' that they are attempting to extend beyond its natural bounds an emotional attitude which, in its origin, is biological. If we are all children of God, then we are all one family.

But in practice those who in theory adopted this creed have always felt that those who did not adopt it were not children of God but children of Satan, and the old mechanism of hatred of those outside the tribe has returned, giving added vigor to the creed, but in a direction which diverted it from its original purpose.

Religion, morality, economic self- interest, the mere pursuit of biological survival, all supply to our intelligence unanswerable arguments in favor of worldwide co-operation, but the old instincts that have come down to us from our tribal ancestors rise up in indignation, feeling that life would lose its savor if there were no one to hate, that anyone who could love such a scoundrel as So-and-so would be a worm, that struggle is the law of life, and that in a world where we all loved one another there would be nothing to live for.

Before the war (World War I) one of the objections commonly urged against votes for women was that women would tend to be pacifists. During the war they gave a large-scale refutation of this charge, and the vote was given to them for their share in the bloody work.

There are many points of view from which the life of man may be considered. There are those who think of him primarily in cultural terms as being capable of lofty art and sublime speculation and discovery of the hidden secrets of nature. There are those who think of him as one of those kinds of animals that are capable of government, though in this respect he is completely outshone by ants and bees. There are those who think of him as the master of war; these include all the men in all countries who decide upon the adornment of public squares, where it is an invariable rule obeyed by all right-thinking public authorities that the most delectable object to be seen by the passers-by is a man on horseback, who is commemorated for his skill in homicide.

Organizations are of two kinds, those, which aim at getting something done, and those which aim at preventing something from being done. The Post Office is an example of the first kind; a fire brigade is an example of the second kind. Neither of these arouses much controversy, because no one objects to letters being carried, and incendiaries dare not avow a desire to see buildings burnt down. But when what is to be prevented is something done by human beings, not by Nature, the matter is otherwise.

The armed forces of one's own nation exist- so each nation asserts- to prevent aggression by other nations. But the armed forces of other nations exist- or so many people believe to promote aggression. If you say anything against the armed forces of your own country, you are a traitor, wishing to see your fatherland ground under the heel of a brutal conqueror. If, on the other hand, you defend a potential enemy State for thinking armed forces necessary to its safety, you malign your own country, whose unalterable devotion to peace only perverse malice could lead you to question. I heard all this said about Germany by a thoroughly virtuous German lady in 1936, in the course of a panegyric on Hitler.

I do not pretend that birth control is the only way in which population can be kept from increasing. There are others, which, one must suppose, opponents of birth control would prefer. War... has hitherto been disappointing in this respect, but perhaps bacteriological war may prove more effective. If a Black Death could be spread throughout the world once in every generation survivors could procreate freely without making the world too full.

There would be nothing in this to offend the consciences of the devout or to restrain the ambitions of nationalists. The state of affairs might be somewhat unpleasant, but what of that? Really high-minded people are indifferent to happiness, especially other people's.

In superstitious moments I am tempted to believe in the myth of the Tower of Babel, and to suppose that in our own day a similar but greater impiety is about to be visited by a more tragic and terrible punishment. Perhaps- so I sometimes allow myself to fancy- God does not intend us to understand the mechanism by which He regulates the material universe. Perhaps the nuclear physicists have come so near to the ultimate secrets that He thinks it time to bring their activities to a stop.

And what simpler method could He devise than to let them carry their ingenuity to the point where they exterminate the human race? If I could think that deer and squirrels, nightingales and larks, would survive, I might view this catastrophe with some equanimity, since man has not shown himself worthy to be the lord of creation. But it is to be feared that the dreadful alchemy of the atomic bomb will destroy all forms of life equally, and that the earth will remain forever a dead clod senselessly whirling round a futile sun. I do not know the immediate precipitating cause of this interesting occurrence.

Perhaps it will be a dispute about Persian oil, perhaps a disagreement as to Chinese trade, perhaps a quarrel between Jews and Mohammedans for the control of Palestine. Any patriotic person can see that these issues are of such importance as to make the extermination of mankind preferable to cowardly conciliation.

Men, quite ordinary men, will compel children to look on while their mothers are raped. In pursuit of political aims men will subm:t their opponents to long years of unspeakable anguish. We know what the Nazis did to Jews at Auschwitz. In mass cruelty, the expulsions of Germans ordered by the Russians fall not very far short of the atrocities perpetrated by the Nazis. And how about our noble selves; We would not do such deeds. Oh no! But we enjoy our juicy steaks and our hot rolls while German children die of hunger because our governments dare not face our indignation if they asked us to forgo some part of our pleasures. If there were a Last Judgment as Christians believe, how do you think our excuses would sound before that final tribunal?

Stalin could neither understand nor respect the point of view, which led Churchill to allow himself to be peaceably dispossessed as a result of a popular vote. I am a firm believer in democratic representative government as the best form for those who have the tolerance and self-restraint that is required to make it workable.

But its advocates make a mistake if they suppose that it can be at once introduced into countries where the average citizen has hitherto lacked all training in the give-and-take that it requires. In a Balkan country, not so many years ago, a party which had been beaten by a narrow margin in a general election retrieved its fortunes by shooting a sufficient number of the representatives of the other side to give it a majority. People in the West thought this characteristic of the Balkans, forgetting that Cromwell and Robespierre had acted likewise.

The American legislators who made the immigration laws consider the Nordics superior to Slavs or Latins or any other white men. But the Nazis, under the stress of war, were led to the conclusion that there are hardly any true Nordics outside Germany; the Norwegians, except Quisling and his few followers, had been corrupted by intermixture with Finns and Lapps and such. Thus politics are a clue to descent. The biologically pure Nordics love Hitler, and if you did not love Hitler, that was proof of tainted blood.

Very little remains of institutions and ways of life that when I was a child appeared as indestructible as granite. I grew up in an atmosphere impregnated with tradition. My parents died before I can remember, and I was brought up by my grandparents.... I was taught a kind of theoretic republicanism which was prepared to tolerate a monarch so long as he recognized that he was an employee of the people and subject to dismissal if he proved unsatisfactory. My grandfather, who was no respecter of persons, used to explain this point of view to Queen Victoria, and she was not altogether sympathetic. She did, however, give him the house in Richmond Park in which I spent all my youth. I imbibed certain political principles and expectations, and have on the whole retained the former in spite of being compelled to reject the latter.

There was to be ordered progress throughout the world, no revolutions, a gradual cessation of war, and an extension of parliamentary government to all those unfortunate regions which did not yet enjoy it.

My grandmother used to laugh about a conversation she had had with the Russian Ambassador She said to him, 'Perhaps some day you will have a parliament in Russia,' and he replied, 'God forbid, my dear Lady John.' The Russian Ambassador of today might give the same answer if he changed the first word. Neither misery nor folly seems to me any part of the inevitable lot of man. And I am convinced that intelligence, patience, and eloquence can, sooner or later, lead the human race out of its self-imposed tortures provided it does not exterminate itself meanwhile.

On the basis of this belief, I have had always a certain degree of optimism, although, as I have grown older, the optimism has grown more sober and the happy issue more distant. But I remain completely incapable of agreeing with those who accept fatalistically the view that man is born to trouble. The causes of unhappiness in the past and in the present are not difficult to ascertain.

There have been poverty, pestilence, and famine, which were due to man's inadequate mastery of nature. There have been wars, oppressions and tortures which have been due to men's hostility to their fellow men. And there have been morbid miseries fostered by gloomy creeds, which have led men into profound inner discords that made all outward prosperity of no avail. All these are unnecessary. In regard to all of them, means are known by which they can be overcome. In the modern world, if communities are unhappy, it is because they choose to be so. Or to speak more precisely, because they have ignorances, habits, beliefs, and passions, which are dearer to them than happiness or even life. I find many men in our dangerous age who seem to be in love with misery and death, and who grow angry when hopes are suggested to them.

How to Become a Man of Genius

If there are among my readers any young men or women who aspire to become leaders of thought in their generation, I hope they will avoid certain errors into which I fell in youth for want of good advice. When I wished to form an opinion upon a subject, I used to study it, weigh the arguments on different sides, and attempt to reach a balanced conclusion. I have since discovered that this is not the way to do things. A man of genius knows it all without the need of study; his opinions are pontifical and depend for their persuasiveness upon literary style rather than argument.

It is necessary to be one-sided, since this facilitates the vehemence that is considered a proof of strength. It is essential to appeal to prejudices and passions of which men have begun to feel ashamed and to do this in the name of some new ineffable ethic. It is well to decry the slow and pettifogging minds which require evidence in order to reach conclusions. Above all, whatever is most ancient should be dished up as the very latest thing.

There is no novelty in this recipe for genius; it was practised by Carlyle in the time of our grandfathers, and by Nietzsche in the time of our fathers, and it has been practised in our own time by D. H. Lawrence. Lawrence is considered by his disciples to have enunciated all sorts of new wisdom about the relations of men and women; in actual fact he has gone back to advocating the domination of the male which one associates with the cave dwellers.

Woman exists, in his philosophy, only as something soft and fat to rest the hero when he returns from his labours. Civilised societies have been learning to see something more than this in women; Lawrence will have nothing of civilisation. He scours the world for what is ancient and dark and loves the traces of Aztec cruelty in Mexico. Young men, who had been learning to behave, naturally read him with delight and go round practising cave-man stuff so far as the usages of polite society will permit. One of the most important elements of success in becoming a man of genius is to learn the art of denunciation. You must always denounce in such a way that your reader thinks that it is the other fellow who is being denounced and not himself; in that case he will be impressed by your noble scorn, whereas if he thinks that it is himself that you are denouncing, he will consider that you are guilty of ill-bred peevishness. Carlyle remarked: "The population of England is twenty millions, mostly fools." Everybody who read this considered himself one of the exceptions, and therefore enjoyed the remark.

You must not denounce well-defined classes, such as persons with more than a certain income, inhabitants of a certain area, or believers in some definite creed; for if you do this, some readers will know that your invective is directed against them. You must denounce persons whose emotions are atrophied, persons to whom only plodding study can reveal the truth, for we all know that these are other people, and we shall therefore view with sympathy your powerful diagnosis of the evils of the age.

Ignore fact and reason, live entirely in the world of your own fantastic and myth-producing passions; do this whole-heartedly and with conviction, and you will become one of the prophets of your age.

OF COOPERATION

In these days, under the influence of democracy, the virtue of co-operation has taken the place formerly held by obedience. The old-fashioned schoolmaster would say of a boy that he was disobedient; the modern schoolmistress says of an infant that he is non-co-operative. It means the same thing: the child, in either case, fails to do what the teacher wishes, but in the first case the teacher acts as the government and in the second as the representative of the People, i.e. of the other children. The result of the new language, as of the old, is to encourage docility, suggestibility, herd-instinct and conventionality, thereby necessarily discouraging originality, initiative and unusual intelligence. Adults who achieve anything of value have seldom been "co-operative" children. As a rule, they have liked solitude: they have tried to slink into a corner with a book and been happiest when they could escape the notice of their barbarian contemporaries. Almost all men who have been distinguished as artists, writers or men of science have in boyhood been objects of derision and contempt to their schoolfellows; and only too often the teachers have sided with the herd, because it annoyed them that a boy should be odd.

It ought to be part of the training of all teachers to be taught to recognise the marks of unusual intelligence in children and to restrain the irritation caused in themselves by anything so unusual. Until this is done, a large proportion of the best talent in America will be persecuted out of existence before the age of fifteen.

Cooperativeness, as an ideal, is defective: it is right to live with reference to the community and not for oneself alone, but living for the community does not mean doing what it does. Suppose you are in a theatre which catches fire, and there is a stampede: the person who has learnt no higher morality than what is called "co-operation" will join in the stampede since he will possess no inner force that would enable him to stand up against the herd. The psychology of a nation embarking on a war is at all points identical.

I do not wish, however, to push the doctrine of individual initiative too far. Godwin, who became Shelley's father-in-law because Shelley so much admired him, asserted that "everything that is usually understood by the term 'co-operation' is in some degree an evil." He admits that, at present, "to pull down a tree, to cut a canal, to navigate a vessel requires the labour of many", but he looks forward to the time when machinery is so perfected that one man unaided will be able to do any of these things.

He thinks also that hereafter there will be no orchestra. "Shall we have concerts of music?" he says. "The miserable state of mechanism of the majority of the performers is so conspicuous as to be even at this day a topic of mortification and ridicule. Will it not be practicable hereafter for one man to perform the whole?" He goes on to suggest that the solitary performer will insist on playing his own productions and refuse to be the slave of composers dead and gone.

All this is, of course, ridiculous, and for my part I find it salutary to see my own opinions thus caricatured. I remain none the less convinced that our age, partly as a result of democratic sentiment, and partly because of the complexity of machine production, is in danger of carrying the doctrine of co-operativeness to lengths which will be fatal to individual excellence, not only in its more anarchic forms, but also in forms which are essential to social progress. Perhaps, therefore, even a man like Godwin may have something to teach those who believe that social conformity is the beginning and end of virtue.

ON ASTROLOGERS

There is always something pathetic about a great and ancient tradition which has fallen on evil days. The astrologer, as one pictures him in the past, is an aged sage with a long white beard, speaking in a slow and trance-like manner, and felt by his auditors and himself to be possessed of mystical lore. In his most glorious days, he controlled the destiny of nations: among the Chaldeans, he stood to the King in the same relation as the Governor of the Bank of England now stands to the Prime Minister. In ancient Rome he was reverenced, except by a few rationalistic Emperors, who banished from the City all "mathematicians", as they were called. The Arabs consulted them on all important occasions; the wisest men of the Renaissance believed in them, and Kepler, the great astronomer, had to become an astrologer in order to win respect and a livelihood. Astrologers still exist; it has been my good fortune to know several. But how different they are from the magnificent beings of former times! They are, so far as I have come across them, hard-working and highly meritorious business men or women, with an aged mother or an invalid husband to support. They follow by rule of thumb the ancient formulae about the House of Life and planets in the ascendant and the rest of it, but their language is sadly modernised, and their horoscopes, instead of being inscribed cabalistically upon parchment, are neatly typed upon the best quarto typing paper. In this, they commit an error of judgment, which makes it difficult to have faith in their power of deciphering the future in the stars.

Do they believe themselves in the sciences that they profess? This is a difficult question. Everything marvellous is believed by some people, and it is not improbable that professional astrologers are of this type. And even if they are aware that their own performances are largely guesswork and inferences from information obtained otherwise, they probably think that there are superior practitioners who never resort to these inferior methods. There was once a worthy man who made a vast fortune by professing to have discovered how to make gold out of sea water. He decamped to South America before it was too late and prepared to live happily ever after. Unfortunately another man professed to have made the same discovery; our friend believed in him, invested all his money in the new process, and lost every penny. This incident shows that people are often less dishonest than they might be thought to be, and probably professional astrologers are in the main honourably convinced of the truth of their doctrines.

That this should be possible is creditable to them but very discreditable to our educational system. In schools and universities information of all sorts is ladled out, but no one is taught to reason, or to consider what is evidence for what. To any person with even the vaguest idea of the nature of scientific evidence, such beliefs as those of astrologers are of course impossible. But so are most of the beliefs upon which governments are based, such as the peculiar merit of persons living in a certain area, or of persons whose income exceeds a certain sum. It would not do to teach people to reason correctly, since the result would be to undermine these beliefs. If these beliefs were to fade, mankind might escape disaster, but politicians could not. At all costs, therefore, we must be kept stupid.

On Modern Uncertainty

There have been four sorts of ages in the world's history. There have been ages when everybody thought they knew everything, ages when nobody thought they knew anything, ages when clever people thought they knew much and stupid people thought they knew little, and ages when stupid people thought they knew much and clever people thought they knew little. The first sort of age is one of stability, the second of slow decay, the third of progress, the fourth of disaster. All primitive ages belong to the first sort: no one has any doubt as to the tribal religion, the wisdom of ancient customs, or the magic by which good crops are to be secured; consequently everyone is happy in the absence of some tangible reason, such as starvation, for being unhappy.

The second sort of age is exemplified by the ancient world before the rise of Christianity but after decadence had begun. In the Roman Empire, tribal religions lost their exclusiveness and force: in proportion as people came to think that there might be truth in religions of others, they also came to think that their might be falsehood in their own. Eastern necromancy was half believed, half disbelieved; the German barbarians were supposed to possess virtues that the more civilised portions of mankind hand lost. Consequently, everybody doubted everything, and doubt paralysed effort.

In the eighteenth and early nineteenth centuries, exactly the opposite happened. Science and scientific technique were a novelty, and gave immense self-confidence to those who understood them.

Their triumphs were obvious and astonishing. Repeatedly, when the Chinese Emperor had decided to persecute the Jesuits, they would turn out to be right about the date of an expected eclipse when the imperial astronomers were wrong, and the Emperor would decide that such clever men, after all, deserved his favours. In England, those who introduced scientific methods in agriculture obtained visibly larger crops than those who adhered to old-time methods, while in manufactures team and machinery put the conservatives to flight. There came, therefore, to be a general belief in educated intelligence. Those who did not possess it allowed themselves to be guided by those who did, and an era of rapid progress resulted. In our age, the exact opposite is the case. Men of science like Eddington are doubtful whether science really knows anything. Economists perceive that the accepted methods of doing the world's business are making everybody poor. Statesmen cannot find any way of securing international co-operation or preventing war. Philosophers have no guidance to offer mankind.

The only people left with positive opinions are those who are too stupid to know when their opinions are absurd. Consequently the world is ruled by fools, and the intelligent count for nothing in the councils of the nations.

This state of affairs, if it continues, must plunge the world more and more deeply into misfortune. The skepticism of the intelligent is the cause of their impotence, and is itself the effect of their laziness: if there is nothing worth doing, that gives an excuse for sitting still. But when disaster is impending, no excuse for sitting still can be valid. The intelligent will have to shed their skepticism, or share responsibility for the evils which all deplore. And they will have to abandon academic grumblings and peevish pedantries, for nothing that they amy say will be of any use unless they learn to speak a language that the democracy can appreciate.

On Sales Resistance

Throughout recent years, a vast amount of money and time and brains has been employed in overcoming sales resistance, i.e. in inducing unoffending persons to waste their money in purchasing objects, which they had no desire to possess. It is characteristic of our age that this sort of thing is considered meritorious: lectures are given on salesmanship, and those who possess the art are highly rewarded. Yet, if a moment's consideration is given to the matter, it is clear that the activity is a noxious one, which does more harm than good. Some hard-working professional man, for example, who has been saving up with a view to giving his family a pleasant summer holiday, is beset in a weak moment by a highly trained bandit who wants to sell him a grand piano.

He points out that that he has no room large enough to house it, but the bandit shows that, by knocking down a bit of wall, the tail of the piano can be made to project from the living room into the best bedroom. Paterfamilias says that he and his wife do not play the piano and his oldest daughter has only just begun to learn scales. "The very reason why you should buy my piano" says the bandit. "On ordinary pianos scales may be tiresome, but on mine they have all the depth of the most exquisite melody." The harassed householder mentions that he has an engagement and cannot stay any longer.

The bandit threatens to come again next day; so, in despair, the victim gives way and his children have to forgo their seaside holiday, while his wife's complaints are a sauce to every meal throughout the summer. In return for all this misery, the salesman has a mere commission and the man whose piano is being sold obtains whatever percentage of the price presents his profits. Yet, both are thought to have deserved well of their country since their enterprise is supposed to be good for business.

All this topsy-turvy Dom is due to the fact that everything economic is looked upon from the standpoint of the producer rather than of the consumer. In former times, it was thought that bread is baked in order to be eaten; nowadays we think that it is eaten in order to be baked. When we spend money, we are expected to do so not with a view to our enjoyment of what we purchase but to enrich those who have manufactured it.

Since the greatest of virtues is business skill and since skill is shown in making people buy what they don't want rather than what they do, the man who is most respected is the one who has caused the most pain to purchasers. All this is connected with a quite elementary mistake, namely, failure to realise that what a man spends in one direction he has to save in another so that bullying is not likely to increase his total expenditure.

But partly also it is connected with the notion that a man's working hours are the only important part of his life and that what he does with the rest of his time is unimportant unless it affects other men's working hours. A few clergymen, it is true, speak of the American home and the joys of family life, but that is regarded merely as *their* professional talk, against which a very considerable sales resistance has grown up. And so everything is done for the sake of something else. We make money not in order to enjoy what it provides but in order that in spending it we may enable others to make money which they will spend in enabling yet others to make money which.... But the end of this is bedlam.

The Philosophy of Logical Analysis

In philosophy ever since the time of Pythagoras there has been an opposition between the men whose thought was mainly inspired by mathematics and those who were more influenced by the empirical sciences. Plato, Thomas Aquinas, Spinoza, and Kant belong to what may be called the mathematical party; Democritus, Aristotle, and the modern empiricist from Locke onwards, belong to the opposite party. In our day a school of philosophy has arisen which sets to work to eliminate Pythagoreanism from the principles of mathematics, and to combine empiricism with an interest in the deductive parts of human knowledge. The aims of this school are less spectacular than those of most philosophersin the past, but some of its achievements are as solid as those of the men of science.

The origin of this philosophy is in the achievements of mathematicians who set to work to purge their subject of fallacies and slipshod reasoning. The great mathematicians of the seventeenth century were optimistic and anxious for quick results; consequently they left the foundations of analytical geometry and the infinitesimal calculus insecure. Leibnitz believed in actual infinitesimals, but although this belief suited his metaphysics it has no sound basis in mathematics. Weierstrass, soon after the middle of the nineteenth century, showed how to establish the calculus without infinite zimals, and thus at last made it logically secure.

Next came Georg Cantor, who developed the theory of continuity and infinite number. "Continuity" had been, until he defined it, a vague word, convenient for philosophers like Hegel, who wished to introduce metaphysical muddles into mathematics. Cantor gave a precise significance to the word, and showed that continuity, as he defined it, was the concept needed by mathematicians and physicist. By this means a great deal of mysticism, such as that of Bergson, was rendered antiquated.

Cantor also overcame the long-standing logical puzzles about infinite number. Take the series of whole numbers from1 onwards; how many of them are there? Clearly the number isnot finite. Up to a thousand, there are a thousand numbers; up to million, a million. Whatever finite number you mention, there are evidently more numbers than that, because from 1 up to the number in question there are just that number of numbers, and then there are others that are greater. The number of finite whole numbers must, therefore, be an infinite number. But now comes a curious fact: The number of even numbers must be the same as the number of all whole numbers. Consider two rows:

There is one entry in the lower row for every one in the top row; therefore the number of terms in the two rows must be the same, although the lower row consists of only half the terms in the top row. Leibnitz, who noticed this, thought it a contradiction, and concluded, though there are infinite collections, there are no infinite numbers. George Cantor, on the contrary, boldly denied that it is a contradiction. He was right; it is only an oddity.

George Cantor defined an "infinite" collection as one which has parts containing as many terms as the whole collection contains. On this basis he was able to built up a most interesting mathematical theory of infinite numbers, thereby taking into realm of exact logic a whole region formerly given over to mysticism and confusion.

The next man of importance was Frege, who published his first work in 1879, and his definition of "number" in 1884;but in spite of the epoch-making nature of his discoveries, he remained wholly without recognition until I drew attention to him in 1903. It is remarkable that, before Frege, every definition of number that had been suggested contained elementary logical blunders. It was customary to identify "number" with "plurality".

But an instance of number is a particular number, say 3, and an instance of 3is a particular triad. The triad is a plurality, but the class of all triads - which Frege identified with the number3 - is a plurality of pluralities, and number in general, of which 3 is an instance, is a plurality of pluralities of pluralities. The elementary grammatical mistake of confounding this with the simple plurality of a given triad made the whole philosophy of number, before Frege, a tissue of nonsense in the strictest sense of the term "nonsense".

From Frege's work it followed that arithmetic, and pure mathematics generally, is nothing but a prolongations of deductive logic. This disproved Kant's theory that arithmetical propositions are "synthetic" and involve a reference to time. The development of pure mathematics from logic was set forth in detail in *Principia Mathematica*, by Whitehead and myself.

It gradually became clear that a great part of philosophy can be reduced to something that may be called "syntax", though the word has to be used in a somewhat wider sense than has hitherto been customary. Some men, notably Carnap, have advanced the theory that all philosophical problems are really syntactical, and that, when errors in syntax are avoided, a philosophical problem is thereby either solved or shown to be insoluble. I think this is an over statement, but there can be no doubt that the utility of philosophical syntax in relation to traditional problems is very great.

I will illustrate its utility by a brief explanation of what is called the theory of descriptions. By a "description" I mean a phrase such as "The present President of the United States", in which a person or thing is designated, not by name, but by some property which is supposed or known to be peculiar to him or it. Such phrases had given a lot of trouble. Suppose I say "The golden mountain does not exist" and suppose you ask "What is it that does not exist?" It would seem that, if I say "It is the golden mountain", I am attributing some sort of existence to it. Obviously I am not making the same statement as if I said, "The round square does not exist". This seemed to imply that the golden mountain is one thing and the round square is another, although neither exists. The theory of descriptions was designed to meet this and other difficulties. According to this theory, when a statement containing a phrase of the form "the so-and-so" is rightly analyzed, the phrase "the so-and-so" disappears. For example, take the statement "Scott was the author of "*Waverley*". The theory interprets this statement as saying:

"One and the only one man wrote *Waverley*, and that man was Scott". Or, more fully:

"There is an entity *c* such that the statement '*x* wrote*Waverley*' is true if *x* is *c* and false otherwise; moreover *c*is Scott".

The first part of this, before the word "moreover", is defined as meaning: "The author of *Waverley* exist (or existedor will exist)". Thus "The golden mountain does not exist" means:

"There is no entity *c* such that '*x* is golden and mountainous' is true when *x* is *c*, but not otherwise".

With this definition the puzzle as to what is meant when we say "The golden mountain does not exist" disappears.

"Existence", according to this theory, can only be asserted of descriptions. We can say "The author of *Waverley* exists", but to say "Scott exists" is bad grammar, or rather bad syntax. This clears up two millennia of muddle-headless about "existence", beginning with Plato's *Theateus*.

One result of the work we have been considering is to dethrone mathematics from the lofty place that it has occupied since Phythagoras and Plato, and to destroy the presumption against empiricism which has been derived from it. Mathematical knowledge, it is true, is not obtained by induction from experience; our reason for believing that 2and 2 are 4 is not that we have so often found, by observation, that one couple and another couple together make a quartet. In this sense, mathematical knowledge is still not empirical. But it is also not *a priori* knowledge about the world. It is, in fact, merely verbal knowledge. "3" means "2+ 1" and "4" means "3 + 1". Hence it follows (though the proof is long) that "4" means the same as "2 + 2". Thus mathematical knowledge ceases to be mysterious. It is all of the same nature as the "great truth" that there are three feet in a yard.

Physics, as well as pure mathematics, has supplied material for the philosophy of logical analysis. This has occurred especially through the theory of relativity and quantum mechanics.

What is important to the philosopher in the theory of relativity is the substitution of space-time for space and time. Common sense thinks of the physical world as composed of "things" which persist through a certain period of time and move in space. Philosophy and physics developed the notion of "thing" into that of "material substance", and thought of material substance as consisting of particles, each very small, and each persisting throughout all time. Einstein substituted events for particles; each event had to each other a relation called "interval", which could be analyzed in various ways into a time-element and space-element. The choice between these various ways was arbitrary and no one of them was theoretically preferable to any other. Given two elements A and B, in different regions, it might happen that according to one convention they were simultaneous, according to another A was earlier than B, and according to yet another B was earlier than A. No physical facts correspond to these different conventions.

From all this it seems to follow that events, not particles, must be the "stuff" of physics. What has been thought of as a particle will have to be thought of as a series of events. The series of events that replaces a particle has certain important physical properties, and therefore demands our attention; but it has no more substantiality than any other series of events that we might arbitrary single out. Thus "matter" is not part of the ultimate material of the world, but merely a convenient way of collecting events into bundles.

Quantum theory reinforces this conclusion, but its chief philosophical importance is that it regards physical phenomena as possibly discontinuous. It suggests that, in an atom (interpreted as above), a certain state of affairs persists for a certain time, and then suddenly is replaced by a finitely different state of affairs. Continuity of motion, which had always been assumed, appears to have been a mere prejudice.

The philosophy appropriate to quantum theory, however, has not yet been adequately developed. I suspect that it will demand even more radical departures from the traditional doctrine of space and time than those demanded by the theory of relativity.

While physics has been making matter less material, psychology has been making mind less mental. We had occasion in a former chapter to compare the association of ideas with the conditioned reflex. The latter, which has replaced the former, is much more physiological. (This is only one illustration; I do not wish to exaggerate the scope of the conditioned reflex).

Thus from both ends physics and psychology have been approaching each other, and making more possible the doctrine of "neutral monism" suggested by William James's criticism of "consciousness". The distinction of mind and matter came into philosophy form religion, although, for a long time, it seemed to have valid grounds. I think that both mind and matter are merely convenient ways of grouping events. Some single events, I should admit, belong only to material groups, but others belong to both kinds of groups, and are therefore at once mental and material. This doctrine effects a great simplification in our picture of the structure of the world.

Modern Physics and physiology throw a new light upon the ancient problem of perception. If there is to be anything that can be called "perception", it must be in some degree an effect of the object perceived, and must more or less resemble the object if it is to be a source of knowledge of the object. The first requisite can only be fulfilled if there are causal chains which are, to a greater or less extent, independent of the rest of the world. According to physics, this is the case. Light-waves travel from the sun to the earth, and in doing so obey their own laws.

This is only roughly true. Einstein has shown that light-rays are affected by gravitation. When they reach our atmosphere, they suffer refraction, and some are more scattered than others. When they reach a human eye, all sorts of things happen which would not happen elsewhere, ending up with what we call "seeing the sun". But although the sun of our visual experience is very different from the sun of the astronomer, it is still a source of knowledge as to the latter, because "seeing the sun" differs from "seeing the moon" in ways that are causally connected with the difference between the astronomer's sun and the astronomer's moon.

What we can know of physical objects in this way, however, is only certain abstract properties of structure. We can know that the sun is round in a sense, though not quite the sense in which what we see is round; but we have no reason to suppose that it is bright or warm, because physics can account for its seeming so without supposing that it is so. Our knowledge of the physical world, therefore, is only abstract and mathematical.

Modern analytical empiricism, of which I have been giving an outline, differs from that of Locke, Berkeley, and Hume by its incorporation of mathematics and its development of powerful logical technique. It is thus able, in regard to certain problems, to achieve definite answers, which have the quality of science rather that of philosophy. It has the advantage, as compared with the philosophies of the system-builders, of being able to tackle its problems one at a time, instead of having to invent at one stroke a block theory of the whole universe. Its methods, in this respect, resemble those of science. I have no doubt that, in so far as philosophical knowledge is possible, it is by such methods, many ancient problems are completely soluble.

There remains, however, a vast field, traditionally included in philosophy, where scientific methods are inadequate. This field includes ultimate questions of value; science alone, for example, cannot prove that it is bad to enjoy the infliction of cruelty. Whatever can be known, can be known by means of science; but things which are legitimately matters of feeling lie outside its province.

Philosophy, throughout its history, has consisted of two parts inharmoniously blended; on the one hand a theory as to the nature of the world, on the other an ethical or political doctrine as to the best way of living. The failure to separate these two with sufficient clarity has been a source of much confused thinking.

Philosophers, from Plato to William James, have allowed their opinions as to the constitution of the universe to be influenced by the desire for edification: knowing, as they supposed, what beliefs would make men virtuous, they have invented arguments, often very sophistical, to prove that these beliefs are true. For my part I reprobate this kind of bias, both on moral and on intellectual grounds. Morally, a philosopher who uses his professional competency for anything except a disinterested search for truth is guilty of a kind of treachery. And when he assumes, in advance of inquiry, that certain beliefs, whether true or false, are such as to promote good behaviour, he is so limiting the scope of philosophical speculation as to make philosophy trivial; the true philosopher is prepared to examine *all* preconceptions.

When any limits are placed, consciously or unconsciously, upon the pursuit of truth, philosophy becomes paralyzed by fear, and the ground is prepared for a government censorship punishing those who utter "dangerous thoughts" - in fact, the philosopher has already places such a censorship over his own investigations.

Intellectually, the effect of mistaken moral considerations upon philosophy has been to impede progress to an extraordinary extent. I do not myself believe that philosophy can either prove or disprove the truth of religious dogmas, but ever since Plato most philosophers have considered it part of their business to produce "proofs" of immortality and the existence of God. They have found fault with the proofs of their predecessors - Saint Thomas rejected Saint Anselm's proofs, and Kant rejected Descartes' – but they have supplied new ones of their own. In order to make their proofs seem valid, they have had to falsify logic, to make mathematics mystical, and to pretend that deep-seated prejudices were heaven-sent intuitions.

All this is rejected by the philosophers who make logical analysis the main business of philosophy. They confess frankly that the human intellect is unable to find conclusive answers to many questions of profound importance to mankind, but they refuse to believe that there are some "higher" way of knowing, by which we can discover truths hidden from science and the intellect. For this renunciation they have been rewarded by the discovery that many questions, formerly obscured by the fog of metaphysics, can be answered with precision, and by objective methods which introduce nothing of the philosopher's temperament except the desire to understand.

Take such questions as: What is number? What are space and time? What is mind, and what is matter? I do not say that a method has been discovered by which, as in science, we can make successive approximations to the truth, in which each new stage results from an improvement, not a rejection, of what has gone before.

In the welter of conflicting fanaticisms, one of the few unifying forces is scientific truthfulness, by which I mean the habit of basing our beliefs upon observations and inferences as impersonal, and as much diverse of local and temperamental bias, as is possible for human beings.

To have insisted upon the introduction of his virtue into philosophy, and to have invented a powerful method by which it can be rendered fruitful, are the chief merits of the philosophical school of which I am a member. The habit of careful veracity acquired in the practice of this philosophical method can be extended to the whole sphere of human activity, producing, wherever it exists, a lessening of fanaticism with an increasing capacity of sympathy and mutual understanding. In abandoning a part of its dogmatic pretensions, philosophy does not cease to suggest and inspire a way of life.

Knowledge and Wisdom

Most people would agree that, although our age far surpasses all previous ages in knowledge, there has been no correlative increase in wisdom. But agreement ceases as soon as we attempt to define 'wisdom' and consider means of promoting it. I want to ask first what wisdom is, and then what can be done to teach it. There are, I think, several factors that contribute to wisdom. Of these I should put first a sense of proportion: the capacity to take account of all the important factors in a problem and to attach to each its due weight. This has become more difficult than it used to be owing to the extent and complexity for the specialized knowledge required of various kinds of technicians. Suppose, for example, that you are engaged in research in scientific medicine. The work is difficult and is likely to absorb the whole of your intellectual energy. You have not time to consider the effect which your discoveries or inventions may have outside the field of medicine. You succeed (let us say), as modern medicine has succeeded, in enormously lowering the infant death-rate, not only in Europe and America, but also in Asia and Africa.

This has the entirely unintended result of making the food supply inadequate and lowering the standard of life in the most populous parts of the world. To take an even more spectacular example, which is in everybody's mind at the present time: You study the composition of the atom from a disinterested desire for knowledge, and incidentally place in the hands of powerful lunatics the means of destroying the human race. In such ways the pursuit of knowledge may become harmful unless it is combined with wisdom; and wisdom in the sense of comprehensive vision is not necessarily present in specialists in the pursuit of knowledge.

Comprehensiveness alone, however, is not enough to constitute wisdom. There must be, also, a certain awareness of the ends of human life. This may be illustrated by the study of history. Many eminent historians have done more harm than good because they viewed facts through the distorting medium of their own passions. Hegel had a philosophy of history which did not suffer from any lack of comprehensiveness, since it started from the earliest times and continued into an indefinite future.

But the chief lesson of history which he sought to inculcate was that from the year 400AD down to his own time Germany had been the most important nation and the standard-bearer of progress in the world. Perhaps one could stretch the comprehensiveness that constitutes wisdom to include not only intellect but also feeling. It is by no means uncommon to find men whose knowledge is wide but whose feelings are narrow. Such men lack what I call wisdom.

It is not only in public ways, but in private life equally, that wisdom is needed. It is needed in the choice of ends to be pursued and in emancipation from personal prejudice. Even an end which it would be noble to pursue if it were attainable may be pursued unwisely if it is inherently impossible of achievement. Many men in past ages devoted their lives to a search for the philosopher's stone and the elixir of life. No doubt, if they could have found them, they would have conferred great benefits upon mankind, but as it was their lives were wasted. To descend to less heroic matters, consider the case of two men, Mr. A and Mr. B, who hate each other and, through mutual hatred, bring each other to destruction. Suppose you go to the Mr. A and say, 'Why do you hate Mr. B?' He will no doubt give you an appalling list of Mr. B's vices, partly true, partly false. And now suppose you go to Mr. B. He will give you an exactly similar list of Mr. A's vices with an equal admixture of truth and falsehood. Suppose you now come back to Mr. A and say, 'You will be surprised too learn that Mr. B says the same things about you as you say about him', and you go to Mr. B and make a similar speech. The first effect, no doubt, will be to increase their mutual hatred, since each will be so horrified by the other's injustice. But perhaps, if you have sufficient patience and sufficient persuasiveness, you may succeed in convincing each that the other has only the normal share of human wickedness, and that their enmity is harmful to both. If you can do this, you will have instilled some fragment of wisdom.

I think the essence of wisdom is emancipation, as fat as possible, from the tyranny of the here and now. We cannot help the egoism of our senses. Sight and sound and touch are bound up with our own bodies and cannot be impersonal. Our emotions start similarly from ourselves. An infant feels hunger or discomfort, and is unaffected except by his own physical condition. Gradually with the years, his horizon widens, and, in proportion as his thoughts and feelings become less personal and less concerned with his own physical states, he achieves growing wisdom.

This is of course a matter of degree. No one can view the world with complete impartiality; and if anyone could, he would hardly be able to remain alive. But it is possible to make a continual approach towards impartiality, on the one hand, by knowing things somewhat remote in time or space, and on the other hand, by giving to such things their due weight in our feelings. It is this approach towards impartiality that constitutes growth in wisdom.

Can wisdom in this sense be taught? And, if it can, should the teaching of it be one of the aims of education? I should answer both these questions in the affirmative. We are told on Sundays that we should love our neighbours as ourselves. On the other six days of the week, we are exhorted to hate. But you will remember that the precept was exemplified by saying that the Samaritan was our neighbour. We no longer have any wish to hate Samaritans and so we are apt to miss the point of the parable.

If you want to get its point, you should substitute Communist or anti-Communist, as the case may be, for Samaritan. It might be objected that it is right to hate those who do harm. I do not think so. If you hate them, it is only too likely that you will become equally harmful; and it is very unlikely that you will induce them to abandon their evil ways. Hatred of evil is itself a kind of bondage to evil. The way out is through understanding, not through hate. I am not advocating non-resistance. But I am saying that resistance, if it is to be effective in preventing the spread of evil, should be combined with the greatest degree of understanding and the smallest degree of force that is compatible with the survival of the good things that we wish to preserve.

It is commonly urged that a point of view such as I have been advocating is incompatible with vigor in action. I do not think history bears out this view. Queen Elizabeth I in England and Henry IV in France lived in a world where almost everybody was fanatical, either on the Protestant or on the

Catholic side. Both remained free from the errors of their time and both, by remaining free, were beneficent and certainly not ineffective. Abraham Lincoln conducted a great war without ever departing from what I have called wisdom.

I have said that in some degree wisdom can be taught. I think that this teaching should have a larger intellectual element than has been customary in what has been thought of as moral instruction. I think that the disastrous results of hatred and narrow-mindedness to those who feel them can be pointed out incidentally in the course of giving knowledge. I do not think that knowledge and morals ought to be too much separated.

It is true that the kind of specialized knowledge which is required for various kinds of skill has very little to do with wisdom. But it should be supplemented in education by wider surveys calculated to put it in its place in the total of human activities. Even the best technicians should also be good citizens; and when I say 'citizens', I mean citizens of the world and not of this or that sect or nation. With every increase of knowledge and skill, wisdom becomes more necessary, for every such increase augments our capacity of realizing our purposes, and therefore augments our capacity for evil, if our purposes are unwise. The world needs wisdom as it has never needed it before; and if knowledge continues to increase, the world will need wisdom in the future even more than it does now.

On Youthful Cynicism

Any person who visits the Universities of the Western world is liable to be struck by the fact that the intelligent young of the present day are cynical to a far greater extent than was the case formerly. This is not true of Russia, India, China or Japan; I believe it is not the case in Czechoslovakia, Jugoslavia, and Poland, nor by any means universally in Germany, but it certainly is a notable characteristic of intelligent youth in England, France and the United States. To understand why youth is cynical in the West, we must also understand why it is not cynical in the East. Young men in Russia are not cynical because they accept, on the whole, the Communist philosophy, and they have a great country full of natural resources, ready to be exploited by the help of intelligence. The young have therefore a career before them which they feel to be worth while. You do not have to consider the ends of life when in the course of creating Utopia you are laying a pipeline, building a railway, or teaching peasants to use Ford tractors simultaneously on a four-mile front. Consequently the Russian youth are vigorous and filled with ardent beliefs.

In India the fundamental belief of the earnest young is in the wickedness of England: from this premise, as from the existence of Descartes, it is possible to deduce a whole philosophy. From the fact that England is Christian, it follows that Hinduism or Mohammedanism, as the case may be, is the only true religion.

From the fact that England is capitalistic and industrial, it follows, according to the temperament of the logician concerned, either that everyone ought to spin with a spinning wheel, or that protective duties ought to be imposed to develop native industrialism and capitalism as the only weapons with which to combat those of the British. From the fact that the British hold India by physical force, it follows that only moral force is admirable.

The persecution of nationalist activities in India is just sufficient to make them heroic, and not sufficient to make them seem futile. In this way the Anglo-Indians save the intelligent youth of India from the blight of cynicism.

In China hatred of England has also played its part, but a much smaller part than in India because the English have never conquered the country. The Chinese youth combine patriotism with genuine enthusiasm for Occidentalism, in the way that was common in Japan fifty years ago. They want the Chinese people to be enlightened, free and prosperous, and they have their work cut out to produce this result. Their ideals are, on the whole, those of the nineteenth century, which in China has not yet begun to seem antiquated.

Cynicism in China was associated with the officials of the Imperial regime and survived among the warring militarists who have distracted the country since 1911, but it has no place in the mentality of the modern intellectuals.

In Japan, the outlook of young intellectuals is not unlike that which prevailed on the Continent of Europe between 1815 and 1848. The watchwords of Liberalism are still potent; parliamentary government, liberty of the subject, free thought and free speech. The struggle against traditional feudalism and autocracy is quite sufficient to keep young men busy and enthusiastic.

To the sophisticated youth of the West all this ardour seems a trifle crude. He is firmly persuaded that having studied everything impartially, he has seen through everything and found that there is 'nothing left remarkable beneath the visiting moon.' There are, of course, plenty of reasons for this in the teachings of the old. I do not think these go to the root of the matter, for in other circumstances the young react against the teaching of the old and achieve a gospel of their own. If the Occidental youth of the present day react only by cynicism, there must be some special reason for this circumstance.

Not only are the young unable to believe what they are told, but they seem also unable to believe anything else. This is a peculiar state of affairs, which deserves investigation. Let us first take some of the old ideals one by one and see why they no longer inspire the old loyalties. We may enumerate among such ideals religion, country, progress, beauty, truth. what is wrong with these in the eyes of the young?

Religion. - The trouble here is partly intellectual, partly social. For intellectual reasons few able men have now the same intensity of religious belief as was possible for, say, St. Thomas Aquinas. The God of most moderns is a little vague, and apt to degenerate into a Life Force or a 'power not ourselves that makes for righteousness'. Even believers are concerned much more with the effects of religion in this world than with that other world they profess to believe in; they are not nearly so sure that this world was created for the glory of God as they are that God is a useful hypothesis for improving this world. By subordinating God to the needs of this sublunary life, they cast suspicion upon the genuineness of their faith. They seem to think that God, like the Sabbath, was made for man. There are also sociological reasons for not accepting the Churches as the basis of modern idealism. The Churches, through their endowments, have become bound up with the defense of property.

Moreover, they are connected with an oppressive ethic, which condemns many pleasures that to the young appear harmless and inflicts many torments that to the sceptical appear unnecessarily cruel. I have known earnest young men who accepted wholeheartedly the teaching of Christ; they found themselves in opposition to official Christianity, outcasts and victims of persecution, quite as much as if they had been militant atheists.

Country. - Patriotism has been in many times and places a passionate belief to which the best minds could give full assent. It was so in England in the time of Shakespeare, in Germany in the time of Fichte, in Italy in the time of Mazzini. It is so still in Poland, China, and Outer Mongolia. In the Western nations it is still immensely powerful: it controls politics, public expenditure, military preparations, and so on. But the intelligent youth are unable to accept it as an adequate ideal; they perceive that it is all very well for oppressed nations, but that as soon as an oppressed nation achieves its freedom, the nationalism which was formerly heroic becomes oppressive.

The Poles, who had the sympathy of idealists ever since Maria Teresa 'wept but took', have used their freedom to organize oppression in Ukrainia. The Irish, upon whom the British had inflicted civilization for eight hundred years, have used their freedom to pass laws preventing the publication of many good books. The spectacle of the Poles murdering Ukrainians and the Irish murdering literature makes nationalism seem a somewhat inadequate ideal even for a small nation. But when it comes to a powerful nation, the argument is even stronger. The Treaty of Versailles was not very encouraging to those who had the luck not to be killed in defending the ideals which their rulers betrayed. Those who during the war averred that they were combating militarism became at its conclusion the leading militarists in their respective countries. Such facts have made it obvious to all intelligent young men that patriotism is the chief curse of our age and will bring civilization to an end if it cannot be mitigated.

Progress. - This is a nineteenth-century ideal which has too much Babbitt about it for the sophisticated youth. Measurable progress is necessarily in unimportant things, such as the number of motor-cars made, or the number of peanuts consumed. The really important things are not measurable and are therefore not suitable for the methods of the booster. Moreover, many modern inventions tend to make people silly. I might instance the radio, the talkies, and poison gas. Shakespeare measured the excellence of an age by its style in poetry, but this mode of measurement is out of date.

Beauty. - There is something that sounds old-fashioned about beauty, though it is hard to say why. A modern painter would be indignant if he were accused of seeking beauty. Most artists nowadays appear to be inspired by some kind of rage against the world so that they wish rather to give significant pain than to afford serene satisfaction. Moreover many kinds of beauty require that a man should take himself more seriously than is possible for an intelligent modern. A prominent citizen in a small city State, such as Athens or Florence, could without difficulty feel himself important. The earth was the center of the Universe, man was the purpose of creation, his own city showed man at his best, and he himself was among the best of his own city. In such circumstances Æschylus or Dante could take his own joys or sorrows seriously.

He could feel that the emotions of the individual matter, and that tragic occurrences deserve to be celebrated in immortal verse. But the modern man, when misfortune assails him, is conscious of himself as a unit in a statistical total; the past and the future stretch before him in a dreary procession of trivial defeats. Man himself appears as a somewhat ridiculous strutting animal, shouting and fussing during a brief interlude between infinite silences. 'Unacommodated man is no more but such a poor, bare, forked animal,' says King Lear, and the idea drives him to madness because it is unfamiliar. But to the modern man the idea is familiar and drives him only to triviality.

Truth. - In old days truth was absolute, eternal and superhuman. Myself when young accepted this view and devoted a misspent youth to the search for truth. But a whole host of enemies have arisen to slay truth: pragmatism, behaviourism, psychologism, relativity-physics. Galileo and the Inquisition disagreed as to whether the earth went round the sun or the sun went round the earth. Both agreed in thinking that there was a great difference between these two opinions. The point on which they agreed was the one on which they were both mistaken: the difference is only one of words. In old days it was possible to worship truth; indeed the sincerity of the worship was demonstrated by the practice of human sacrifice. But it is difficult to worship a merely human and relative truth. The law of gravitation, according to Eddington, is only a convenient convention of measurement. It is not truer than other views, any more than the metric system is truer than feet and yards.

Nature and Nature's law lay hid in night;
God said, 'Let Newton be,; and measurement was facilitated.

This sentiment seems lacking in sublimity. When Spinoza believed anything, he considered that he was enjoying the intellectual love of God. The modern man believes with Marx that he is swayed by economic motives, or with Freud that some sexual motive underlies his belief in the exponential theorem or in the distribution of fauna in the Red Sea. In neither case can he enjoy Spinoza's exaltation.

So far we have been considering modern cynicism in a rationalistic manner, as something that has intellectual causes. Belief, however, as modern psychologists never weary of telling us, is seldom determined by rational motives, and the same is true of disbelief, though skeptics often overlook this fact. The causes of any widespread skepticism are likely to be sociological rather than intellectual.

The main cause is always comfort without power. The holders of power are not cynical, since they are able to enforce their ideals. Victims of oppression are not cynical, since they are filled with hate, and hate, like any other strong passion, brings with it a train of attendant beliefs. Until the advent of education, democracy, and mass production, intellectuals had everywhere a considerable influence upon the march of affairs, which was by no means diminished if their heads were cut off. The modern intellectual finds himself in a quite different situation. It is by no means difficult for him to obtain a fat job and a good income provided he is willing to sell his services to the stupid rich either as propagandist or as Court jester. The effect of mass production and elementary education is that stupidity is more firmly entrenched than at any other time since the rise of civilization. When the Czarist Government killed Lenin's brother, it did not turn Lenin into a cynic, since hatred inspired a lifelong activity in which he was finally successful.

But in the more solid countries of the West there is seldom such potent cause for hatred, or such opportunity for spectacular revenge. The work of intellectuals is ordered and paid for by Governments or rich men, whose aims probably seem absurd, if not pernicious, to the intellectuals concerned. But a dash of cynicism enables them to adjust their consciences to the situation. There are, it is true, some activities in which wholly admirable work is desired by the powers that be; the chief of these is science, and the next is public architecture in America. But if a man's education has been literary, as is still too often the case, he finds himself at the age of twenty-two with a considerable skill that he cannot exercise in any manner that appear important to himself. Men of science are not cynical even in the West, because they can exercise their best brains with the full approval of the community; but in this they are exceptionally fortunate among modern intellectuals.

If this diagnosis is right, modern cynicism cannot be cured merely by preaching, or by putting better ideals before the young than those that their pastors and masters fish out from the rusty armory of outworn superstitions. The cure will only come when intellectuals can find a career that embodies their creative impulses. I do not see any prescription except the old one advocated by Disraeli: 'Educate our masters.' But it will have to be a more real education than is commonly given at the present day to either proletarians or plutocrats, and it will have to be an education taking some account of real cultural values and not only of the utilitarian desire to produce so many goods that nobody have time to enjoy them. A man is not allowed to practice medicine unless he knows something of the human body, but a financier is allowed to operate freely without any knowledge at all of the multifarious effects of his activities, with the sole exception of the effect upon his bank account.

How pleasant a world would be in which no man was allowed to operate on the Stock Exchange unless he could pass an examination in economics and Greek poetry, and in which politicians were obliged to have a competent knowledge of history and modern novels! Imagine a magnate confronted with the question: 'If you were to make a corner in wheat, what effect would this have upon German poetry?' Causation in the modern world is more complex and remote in its ramifications than it ever was before, owing to the increase in large organizations; but those who control these organizations are ignorant men who do not know the hundredth part of the consequences of their actions. Rabelais published his book anonymously for fear of losing his University post.

A modern Rabelais would never write the book, because he would be aware that his anonymity would be penetrated by the perfected methods of publicity. The rulers of the world have always been stupid, but they have not in the past been so powerful as they are now. It is therefore more important than it used to be to find some way of securing that they shall be intelligent. Is this problem insoluble? I do not think so, but I should be the last to maintain that it is easy.

Philosophical Consequences Of Relativity

[The mathematician, philosopher, and social thinker Bertrand Russell was at work on his classic exposition of Einstein's theory of relativity, The A. B. C. of Relativity, when he agreed to write this piece for the Thirteenth Edition of

Britannica. It makes for an unusual encyclopadia article—it is tentative, somewhat speculative—but it provides an interesting counterpoint to Einstein's own, more technical article.]

Relativity: Philosophical Consequences.

Of the consequences in philosophy, which may be supposed to follow from the theory of relativity, some are fairly certain, while others are open to question. There has been a tendency, not uncommon in the case of a new scientific theory, for every philosopher to interpret the work of Einstein in accordance with his own metaphysical system, and to suggest that the outcome is a great accession of strength to the views, which the philosopher in question previously held. This cannot be true in all cases; and it may be hoped that it is true in none. It would be disappointing if so fundamental a change as Einstein has introduced involved no philosophical novelty.

Space-Time.—For philosophy, the most important novelty was present already in the special theory of relativity; that is, the substitution of space-time for space and time. In Newtonian dynamics, two events were separated by two kinds of interval, one being distance in space, the other lapse of time. As soon as it was realised that all motion is relative (which happened long before Einstein), distance in space became ambiguous except in the case of simultaneous events, but it was still thought that there was no ambiguity about simultaneity in different places.

The special theory of relativity showed, by experimental arguments which were new, and by logical arguments which could have been discovered any time after it became known that light travels with a finite velocity, that simultaneity is only definite when it applies to events in the same place, and becomes more and more ambiguous as the events are more widely removed from each other in space.

This statement is not quite correct, since it still uses the notion of "space." The correct statement is this: Events have a four-dimensional order, by means of which we can say that an event A is nearer to an event B than to an event C; this is a purely ordinal matter, not involving anything quantitative. But, in addition, there is between neighbouring events a quantitative relation called "interval," which fulfils the functions both of distance in space and of lapse of time in the traditional dynamics, but fulfils them with a difference. If a body can move so as to be present at both events, the interval is time-like.

If a ray of light can move so as to be present at both events, the interval is zero. If neither can happen, the interval is space-like. When we speak of a body being present "at" an event, we mean that the event occurs in the same place in space-time as one of the events which make up the history of the body; and when we say that two events occur at the same place in space-time, we mean that there is no event between them in the four-dimensional space-time order. All the events which happen to a man at a given moment (in his own time) are, in this sense, in one place; for example, if we hear a noise and see a colour simultaneously, our two perceptions are both in one place in space-time.

When one body can be present at two events which are not in one place in space-time, the time-order of the two events is not ambiguous, though the magnitude of the time-interval will be different in different systems of measurement. But whenever the interval between two events is space-like, their time-order will be different in different equally legitimate systems of measurement; in this case, therefore, the time-order does not represent a physical fact.

It follows that, when two bodies are in relative motion, like the sun and a planet, there is no such physical fact as "the distance between the bodies at a given time"; this alone shows that Newton's law of gravitation is logically faulty. Fortunately, Einstein has not only pointed out the defect, but remedied it. His arguments against Newton, however, would have remained valid even if his own law of gravitation had not proved right.

Time not a Single Cosmic Order.—The fact that time is private to each body, not a single cosmic order, involves changes in the notions of substance and cause, and suggests the substitution of a series of events for a substance with changing states.

The controversy about the aether thus becomes rather unreal. Undoubtedly, when light-waves travel, events occur, and it used to be thought that these events must be "in" something; the something in which they were was called the aether. But there seems no reason except a logical prejudice to suppose that the events are "in" anything. Matter, also, may be reduced to a law according to which events succeed each other and spread out from centres; but here we enter upon more speculative considerations.

Physical Laws.—Prof. Eddington has emphasised an aspect of relativity theory which is of great philosophical importance, but difficult to make clear without somewhat abstruse mathematics. The aspect in question is the reduction of what used to be regarded as physical laws to the status of truisms or definitions. Prof. Eddington, in a profoundly interesting essay on "The Domain of Physical Science," states the matter as follows:—

In the present stage of science the laws of physics appear to be divisible into three classes—the identical, the statistical and the transcendental. The "identical laws" include the great field-laws which are commonly quoted as typical instances of natural law—the law of gravitation, the law of conservation of mass and energy, the laws of electric and magnetic force and the conservation of electric charge.

These are seen to be identities, when we refer to the cycle so as to understand the constitution of the entities obeying them; and unless we have misunderstood this constitution, violation of these laws is inconceivable. They do not in any way limit the actual basal structure of the world, and are not laws of governance.

It is these identical laws that form the subject-matter of relativity theory; the other laws of physics, the statistical and transcendental, lie outside its scope. Thus the net result of relativity theory is to show that the traditional laws of physics, rightly understood, tell us almost nothing about the course of nature, being rather of the nature of logical truisms.

This surprising result is an outcome of increased mathematical skill. As the same author [Footnote 2] says elsewhere:—

In one sense, deductive theory is the enemy of experimental physics. The latter is always striving to settle by crucial tests the nature of the fundamental things; the former strives to minimise the successes obtained by showing how wide a nature of things is compatible with all experimental results.

The suggestion is that, in almost any conceivable world, something will be conserved; mathematics gives us the means of constructing a variety of mathematical expressions having this property of conservation. It is natural to suppose that it is useful to have senses, which notice these conserved entities; hence mass, energy, and so on seem to have a basis in our experience, but are in fact merely certain quantities which are conserved and which we are adapted for noticing. If this view is correct, physics tells us much less about the real world than was formerly supposed.

Force and Gravitation.—An important aspect of relativity is the elimination of "force." This is not new in idea; indeed, it was already accepted in rational dynamics. But there remained the outstanding difficulty of gravitation, which Einstein has overcome. The sun is, so to speak, at the summit of a hill, and the planets are on the slopes.

They move as they do because of the slope where they are, not because of some mysterious influence emanating from the summit. Bodies move as they do because that is the easiest possible movement in the region of space-time in which they find themselves, not because "forces" operate upon them. The apparent need of forces to account for observed motions arises from mistaken insistence upon Euclidean geometry; when once we have overcome this prejudice, we find that observed motions, instead of showing the presence of forces, show the nature of the geometry applicable to the region concerned. Bodies thus become far more independent of each other than they were in Newtonian physics: there is an increase of individualism and a diminution of central government, if one may be permitted such metaphorical language. This may, in time, considerably modify the ordinary educated man's picture of the universe, possibly with far-reaching results.

Realism in Relativity.—It is a mistake to suppose that relativity adopts an idealistic picture of the world—using "idealism" in the technical sense, in which it implies that there can be nothing which is not experience. The "observer" who is often mentioned in expositions of relativity need not be a mind, but may be a photographic plate or any kind of recording instrument.

The fundamental assumption of relativity is realistic, namely, that those respects in which all observers agree when they record a given phenomenon may be regarded as objective, and not as contributed by the observers. This assumption is made by common sense.

The apparent sizes and shapes of objects differ according to the point of view, but common sense discounts these differences. Relativity theory merely extends this process. By taking into account not only human observers, who all share the motion of the earth, but also possible "observers" in very rapid motion relatively to the earth, it is found that much more depends upon the point of view of the observer than was formerly thought. But there is found to be a residue which is not so dependent; this is the part which can be expressed by the method of "tensors." The importance of this method can hardly be exaggerated; it is, however, quite impossible to explain it in non-mathematical terms.

Relativity Physics.—Relativity physics is, of course, concerned only with the quantitative aspects of the world. The picture, which it suggests, is somewhat as follows:—In the four-dimensional space-time frame there are events everywhere, usually many events in a single place in space-time.

The abstract mathematical relations of these events proceed according to the laws of physics, but the intrinsic nature of the events is wholly and inevitably unknown except when they occur in a region where there is the sort of structure we call a brain.

Then they become the familiar sights and sounds and so on of our daily life. We know what it is like to see a star, but we do not know the nature of the events, which constitute the ray of light that travels from the star to our eye. And the space-time frame itself is known only in its abstract mathematical properties; there is no reason to suppose it similar in intrinsic character to the spatial and temporal relations of our perceptions as known in experience.

There does not seem any possible way of overcoming this ignorance, since the very nature of physical reasoning allows only the most abstract inferences, and only the most abstract properties of our perceptions can be regarded as having objective validity. Whether any other science than physics can tell us more, does not fall within the scope of the present article.

Meanwhile, it is a curious fact that this meager kind of knowledge is sufficient for the practical uses of physics. From a practical point of view, the physical world only matters in so far as it affects us, and the intrinsic nature of what goes on in our absence is irrelevant, provided we can predict the effects upon ourselves.

This we can do, just as a person can use a telephone without understanding electricity. Only the most abstract knowledge is required for practical manipulation of matter. But there is a grave danger when this habit of manipulation based upon mathematical laws is carried over into our dealings with human beings, since they, unlike the telephone wire, are capable of happiness and misery, desire and aversion. It would therefore be unfortunate if the habits of mind which are appropriate and right in dealing with material mechanisms were allowed to dominate the administrator's attempts at social constructiveness.

The Russell-Einstein Manifesto

IN the tragic situation which confronts humanity, we feel that scientists should assemble in conference to appraise the perils that have arisen as a result of the development of weapons of mass destruction, and to discuss a resolution in the spirit of the appended draft. We are speaking on this occasion, not as members of this or that nation, continent, or creed, but as human beings, members of the species Man, whose continued existence is in doubt. The world is full of conflicts; and, overshadowing all minor conflicts, the titanic struggle between Communism and anti-Communism.

Almost everybody who is politically conscious has strong feelings about one or more of these issues; but we want you, if you can, to set aside such feelings and consider yourselves only as members of a biological species which has had a remarkable history, and whose disappearance none of us can desire. We shall try to say no single word which should appeal to one group rather than to another.

All, equally, are in peril, and, if the peril is understood, there is hope that they may collectively avert it. We have to learn to think in a new way. We have to learn to ask ourselves, not what steps can be taken to give military victory to whatever group we prefer, for there no longer are such steps; the question we have to ask ourselves is: what steps can be taken to prevent a military contest of which the issue must be disastrous to all parties?

The general public, and even many men in positions of authority, have not realized what would be involved in a war with nuclear bombs. The general public still thinks in terms of the obliteration of cities. It is understood that the new bombs are more powerful than the old, and that, while one A-bomb could obliterate Hiroshima, one H-bomb could obliterate the largest cities, such as London, New York, and Moscow.

No doubt in an H-bomb war great cities would be obliterated. But this is one of the minor disasters that would have to be faced. If everybody in London, New York, and Moscow were exterminated, the world might, in the course of a few centuries, recover from the blow.

But we now know, especially since the Bikini test, that nuclear bombs can gradually spread destruction over a very much wider area than had been supposed. It is stated on very good authority that a bomb can now be manufactured which will be 2,500 times as powerful as that which destroyed Hiroshima. Such a bomb, if exploded near the ground or under water, sends radio-active particles into the upper air. They sink gradually and reach the surface of the earth in the form of a deadly dust or rain. It was this dust which infected the Japanese fishermen and their catch of fish. No one knows how widely such lethal radio-active particles might be diffused, but the best authorities are unanimous in saying that a war with H-bombs might possibly put an end to the human race. It is feared that if many H-bombs are used there will be universal death, sudden only for a minority, but for the majority a slow torture of disease and disintegration.

Many warnings have been uttered by eminent men of science and by authorities in military strategy. None of them will say that the worst results are certain. What they do say is that these results are possible, and no one can be sure that they will not be realized. We have not yet found that the views of experts on this question depend in any degree upon their politics or prejudices. They depend only, so far as our researches have revealed, upon the extent of the particular expert's knowledge. We have found that the men who know most are the most gloomy.

Here, then, is the problem which we present to you, stark and dreadful and inescapable: Shall we put an end to the human race; or shall mankind renounce war? People will not face this alternative because it is so difficult to abolish war.

The abolition of war will demand distasteful limitations of national sovereignty. But what perhaps impedes understanding of the situation more than anything else is that the term "mankind" feels vague and abstract. People scarcely realize in imagination that the danger is to themselves and their children and their grandchildren, and not only to a dimly apprehended humanity. They can scarcely bring themselves to grasp that they, individually, and those whom they love are in imminent danger of perishing agonizingly. And so they hope that perhaps war may be allowed to continue provided modern weapons are prohibited.

This hope is illusory. Whatever agreements not to use H-bombs had been reached in time of peace, they would no longer be considered binding in time of war, and both sides would set to work to manufacture H-bombs as soon as war broke out, for, if one side manufactured the bombs and the other did not, the side that manufactured them would inevitably be victorious.

Although an agreement to renounce nuclear weapons as part of a general reduction of armaments would not afford an ultimate solution, it would serve certain important purposes. First, any agreement between East and West is to the good in so far as it tends to diminish tension. Second, the abolition of thermo-nuclear weapons, if each side believed that the other had carried it out sincerely, would lessen the fear of a sudden attack in the style of Pearl Harbour, which at present keeps both sides in a state of nervous apprehension. We should, therefore, welcome such an agreement though only as a first step. Most of us are not neutral in feeling, but, as human beings, we have to remember that, if the issues between East and West are to be decided in any manner that can give any possible satisfaction to anybody, whether Communist or anti-Communist, whether Asian or European or American, whether White or Black, then these issues must not be decided by war. We should wish this to be understood, both in the East and in the West. There lies before us, if we choose, continual progress in happiness, knowledge, and wisdom. Shall we, instead, choose death, because we cannot forget our quarrels? We appeal as human beings to human beings: Remember your humanity, and forget the rest. If you can do so, the way lies open to a new Paradise; if you cannot, there lies before you the risk of universal death.

Resolution

WE invite this Congress, and through it the scientists of the world and the general public, to subscribe to the following resolution:

"In view of the fact that in any future world war nuclear weapons will certainly be employed, and that such weapons threaten the continued existence of mankind, we urge the governments of the world to realize, and to acknowledge publicly, that their purpose cannot be furthered by a world war, and we urge them, consequently, to find peaceful means for the settlement of all matters of dispute between them.".

What is an Agnostic

An agnostic thinks it impossible to know the truth in matters such as God and the future life with which Christianity and other religions are concerned. Or, if not impossible, at least impossible at the present time.

Are agnostics Atheists

No. An atheist, like a Christian, holds that we *can* know whether or not there is a God. The Christian holds that we can know there is a God; the atheist, that we can know there is not. The Agnostic suspends judgment, saying that there are not sufficient grounds either for affirmation or for denial. At the same time, an Agnostic may hold that the existence of God, though not impossible, is very improbable; he may even hold it so improbable that it is not worth considering in practice. In that case, he is not far removed from atheism. His attitude may be that which a careful philosopher would have towards the gods of ancient Greece. If I were asked to *prove* that Zeus and Poseidon and Hera and the rest of the Olympians do not exist, I should be at a loss to find conclusive arguments. An Agnostic may think the Christian God as improbable as the Olympians; in that case, he is, for practical purposes, at one with the atheists.

Since you deny 'God's Law', what authority do you accept as a guide to Conduct

An Agnostic does not accept any 'authority' in the sense in which religious people do. He holds that a man should think out questions of conduct for himself. Of course, he will seek to profit by the wisdom of others, but he will have to select for himself the people he is to consider wise, and he will not regard even what they say as unquestionable. He will observe that what passes as 'God's law' varies from time to time. The Bible says both that a woman must not marry her deceased husband's brother, and that, in certain circumstances, she must do so. If you have the misfortune to be a childless widow with an unmarried brother-in-law, it is logically impossible for you to avoid disobeying 'God's law'.

How do you know what is good and what is evil? What does An agnostic Consider a sin

The Agnostic is not quite so certain as some Christians are as to what is good and what is evil. He does not hold, as most Christians in the past held, that people who disagree with the government on abstruse points of theology ought to suffer a painful death. He is against persecution, and rather chary of moral condemnation.

As for 'sin', he thinks it not a useful notion. He admits, of course, that some kinds of conduct are desirable and some undesirable, but he holds that the punishment of undesirable kinds is only to be commended when it is deterrent or reformatory, not when it is inflicted because it is thought a good thing on its own account that the wicked should suffer. It was this belief in vindictive punishment that made men accept Hell. This is part of the harm done by the notion of 'sin'.

Does an Agnostic do whatever he Pleases

In one sense, no; in another sense, everyone does whatever he pleases. Suppose, for example, you hate someone so much that you would like to murder him. Why do you not do so? You may reply: "Because religion tells me that murder is a sin." But as a statistical fact, agnostics are not more prone to murder than other people, in fact, rather less so. They have the same motives for abstaining from murder as other people have. Far and away the most powerful of these motives is the fear of punishment. In lawless conditions, such as a gold rush, all sorts of people will commit crimes, although in ordinary circumstances they would have been law-abiding. There is not only actual legal punishment; there is the discomfort of dreading discovery, and the loneliness of knowing that, to avoid being hated, you must wear a mask with even your closest intimates. And there is also what may be called "conscience": If you ever contemplated a murder, you would dread the horrible memory of your victim's last moments or lifeless corpse. All this, it is true, depends upon your living in a law-abiding community, but there are abundant secular reasons for creating and preserving such a community.

I said that there is another sense in which every man does as he pleases. No one but a fool indulges every impulse, but what holds a desire in check is always some other desire. A man's anti-social wishes may be restrained by a wish to please God, but they may also be restrained by a wish to please his friends, or to win the respect of his community, or to be able to contemplate himself without disgust. But if he has no such wishes, the mere abstract concepts of morality will not keep him straight.

How does an Agnostic Regard the Bible

An agnostic regards the Bible exactly as enlightened clerics regard it. He does not think that it is divinely inspired; he thinks its early history legendary, and no more exactly true than that in Homer; he thinks its moral teaching sometimes good, but sometimes very bad. For example: Samuel ordered Saul, in a war, to kill not only every man, woman, and child of the enemy, but also all the sheep and cattle. Saul, however, let the sheep and the cattle live, and for this we are told to condemn him. I have never been able to admire Elisha for cursing the children who laughed at him, or to believe (what the Bible asserts) that a benevolent Deity would send two she-bears to kill the children.

How Does an Agnostic Regard Jesus, the Virgin Birth, and the Holy Trinity

Since an agnostic does not believe in God, he cannot think that Jesus was God. Most agnostics admire the life and moral teachings of Jesus as told in the Gospels, but not necessarily more than those of certain other men. Some would place him on a level with Buddha, some with Socrates and some with Abraham Lincoln. Nor do they think that what He said is not open to question, since they do not accept any authority as absolute. They regard the Virgin Birth as a doctrine taken over from pagan mythology, where such births were not uncommon. (Zoroaster was said to have been born of a virgin; Ishtar, the Babylonian goddess, is called the Holy Virgin.) They cannot give credence to it, or to the doctrine of the Trinity, since neither is possible without belief in God.

Can an Agnostic be a Christian

The word "Christian" has had various different meanings at different times. Throughout most of the centuries since the time of Christ, it has meant a person who believed God and immortality and held that Christ was God. But Unitarians call themselves Christians, although they do not believe in the divinity of Christ, and many people nowadays use the word "God" in a much less precise sense than that which it used to bear. Many people who say they believe in God no longer mean a person, or a trinity of persons, but only a vague tendency or power or purpose immanent in evolution. Others, going still further, mean by "Christianity" merely a system of ethics which, since they are ignorant of history, they imagine to be characteristic of Christians only.

When, in a recent book, I said that what the world needs is "love, Christian love, or compassion," many people thought this showed some changes in my views, although in fact, I might have said the same thing at any time. If you mean by a "Christian" a man who loves his neighbour, who has wide sympathy with suffering, and who ardently desires a world freed from the cruelties and abominations which at present disfigure it, then, certainly, you will be justified in calling me a Christian. And, in this sense, I think you will find more "Christians" among agnostics than among the orthodox. But, for my part, I cannot accept such a definition. Apart from other objections to it, it seems rude to Jews, Buddhists, Mohammedans, and other non-Christians, who, so far as history shows, have been at least as apt as Christians to practice the virtues which some modern Christians arrogantly claim as distinctive of their own religion.

I think also that all who called themselves Christians in an earlier time, and a great majority of those who do so at the present day, would consider that belief in God and immortality is essential to a Christian. On these grounds, I should not call myself a Christian, and I should say that an agnostic cannot be a Christian. But, if the word "Christianity" comes to be generally used to mean merely a kind of morality, then it will certainly be possible for an agnostic to be a Christian.

Does an Agnostic Deny that Man has a Soul

This question has no precise meaning unless we are given a definition of the word "soul." I suppose what is meant is, roughly, something nonmaterial which persists throughout a person's life and even, for those who believe in immortality, throughout all future time.

If this is what is meant, an agnostic is not likely to believe that man has a soul. But I must hasten to add that this does not mean that an agnostic must be a materialist. Many agnostics (including myself) are quite as doubtful of the body as they are of the soul, but this is a long story taking one into difficult metaphysics. Mind and matter alike, I should say, are only convenient symbols in discourse, not actually existing things.

Does an Agnostic Believe in a Hereafter, in Heaven or Hell

The question whether people survive death is one as to which evidence is possible. Psychical research and spiritualism are thought by many to supply such evidence. An agnostic, as such, does not take a view about survival unless he thinks that there is evidence one way or the other. For my part, I do not think there is any good reason to believe that we survive death, but I am open to conviction if adequate evidence should appear. Heaven and hell are a different matter. Belief in hell is bound up with the belief that the vindictive punishment of sin is a good thing, quite independently of any reformative or deterrent effect that it may have.

Hardly an agnostic believes this. As for heaven, there might conceivably someday be evidence of its existence through spiritualism, but most agnostics do not think that there is such evidence, and therefore do not believe in heaven.

Are you Never Afraid of God's Judgment in Denying Him

Most certainly not. I also deny Zeus and Jupiter and Odin and Brahma, but this causes me no qualms. I observe that a very large portion of the human race does not believe in God and suffers no visible punishment in consequence. And if there were a God, I think it very unlikely that He would have such an uneasy vanity as to be offended by those who doubt His existence.

How do Agnostics Explain the Beauty and Harmony of Nature

I do not understand where this "beauty" and "harmony" are supposed to be found. Throughout the animal kingdom, animals ruthlessly prey upon each other. Most of them are either cruelly killed by other animals or slowly die of hunger. For my part, I am unable to see any great beauty or harmony in the tapeworm. Let it not be said that this creature is sent as a punishment for our sins, for it is more prevalent among animals than among humans.

I suppose the questioner is thinking of such things as the beauty of the starry heavens. But one should remember that stars every now and again explode and reduce everything in their neighbourhood to a vague mist. Beauty, in any case, is subjective and exists only in the eye of the beholder.

How do Aagnostics Explain Miracles and other Revelations of God's Omnipotence

Agnostics do not think that there is any evidence of "miracles" in the sense of happenings contrary to natural law. We know that faith healing occurs and is in no sense miraculous. At Lourdes, certain diseases can be cured and others cannot. Those that can be cured at Lourdes can probably be cured by any doctor in whom the patient has faith. As for the records of other miracles, such as Joshua commanding the sun to stand still, the agnostic dismisses them as legends and points to the fact that all religions are plentifully supplied with such legends. There is just as much miraculous evidence for the Greek gods in Homer as for the Christian God in the Bible. There have been base and cruel passions, which religion opposes.

If you Abandon Religious Principles, Could Mankind Exist

The existence of base and cruel passions is undeniable, but I find no evidence in history that religion has opposed these passions. On the contrary, it has sanctified them, and enabled people to indulge them without remorse. Cruel persecutions have been commoner in Christendom than anywhere else. What appears to justify persecution is dogmatic belief. Kindliness and tolerance only prevail in proportion as dogmatic belief decays. In our day, a new dogmatic religion, namely, communism, has arisen.

To this, as to other systems of dogma, the agnostic is opposed. The persecuting character of present day communism is exactly like the persecuting character of Christianity in earlier centuries. In so far as Christianity has become less persecuting, this is mainly due to the work of freethinkers who have made dogmatists rather less dogmatic. If they were as dogmatic now as in former times, they would still think it right to burn heretics at the stake. The spirit of tolerance which some modern Christians regard as essentially Christian is, in fact, a product of the temper which allows doubt and is suspicious of absolute certainties. I think that anybody who surveys past history in an impartial manner will be driven to the conclusion that religion has caused more suffering than it has prevented.

What is the Meaning of Life to the Agnostic

I feel inclined to answer by another question: What is the meaning of 'the meaning of life'? I suppose what is intended is some general purpose. I do not think that life in general has any purpose.

It just happened. But individual human beings have purposes, and there is nothing in agnosticism to cause them to abandon these purposes. They cannot, of course, be certain of achieving the results at which they aim; but you would think ill of a soldier who refused to fight unless victory was certain. The person who needs religion to bolster up his own purposes is a timorous person, and I cannot think as well of him as of the man who takes his chances, while admitting that defeat is not impossible.

Does not the Denial of Religion Mean the Denial of Marriage and Chastity

Here again, one must reply by another question: Does the man who asks this question believe that marriage and chastity contribute to earthly happiness here below, or does he think that, while they cause misery here below, they are to be advocated as means of getting to heaven? The man who takes the latter view will no doubt expect agnosticism to lead to a decay of what he calls virtue, but he will have to admit that what he calls virtue is not what ministers to the happiness of the human race while on earth.

If, on the other hand, he takes the former view, namely, that there are terrestrial arguments in favor of marriage and chastity, he must also hold that these arguments are such as should appeal to the agnostic. Agnostics, as such, have no distinctive views about sexual morality. But most of them would admit that there are valid arguments against the unbridled indulgence of sexual desires. They would derive these arguments, however, from terrestrial sources and not from supposed divine commands.

Is not Faith in Reason Alone a Dangerous Creed? Is not Reason Imperfect and Inadequate Without Spiritual and Moral Law

No sensible man, however agnostic, has "faith in reason alone." Reason is concerned with matters of fact, some observed, some inferred. The question whether there is a future life and the question whether there is a God concern matters of fact, and the agnostic will hold that they should be investigated in the same way as the question, "Will there be an eclipse of the moon tomorrow?" But matters of fact alone are not sufficient to determine action, since they do not tell us what ends we ought to pursue. In the realm of ends, we need something other than reason. The agnostic will find his ends in his own heart and not in an external command. Let us take an illustration: Suppose you wish to travel by train from New York to Chicago; you will use reason to discover when the trains run, and a person who though that there was some faculty of insight or intuition enabling him to dispense with the timetable would be thought rather silly.

But no timetable will tell him that it is wise, he will have to take account of further matters of fact; but behind all the matters of fact, there will be the ends that he thinks fitting to pursue, and these, for an agnostic as for other men, belong to a realm which is not that of reason, though it should be in no degree contrary to it. The realm I mean is that of emotion and feeling and desire.

Do you Regard all Religions as forms of Superstition or Dogma? Which of the Existing Religions do you most Respect, and why

All the great organized religions that have dominated large populations have involved a greater or less amount of dogma, but "religion" is a word of which the meaning is not very definite. Confucianism, for instance, might be called a religion, although it involves no dogma. And in some forms of liberal Christianity, the element of dogma is reduced to a minimum.

Of the great religions of history, I prefer Buddhism, especially in its earliest forms, because it has had the smallest element of persecution.

Communism like Agnosticism Opposes Religion, are Agnostics Communists

Communism does not oppose religion. It merely opposes the Christian religion, just as Mohammedanism does. Communism, at least in the form advocated by the Soviet Government and the Communist Party, is a new system of dogma of a peculiarly virulent and persecuting sort. Every genuine Agnostic must therefore be opposed to it.

Do Agnostics think that Science and Religion are Impossible to Reconcile

The answer turns upon what is meant by 'religion'. If it means merely a system of ethics, it can be reconciled with science. If it means a system of dogma, regarded as unquestionably true, it is incompatible with the scientific spirit, which refuses to accept matters of fact without evidence, and also holds that complete certainty is hardly ever impossible.

What kind of Evidence could Convince you that God exists

I think that if I heard a voice from the sky predicting all that was going to happen to me during the next twenty-four hours, including events that would have seemed highly improbable, and if all these events then produced to happen, I might perhaps be convinced at least of the existence of some superhuman intelligence. I can imagine other evidence of the same sort which might convince me, but so far as I know, no such evidence exists.

What Is the Soul

One of the most painful circumstances of recent advances in science is that each one makes us know less than we thought we did. When I was young we all knew, or thought we knew, that a man consists of a soul and a body; that the body is in time and space, but the soul is in time only.

Whether the soul survives death was a matter as to which opinions might differ, but that there is a soul was thought to be indubitable. As for the body, the plain man of course considered its existence self-evident, and so did the man of science, but the philosopher was apt to analyse it away after one fashion or another, reducing it usually to ideas in the mind of the man who had the body and anybody else who happened to notice him.

The philosopher, however, was not taken seriously, and science remained comfortably materialistic, even in the hands of quite orthodox scientists.

Nowadays these fine old simplicities are lost: physicists assure us that there is no such thing as matter, and psychologists assure us that there is no such thing as mind. This is an unprecedented occurrence. Who ever heard of a cobbler saying that there was no such thing as boots, or a tailor maintaining that all men are really naked? Yet that would have been no odder than what physicists and certain psychologists have been doing.

To begin with the latter, some of them attempt to reduce everything that seems to be mental activity to an activity of the body. There are, however, various difficulties in the way of reducing mental activity to physical activity. I do not think we can yet say with any assurance whether these difficulties are or are not insuperable. What we can say, on the basis of physics itself, is that what we have hitherto called our body is really an elabourate scientific construction not corresponding to any physical reality.

The modern would-be materialist thus finds himself in a curious position, for, while he may with a certain degree of success reduce the activities of the mind to those of the body, he cannot explain away the fact that the body itself is merely a convenient concept invented by the mind. We find ourselves thus going round and round in a circle: mind is an emanation of body, and body is an invention of mind. Evidently this cannot be quite right, and we have to look for something that is neither mind nor body, out which both can spring.

Let us begin with the body. The plain man thinks that material objects must certainly exist, since they are evident to the senses. Whatever else may be doubted, it is certain that anything you can bump into must be real; this is the plain man's metaphysic.

This is all very well, but the physicist comes along and shows that you never bump into anything: even when you run your hand along a stone wall, you do not really touch it. When you think you touch a thing, there are certain electrons and protons, forming part of your body, which are attracted and repelled by certain electrons and protons in the thing you think you are touching, but there is no actual contact. The electrons and protons in your body, becoming agitated by nearness to the other electrons and protons are disturbed, and transmit a disturbance along your nerves to the brain; the effect in the brain is what is necessary to your sensation of contact, and by suitable experiments this sensation can be made quite deceptive. The electrons and protons themselves, however, are only crude first approximations, a way of collecting into a bundle either trains of waves or the statistical probabilities of various different kinds of events. Thus matter has become altogether too ghostly to be used as an adequate stick with which to beat the mind. Matter in motion, which used to seem so unquestionable, turns out to be a concept quite inadequate for the needs of physics.

Nevertheless modern science gives no indication whatever of the existence of the soul or mind as an entity; indeed the reasons for disbelieving in it are very much of the same kind as the reasons for disbelieving in matter. Mind and matter were something like the lion and the unicorn fighting for the crown; the end of the battle is not the victory of one or the other, but the discovery that both are only heraldic inventions. The world consists of events, not of things that endure for a long time and have changing properties. Events can be collected into groups by their causal relations.

If the causal relations are of one sort, the resulting group of events may be called a physical object, and if the causal relations are of another sort, the resulting group may be called a mind. Any event that occurs inside a man's head will belong to groups of both kinds; considered as belonging to a group of one kind, it is a constituent of his brain, and considered as belonging to a group of the other kind, it is a constituent of his mind.

Thus both mind and matter are merely convenient ways of organizing events. There can be no reason for supposing that either a piece of mind or a piece of matter is immortal. The sun is supposed to be losing matter at the rate of millions of tons a minute. The most essential characteristic of mind is memory, and there is no reason whatever to suppose that the memory associated with a given person survives that person's death. Indeed there is every reason to think the opposite, for memory is clearly connected with a certain kind of brain structure, and since this structure decays at death, there is every reason to suppose that memory also must cease.

Although metaphysical materialism cannot be considered true, yet emotionally the world is pretty much the same as I would be if the materialists were in the right. I think the opponents of materialism have always been actuated by two main desires: the first to prove that the mind is immortal, and the second to prove that the ultimate power in the universe is mental rather than physical.

In both these respects, I think the materialists were in the right. Our desires, it is true, have considerable power on the earth's surface; the greater part of the land on this planet has a quite different aspect from that which it would have if men had not utilized it to extract food and wealth. But our power is very strictly limited. We cannot at present do anything whatever to the sun or moon or even to the interior of the earth, and there is not the faintest reason to suppose that what happens in regions to which our power does not extend has any mental causes.

That is to say, to put the matter in a nutshell, there is no reason to think that except on the earth's surface anything happens because somebody wishes it to happen. And since our power on the earth's surface is entirely dependent upon the sun, we could hardly realize any of our wishes if the sun grew could. It is of course rash to dogmatize as to what science may achieve in the future. We may learn to prolong human existence longer than now seems possible, but if there is any truth in modern physics, more particularly in the second law of thermodynamics, we cannot hope that the human race will continue for ever.

Some people may find this conclusion gloomy, but if we are honest with ourselves, we shall have to admit that what is going to happen many millions of years hence has no very great emotional interest for us here and now. And science, while it diminishes our cosmic pretensions, enormously increases our terrestrial comfort. That is why, in spite of the horror of the theologians, science has on the whole been tolerated.

Why I am A Rationalist

The Rational Habit Of Mind Is A Rare One: I am, in this age when there are a great many appeals to unreason, an unrepentant Rationalist. I have been a Rationalist ever since I can remember, and I do not propose to cease to be so whatever appeals to unreason may be made. We have listened to a speech, by which I think we were all much moved, about the pioneers in the past who have done what they could to promote the cause of freedom of thought.

I suppose it is for me to speak about the great need of continuing this work in our own day, and about how much there is that remains for all who sympathize with its objects to accomplish. We are not yet, and I suppose men and women never will be, completely rational. Perhaps, if we were, we should not have all the pleasures that we have at present; but I think complete rationality is so distant a prospect that we need not be much alarmed by it, and the nearest approach that we are likely to get is sure to be all to the good. I certainly find that there is a very great deal of irrationality still about in the world.

While Professor Graham Wallas was speaking about the bequests that have been made to the Rationalist Press Association I was thinking: What is its creed, what is its dogma, and what is going to be the, so to speak, doctrine that these benefactions are going to be devoted to propagating? You have, of course, to be a little careful, when you find yourself landed with endowments and benefactions, lest you should become another endowed church. (*Laughter.*) As far as I can see, the view to which we are committed, one which I have stated on a former occasion, is that we ought not to believe, and we ought not to try to cause others to believe, any proposition for which there is no evidence whatever.

That seems a modest proposition, and if you can stick to that you will be fairly sure that you are not going to become a sort of ossified endowed church. We ought not to commit ourselves to dogmatic negations any more than to dogmatic affirmations; we ought merely to say that there are a great many propositions about which men and women feel pretty certain, but, concerning which they have no right to feel certain, and it is our business as Rationalists to try to make them see that those things are not certain. I am told that that is a very wicked position to maintain. I have here a book recently published which I commend to your attention.

You may or may not know that some little time ago, under the auspices of the National Secular Society, I delivered a lecture on "Why I am Not a Christian." Now, It appears that I did not know why it is that I am not a Christian; and here is a book which will tell you why I am not — by Mr.. H. G. Wood, who is a somewhat eminent member of the Society of Friends, a body for which I have the greatest respect. His book is called *Why Mr.. Bertrand Russell is Not a Christian*. It seems that the reasons are not those which I thought they were. He says in one sentence: "The main reason why he is not a Christian is that he simply does not know what religion is." One might say that Mr. Wood is not an Agnostic because he does not know what Agnosticism is. After all, I had all the benefits of a Christian education, and he did not have the benefits of an Agnostic education; so that possibly the argument might be considered two-edged. Nevertheless, I commend the book to your attention, and you will then know why it is that I am not a Christian.

There is a very large amount of Rationalist work required in the world. I think the battle is quite as fierce as ever it was. Take, for example America. America is a very important country. What America thinks today the rest of the world will be forced to think tomorrow, and therefore what America thinks is important. There are some hopeful features about America.

I was recently on a boat going to America, and a minister of religion on the boat invited me to speak to his congregation about my views on religion. I said: "Yours must be a very broad-minded congregation"; and this minister of religion, somewhat to my surprise, replied: "Oh, of course, I do not believe in God." I met other ministers of religion in America who took the same line. That, I must say, somewhat surprised me; but they are, I am afraid, rather a small minority, and the great bulk of Americans are still extremely theological. Moreover, we have to face the very serious position due to the growth of the Roman Catholic Church in America, because, as far as I can see, the Roman Catholic Church is likely to dominate America in another fifty or a hundred years by the sheer increase of numbers, and not by rational propaganda.

That is a very grave matter, and a matter which I think will affect the whole of the civilized world very much. Of course, you know that already in Boston, which was once the home of advanced Protestantism, the Roman Catholics rule the whole place; and there is a censorship upon literature more severe than in any other part of America. I expect you know that in America men are still sent to prison for Atheism, not only in Fundamentalist States, but even in States of the East, and altogether there is in that part of the world an enormous need of propaganda on these matters.

It is very important to all of us, because the Americans tend more and more to rule the world, and we shall find ourselves in a very difficult position unless we can more or less liberalize them — a mission, I may say, in which I have done what I can, and my wife has also.

We have to realize that the attitude of Rationalism, which I defined as that of not believing a proposition or causing others to believe it unless there is at least some reason for supposing it to be true, is by no means widespread. Take the matter of education, concerning which Professor Graham Wallas spoke. In most countries of the world a great many extremely dubious propositions are taught to the young with great emphasis, and the young grow up accepting those extremely dubious propositions. If by any chance you attempt, as my wife and I are attempting at this moment, to bring up a small number of young people free from superstition, you find yourself in a very difficult situation. You find, of course, that the public money which goes to education will not be given to any education that involves no element of superstition.

You find that support is extremely difficult to obtain; you find that altogether it is thought that, whatever grown men and women may be allowed to think, the young, at any rate, ought to believe a whole lot of absurdities. That it is quite impossible for the young to attain the necessary minimum of virtues unless you produce an extremely large number of very bad arguments in favor of those virtue-arguments, which, of course, they will see through as soon as they get a little older. But it is thought that what they do then when they see through them does not so much matter. I cannot quite take that view.

I think that any virtue that you may believe in should be one that you can support from the very first without appealing to anything that you do not yourself believe. Education will have to be quite enormously transformed if that view is accepted. I believe that it is at present illegal in every country of the world except Russia to teach children in the kind of way which skilled medical practitioners would consider the best for their mental health.

That is one point upon which irrational convictions as generally held interfere, and there are a number of ways in which it is at present impossible to educate rationally without coming up against the authorities. The authorities are organized upon a basis of certain irrational dogmas, and those dogmas are not all of them theological. Some are theological, and some are of other sorts; but the rational habit of mind is a very rare one.

I think that we ought to do all that we can to bring before the world the importance of the attitude that we are not going to believe a thing unless there is some reason to think that it is true. I know that that is thought to be very shocking. It is supposed that there are a lot of things that you ought to believe because good people believe them, and not because there is any reason for them. I do not take that view. I think anything that is worth believing must have some positive ground in its favor. There are always new grounds being alleged in favor of irrationality; perpetually new things come up. Take, for example, the kind of use that has been made by some people of psycho-analysis. If you read the works of the founder of psycho-analysis, you find an entirely rationalist attitude; but if you listen to some of the minor disciples you will imagine that this doctrine has swept away the idea that opinions can be based upon reason at all. That, of course, is not the truth of it. You will always find a number of clever people engaged in perversions of anything that comes up — engaged in saying that the latest results of science prove that the people who always opposed science are after all in the right. That is where there is always humbug. Anybody who tells you that the latest results of science prove something, he himself not being a scientist, you may be pretty sure is talking nonsense.

Why I am Not a Christian

Introductory note: Russell delivered this lecture on March 6, 1927 to the National Secular Society, South London Branch, at Battersea Town Hall. Published in pamphlet form in that same year, the essay subsequently achieved new fame with Paul Edwards' edition of Russell's book, *Why I Am Not a Christian and Other Essays...* (1957).

As your Chairman has told you, the subject about which I am going to speak to you tonight is "Why I Am Not a Christian." Perhaps it would be as well, first of all, to try to make out what one means by the word *Christian*. It is used these days in a very loose sense by a great many people. Some people mean no more by it than a person who attempts to live a good life. In that sense I suppose there would be Christians in all sects and creeds; but I do not think that that is the proper sense of the word, if only because it would imply that all the people who are not Christians — all the Buddhists, Confucians, Mohammedans, and so on — are not trying to live a good life.

I do not mean by a Christian any person who tries to live decently according to his lights. I think that you must have a certain amount of definite belief before you have a right to call yourself a Christian. The word does not have quite such a full-blooded meaning now as it had in the times of St. Augustine and St. Thomas Aquinas. In those days, if a man said that he was a Christian it was known what he meant. You accepted a whole collection of creeds, which were set out with great precision, and every single syllable of those creeds you believed with the whole strength of your convictions.

What Is a Christian

Nowadays it is not quite that. We have to be a little more vague in our meaning of Christianity. I think, however, that there are two different items which are quite essential to anybody calling himself a Christian. The first is one of a dogmatic nature — namely, that you must believe in God and immortality. If you do not believe in those two things, I do not think that you can properly call yourself a Christian. Then, further than that, as the name implies, you must have some kind of belief about Christ.

The Mohammedans, for instance, also believe in God and in immortality, and yet they would not call themselves Christians. I think you must have at the very lowest the belief that Christ was, if not divine, at least the best and wisest of men. If you are not going to believe that much about Christ, I do not think you have any right to call yourself a Christian. Of course, there is another sense, which you find in *Whitaker's Almanack* and in geography books, where the population of the world is said to be divided into Christians, Mohammedans, Buddhists, fetish worshipers, and so on; and in that sense we are all Christians.

The geography books count us all in, but that is a purely geographical sense, which I suppose we can ignore. Therefore, I take it that when I tell you why I am not a Christian I have to tell you two different things: first, why I do not believe in God and in immortality; and, secondly, why I do not think that Christ was the best and wisest of men, although I grant him a very high degree of moral goodness.

But for the successful efforts of unbelievers in the past, I could not take so elastic a definition of Christianity as that. As I said before, in olden days it had a much more full-blooded sense. For instance, it included he belief in hell. Belief in eternal hell-fire was an essential item of Christian belief until pretty recent times. In this country, as you know, it ceased to be an essential item because of a decision of the Privy Council, and from that decision the Archbishop of Canterbury and the Archbishop of York dissented. But in this country our religion is settled by Act of Parliament, and therefore the Privy Council was able to override their Graces and hell was no longer necessary to a Christian. Consequently, I shall not insist that a Christian must believe in hell.

The Existence of God

To come to this question of the existence of God: it is a large and serious question, and if I were to attempt to deal with it in any adequate manner I should have to keep you here until Kingdom Come, so that you will have to excuse me if I deal with it in a somewhat summary fashion. You know, of course, that the Catholic Church has laid it down as a dogma that the existence of God can be proved by the unaided reason.

That is a somewhat curious dogma, but it is one of their dogmas. They had to introduce it because at one time the freethinkers adopted the habit of saying that there were such and such arguments which mere reason might urge against the existence of God, but of course they knew as a matter of faith that God did exist. The arguments and the reasons were set out at great length, and the Catholic Church felt that they must stop it. Therefore they laid it down that the existence of God can be proved by the unaided reason and they had to set up what they considered were arguments to prove it. There are, of course, a number of them, but I shall take only a few.

The First-cause Argument

Perhaps the simplest and easiest to understand is the argument of the First Cause. (It is maintained that everything we see in this world has a cause, and as you go back in the chain of causes further and further you must come to a First Cause, and to that First Cause you give the name of God.) That argument, I suppose, does not carry very much weight nowadays, because, in the first place, cause is not quite what it used to be.

The philosophers and the men of science have got going on cause, and it has not anything like the vitality it used to have; but, apart from that, you can see that the argument that there must be a First Cause is one that cannot have any validity. I may say that when I was a young man and was debating these questions very seriously in my mind, I for a long time accepted the argument of the First Cause, until one day, at the age of eighteen, I read John Stuart Mill's Autobiography, and I there found this sentence: "My father taught me that the question 'Who made me?' cannot be answered, since it immediately suggests the further question `Who made god?'" That very simple sentence showed me, as I still think, the fallacy in the argument of the First Cause.

If everything must have a cause, then God must have a cause. If there can be anything without a cause, it may just as well be the world as God, so that there cannot be any validity in that argument. It is exactly of the same nature as the Hindu's view, that the world rested upon an elephant and the elephant rested upon a tortoise; and when they said, "How about the tortoise?" the Indian said, "Suppose we change the subject." The argument is really no better than that. There is no reason why the world could not have come into being without a cause; nor, on the other hand, is there any reason why it should not have always existed. There is no reason to suppose that the world had a beginning at all. The idea that things must have a beginning is really due to the poverty of our imagination. Therefore, perhaps, I need not waste any more time upon the argument about the First Cause.

The Natural-law Argument

Then there is a very common argument from natural law. That was a favorite argument all through the eighteenth century, especially under the influence of Sir Isaac Newton and his cosmogony. People observed the planets going around the sun according to the law of gravitation, and they thought that God had given a behest to these planets to move in that particular fashion, and that was why they did so.

That was, of course, a convenient and simple explanation that saved them the trouble of looking any further for explanations of the law of gravitation. Nowadays we explain the law of gravitation in a somewhat complicated fashion that Einstein has introduced. I do not propose to give you a lecture on the law of gravitation, as interpreted by Einstein, because that again would take some time; at any rate, you no longer have the sort of natural law that you had in the Newtonian system, where, for some reason that nobody could understand, nature behaved in a uniform fashion.

We now find that a great many things we thought were natural laws are human conventions. You know that even in the remotest depths of stellar space there are still three feet to a yard. That is, no doubt, a very remarkable fact, but you would hardly call it a law of nature. And a great many things that have been regarded as laws of nature are of that kind. On the other hand, where you can get down to any knowledge of what atoms actually do, you will find they are much less subject to law than people thought, and that the laws at which you arrive are statistical averages of just the sort that would emerge from chance. There is, as we all know, a law that if you throw dice you will get double sixes only about once in thirty-six times, and we do not regard that as evidence that the fall of the dice is regulated by design; on the contrary, if the double sixes came every time we should think that there was design. The laws of nature are of that sort as regards a great many of them.

They are statistical averages such as would emerge from the laws of chance; and that makes this whole business of natural law much less impressive than it formerly was. Quite apart from that, which represents the momentary state of science that may change tomorrow, the whole idea that natural laws imply a lawgiver is due to a confusion between natural and human laws. Human laws are behests commanding you to behave a certain way, in which you may choose to behave, or you may choose not to behave.

But natural laws are a description of how things do in fact behave, and being a mere description of what they in fact do, you cannot argue that there must be somebody who told them to do that, because even supposing that there were, you are then faced with the question "Why did God issue just those natural laws and no others?" If you say that he did it simply from his own good pleasure, and without any reason, you then find that there is something which is not subject to law, and so your train of natural law is interrupted. If you say, as more orthodox theologians do, that in all the laws which God issues he had a reason for giving those laws rather than others — the reason, of course, being to create the best universe, although you would never think it to look at it — if there were a reason for the laws which God gave, then God himself was subject to law, and therefore you do not get any advantage by introducing God as an intermediary.

You really have a law outside and anterior to the divine edicts, and God does not serve your purpose, because he is not the ultimate lawgiver. In short, this whole argument about natural law no longer has anything like the strength that it used to have.

I am traveling on in time in my review of the arguments. The arguments that are used for the existence of God change their character as time goes on. They were at first hard intellectual arguments embodying certain quite definite fallacies. As we come to modern times they become less respectable intellectually and more and more affected by a kind of moralizing vagueness.

The Argument from Design

The next step in the process brings us to the argument from design. You all know the argument from design: everything in the world is made just so that we can manage to live in the world, and if the world was ever so little different, we could not manage to live in it. That is the argument from design. It sometimes takes a rather curious form; for instance, it is argued that rabbits have white tails in order to be easy to shoot. I do not know how rabbits would view that application. It is an easy argument to parody. You all know Voltaire's remark, that obviously the nose was designed to be such as to fit spectacles.

That sort of parody has turned out to be not nearly so wide of the mark as it might have seemed in the eighteenth century, because since the time of Darwin we understand much better why living creatures are adapted to their environment. It is not that their environment was made to be suitable to them but that they grew to be suitable to it, and that is the basis of adaptation. There is no evidence of design about it.

When you come to look into this argument from design, it is a most astonishing thing that people can believe that this world, with all the things that are in it, with all its defects, should be the best that omnipotence and omniscience have been able to produce in millions of years. I really cannot believe it. Do you think that, if you were granted omnipotence and omniscience and millions of years in which to perfect your world, you could produce nothing better than the Ku Klux Klan or the Fascists? Moreover, if you accept the ordinary laws of science, you have to suppose that human life and life in general on this planet will die out in due course: it is a stage in the decay of the solar system; at a certain stage of decay you get the sort of conditions of temperature and so forth which are suitable to protoplasm, and there is life for a short time in the life of the whole solar system. You see in the moon the sort of thing to which the earth is tending — something dead, cold, and lifeless. I am told that that sort of view is depressing, and people will sometimes tell you that if they believed that, they would not be able to go on living. Do not believe it; it is all nonsense. Nobody really worries about much about what is going to happen millions of years hence. Even if they think they are worrying much about that, they are really deceiving themselves.

They are worried about something much more mundane, or it may merely be a bad digestion; but nobody is really seriously rendered unhappy by the thought of something that is going to happen to this world millions and millions of years hence. Therefore, although it is of course a gloomy view to suppose that life will die out — at least I suppose we may say so, although sometimes when I contemplate the things that people do with their lives I think it is almost a consolation — it is not such as to render life miserable. It merely makes you turn your attention to other things.

The Moral Arguments for Deity

Now we reach one stage further in what I shall call the

intellectual descent that the Theists have made in their argumentations, and we come to what are called the moral arguments for the existence of God. You all know, of course, that there used to be in the old days three intellectual arguments for the existence of God, all of which were disposed of by Immanuel Kant in the *Critique of Pure Reason*; but no sooner had he disposed of those arguments than he invented a new one, a moral argument, and that quite convinced him. He was like many people: in intellectual matters he was skeptical, but in moral matters he believed implicitly in the maxims that he had imbibed at his mother's knee. That illustrates what the psychoanalysts so much emphasize — the immensely stronger hold upon us that our very early associations have than those of later times.

Kant, as I say, invented a new moral argument for the existence of God, and that in varying forms was extremely popular during the nineteenth century. It has all sorts of forms. One form is to say there would be no right or wrong unless God existed. I am not for the moment concerned with whether there is a difference between right and wrong, or whether there is not: that is another question.

The point I am concerned with is that, if you are quite sure there is a difference between right and wrong, then you are in this situation: Is that difference due to God's fiat or is it not? If it is due to God's fiat, then for God himself there is no difference between right and wrong, and it is no longer a significant statement to say that God is good.

If you are going to say, as theologians do, that God is good, you must then say that right and wrong have some meaning which is independent of God's fiat, because God's fiats are good and not bad independently of the mere fact that he made them. If you are going to say that, you will then have to say that it is not only through God that right and wrong came into being, but that they are in their essence logically anterior to God.

You could, of course, if you liked, say that there was a superior deity who gave orders to the God that made this world, or could take up the line that some of the gnostics took up a line which I often thought was a very plausible one that as a matter of fact this world that we know was made by the devil at a moment when God was not looking. There is a good deal to be said for that, and I am not concerned to refute it.

The Argument for the Remedying of Injustice

Then there is another very curious form of moral argument, which is this: they say that the existence of God is required in order to bring justice into the world. In the part of this universe that we know there is great injustice, and often the good suffer, and often the wicked prosper, and one hardly knows which of those is the more annoying; but if you are going to have justice in the universe as a whole you have to suppose a future life to redress the balance of life here on earth. So they say that there must be a God, and there must be Heaven and Hell in order that in the long run there may be justice. That is a very curious argument. If you looked at the matter from a scientific point of view, you would say, "After all, I only know this world.

I do not know about the rest of the universe, but so far as one can argue at all on probabilities one would say that probably this world is a fair sample, and if there is injustice here the odds are that there is injustice elsewhere also." Supposing you got a crate of oranges that you opened, and you found all the top layer of oranges bad, you would not argue, "The underneath ones must be good, so as to redress the balance." You would say, "Probably the whole lot is a bad consignment"; and that is really what a scientific person would argue about the universe.

He would say, "Here we find in this world a great deal of injustice, and so far as that goes that is a reason for supposing that justice does not rule in the world; and therefore so far as it goes it affords a moral argument against deity and not in favor of one." Of course I know that the sort of intellectual arguments that I have been talking to you about are not what really moves people. What really moves people to believe in God is not any intellectual argument at all. Most people believe in God because they have been taught from early infancy to do it, and that is the main reason.

Then I think that the next most powerful reason is the wish for safety, a sort of feeling that there is a big brother who will look after you. That plays a very profound part in influencing people's desire for a belief in God.

The Character of Christ

I now want to say a few words upon a topic which I often think is not quite sufficiently dealt with by Rationalists, and that is the question whether Christ was the best and the wisest of men. It is generally taken for granted that we should all agree that that was so.

I do not myself. I think that there are a good many points upon which I agree with Christ a great deal more than the professing Christians do. I do not know that I could go with Him all the way, but I could go with Him much further than most professing Christians can.

You will remember that He said, "Resist not evil: but whosoever shall smite thee on thy right cheek, turn to him the other also." That is not a new precept or a new principle. It was used by Lao-tse and Buddha some 500 or 600 years before Christ, but it is not a principle which as a matter of fact Christians accept. I have no doubt that the present prime minister [Stanley Baldwin], for instance, is a most sincere Christian, but I should not advise any of you to go and smite him on one cheek. I think you might find that he thought this text was intended in a figurative sense.

Then there is another point which I consider excellent. You will remember that Christ said, "Judge not lest ye be judged." That principle I do not think you would find was popular in the law courts of Christian countries. I have known in my time quite a number of judges who were very earnest Christians, and none of them felt that they were acting contrary to Christian principles in what they did. Then Christ says, "Give to him that asketh of thee, and from him that would borrow of thee turn not thou away." That is a very good principle. Your Chairman has reminded you that we are not here to talk politics, but I cannot help observing that the last general election was fought on the question of how desirable it was to turn away from him that would borrow of thee, so that one must assume that the Liberals and Conservatives of this country are composed of people who do not agree with the teaching of Christ, because they certainly did very emphatically turn away on that occasion.

Then there is one other maxim of Christ which I think has a great deal in it, but I do not find that it is very popular among some of our Christian friends. He says, "If thou wilt be perfect, go and sell that which thou hast, and give to the poor." That is a very excellent maxim, but, as I say, it is not much practised. All these, I think, are good maxims, although they are a little difficult to live up to. I do not profess to live up to them myself; but then, after all, it is not quite the same thing as for a Christian.

Defects in Christ's Teaching

Having granted the excellence of these maxims, I come to certain points in which I do not believe that one can grant either the superlative wisdom or the superlative goodness of Christ as depicted in the Gospels; and here I may say that one is not concerned with the historical question. Historically it is quite doubtful whether Christ ever existed at all, and if He did we do not know anything about him, so that I am not concerned with the historical question, which is a very difficult one. I am concerned with Christ as He appears in the Gospels, taking the Gospel narrative as it stands, and there one does find some things that do not seem to be very wise. For one thing, he certainly thought that His second coming would occur in clouds of glory before the death of all the people who were living at that time.

There are a great many texts that prove that. He says, for instance, "Ye shall not have gone over the cities of Israel till the Son of Man be come." Then he says, "There are some standing here which shall not taste death till the Son of Man comes into His kingdom"; and there are a lot of places where it is quite clear that He believed that His second coming would happen during the lifetime of many then living. That was the belief of His earlier followers, and it was the basis of a good deal of His moral teaching. When He said, "Take no thought for the morrow," and things of that sort, it was very largely because He thought that the second coming was going to be very soon, and that all ordinary mundane affairs did not count. I have, as a matter of fact, known some Christians who did believe that the second coming was imminent. I knew a parson who frightened his congregation terribly by telling them that the second coming was very imminent indeed, but they were much consoled when they found that he was planting trees in his garden. The early Christians did really believe it, and they did abstain from such things as planting trees in their gardens, because they did accept from Christ the belief that the second coming was imminent. In that respect, clearly He was not so wise as some other people have been, and He was certainly not superlatively wise.

The Moral Problem

Then you come to moral questions. There is one very serious defect to my mind in Christ's moral character, and that is that He believed in hell. I do not myself feel that any person who is really profoundly humane can believe in everlasting punishment. Christ certainly as depicted in the Gospels did believe in everlasting punishment, and one does find repeatedly a vindictive fury against those people who would not listen to His preaching — an attitude which is not uncommon with preachers, but which does somewhat detract from superlative excellence. You do not, for instance find that attitude in Socrates. You find him quite bland and urbane toward the people who would not listen to him; and it is, to my mind, far more worthy of a sage to take that line than to take the line of indignation. You probably all remember the sorts of things that Socrates was saying when he was dying, and the sort of things that he generally did say to people who did not agree with him.

You will find that in the Gospels Christ said, "Ye serpents, ye generation of vipers, how can ye escape the damnation of

Hell." That was said to people who did not like His preaching. It is not really to my mind quite the best tone, and there are a great many of these things about Hell. There is, of ccurse, the familiar text about the sin against the Holy Ghost: "Whosoever speaketh against the Holy Ghost it shall not be forgiven him neither in this World nor in the world to come." That text has caused an unspeakable amount of misery in the world, for all sorts of people have imagined that they have committed the sin against the Holy Ghost, and thought that it would not be forgiven them either in this world or in the world to come. I really do not think that a person with a proper degree of kindliness in his nature would have put fears and terrors of that sort into the world.

Then Christ says, "The Son of Man shall send forth his His angels, and they shall gather out of His kingdom all things that offend, and them which do iniquity, and shall cast them into a furnace of fire; there shall be wailing and gnashing of teeth"; and He goes on about the wailing and gnashing of teeth. It comes in one verse after another, and it is quite manifest to the reader that there is a certain pleasure in contemplating wailing and gnashing of teeth, or else it would not occur so often.

Then you all, of course, remember about the sheep and the goats; how at the second coming He is going to divide the sheep from the goats, and He is going to say to the goats, "Depart from me, ye cursed, into everlasting fire." He continues, "And these shall go away into everlasting fire." Then He says again, "If thy hand offend thee, cut it off; it is better for thee to enter into life maimed, than having two hands to go into Hell, into the fire that never shall be quenched; where the worm dieth not and the fire is not quenched." He repeats that again and again also. I must say that I think all this doctrine, that hell-fire is a punishment for sin, is a doctrine of cruelty. It is a doctrine that put cruelty into the world and gave the world generations of cruel torture; and the Christ of the Gospels, if you could take Him as His chroniclers represent Him, would certainly have to be considered partly responsible for that. There are other things of less importance. There is the instance of the Gadarene swine, where it certainly was not very kind to the pigs to put the devils into them and make them rush down the hill into the sea. You must remember that He was omnipotent, and He could have made the devils simply go away; but He chose to send them into the pigs. Then there is the curious story of the fig tree, which always rather puzzled me. You remember what happened about the fig tree. "He was hungry; and seeing a fig tree afar off having leaves, He came if haply He might find anything thereon; and when He came to it He found nothing but leaves, for the time of figs was not yet. And Jesus answered and said unto it: 'No man eat fruit of thee hereafter for ever'... and Peter... saith unto Him: 'Master, behold the fig tree which thou cursedst is withered away.'" This is a very curious story, because it was not the right time of year for figs, and you really could not blame the tree. I cannot myself feel that either in the matter of wisdom or in the matter of virtue Christ stands quite as high as some other people known to history. I think I should put Buddha and Socrates above Him in those respects.

The Emotional Factor

As I said before, I do not think that the real reason why people accept religion has anything to do with argumentation. They accept religion on emotional grounds. One is often told that it is a very wrong thing to attack religion, because religion makes men virtuous. So I am told; I have not noticed it. You know, of course, the parody of that argument in Samuel Butler's book, *Erewhon Revisited*.

You will remember that in *Erewhon* there is a certain Higgs who arrives in a remote country, and after spending some time there he escapes from that country in a balloon. Twenty years later he comes back to that country and finds a new religion in which he is worshiped under the name of the "Sun Child," and it is said that he ascended into heaven. He finds that the Feast of the Ascension is about to be celebrated, and he hears Professors Hanky and Panky say to each other that they never set eyes on the man Higgs, and they hope they never will; but they are the high priests of the religion of the Sun Child. He is very indignant, and he comes up to them, and he says, "I am going to expose all this humbug and tell the people of Erewhon that it was only I, the man Higgs, and I went up in a balloon." He was told, "You must not do that, because all the morals of this country are bound round this myth, and if they once know that you did not ascend into Heaven they will all become wicked"; and so he is persuaded of that and he goes quietly away.

That is the idea — that we should all be wicked if we did not hold to the Christian religion. It seems to me that the people who have held to it have been for the most part extremely wicked. You find this curious fact, that the more intense has been the religion of any period and the more profound has been the dogmatic belief, the greater has been the cruelty and the worse has been the state of affairs. In the so-called ages of faith, when men really did believe the Christian religion in all its completeness, there was the Inquisition, with all its tortures; there were millions of unfortunate women burned as witches; and there was every kind of cruelty practiced upon all sorts of people in the name of religion.

You find as you look around the world that every single bit of progress in humane feeling, every improvement in the criminal law, every step toward the diminution of war, every step toward better treatment of the coloured races, or every mitigation of slavery, every moral progress that there has been in the world, has been consistently opposed by the organized churches of the world. I say quite deliberately that the Christian religion, as organized in its churches, has been and still is the principal enemy of moral progress in the world.

How the Churches Have Retarded Progress

You may think that I am going too far when I say that that is still so. I do not think that I am. Take one fact. You will bear with me if I mention it. It is not a pleasant fact, but the churches compel one to mention facts that are not pleasant. Supposing that in this world that we live in today an inexperienced girl is married to a syphilitic man; in that case the Catholic Church says, "This is an indissoluble sacrament.

You must endure celibacy or stay together. And if you stay together, you must not use birth control to prevent the birth of syphilitic children." Nobody whose natural sympathies have not been warped by dogma, or whose moral nature was not absolutely dead to all sense of suffering, could maintain that it is right and proper that that state of things should continue.

That is only an example. There are a great many ways in which, at the present moment, the church, by its insistence upon what it chooses to call morality, inflicts upon all sorts of people undeserved and unnecessary suffering. And of course, as we know, it is in its major part an opponent still of progress and improvement in all the ways that diminish suffering in the world, because it has chosen to label as morality a certain narrow set of rules of conduct which have nothing to do with human happiness; and when you say that this or that ought to be done because it would make for human happiness, they think that has nothing to do with the matter at all. "What has human happiness to do with morals? The object of morals is not to make people happy."

Fear, the Foundation of Religion

Religion is based, I think, primarily and mainly upon fear. It is partly the terror of the unknown and partly, as I have said, the wish to feel that you have a kind of elder brother who will stand by you in all your troubles and disputes. Fear is the basis of the whole thing — fear of the mysterious, fear of defeat, fear of death.

Fear is the parent of cruelty, and therefore it is no wonder if cruelty and religion have gone hand in hand. It is because fear is at the basis of those two things. In this world we can now begin a little to understand things, and a little to master them by help of science, which has forced its way step by step against the Christian religion, against the churches, and against the opposition of all the old precepts. Science can help us to get over this craven fear in which mankind has lived for so many generations.

Science can teach us, and I think our own hearts can teach

us, no longer to look around for imaginary supports, no longer to invent allies in the sky, but rather to look to our own efforts here below to make this world a better place to live in, instead of the sort of place that the churches in all these centuries have made it.

What We Must Do?

We want to stand upon our own feet and look fair and square at the world — its good facts, its bad facts, its beauties, and its ugliness; see the world as it is and be not afraid of it. Conquer the world by intelligence and not merely by being slavishly subdued by the terror that comes from it. The whole conception of God is a conception derived from the ancient Oriental despotisms.

It is a conception quite unworthy of free men. When you hear people in church debasing themselves and saying that they are miserable sinners, and all the rest of it, it seems contemptible and not worthy of self-respecting human beings. We ought to stand up and look the world frankly in the face. We ought to make the best we can of the world, and if it is not so good as we wish, after all it will still be better than what these others have made of it in all these ages. A good world needs knowledge, kindliness, and courage; it does not need a regretful hankering after the past or a fettering of the free intelligence by the words uttered long ago by ignorant men. It needs a fearless outlook and a free intelligence. It needs hope for the future, not looking back all the time toward a past that is dead, which we trust will be far surpassed by the future that our intelligence can create.

Vagueness

Reflection on philosophical problems has convinced me that a much larger number than I used to think, or than is generally thought, are connected with the principles of symbolism, that is to say, with the relation between what means and what is meant. In dealing with highly abstract matters it is much easier to grasp the symbols (usually words) than it is to grasp what they stand for. The result of this is that almost all thinking that purports to be philosophical or logical consists in attributing to the world the properties of language. Since language really occurs, it obviously has all the properties common to all occurrences, and to that extent the metaphysic based upon linguistic considerations may not be erroneous.

But language has many properties which are not shared by things in general, and when these properties intrude into our metaphysic it becomes altogether misleading. I do not think that the study of the principles of symbolism will yield any *positive* results in metaphysics, but I do think it will yield a great many negative results by enabling us to avoid fallacious inferences from symbols to things. The influence of symbolism on philosophy is mainly unconscious; if it were conscious it would do less harm. By studying the principles of symbolism we can learn not to be unconsciously influenced by language, and in this way can escape a host of erroneous notions.

Vagueness, which is my topic tonight, illustrates these remarks. You will no doubt think that, in the words of the poet: "Who speaks of vagueness should himself be vague." I propose to prove that all language is vague, and that therefore my language is vague, but I do not wish this conclusion to be one that you could derive without the help of the symbolism. I shall be as little vague as I know how to be if I am to employ the English language. You all know that I invented a special language with a view to avoiding vagueness, but unfortunately it is unsuited for public occasions. I shall, therefore, though regretfully, address you in English, and whatever vagueness is to be found in my words must be attributed to our ancestors for not having been predominantly interested in logic.

There is a certain tendency in those who have realized that words are vague to infer that things also are vague. We hear a great deal about the flux and the continuum and the unanalysability of the Universe, and it is often suggested that as our language becomes more precise, it becomes less adapted to represent the primitive chaos out of which man is supposed to have evolved the cosmos. This seems to me precisely a case of the fallacy of verbalism — the fallacy that consists in mistaking the properties of words for the properties of things.

Vagueness and precision alike are characteristics which can only belong to a representation, of which language is an example. The have to do with the relation between a representation and that which it represents. Apart from representation, whether cognitive or mechanical, there can be no such thing as vagueness or precision; things are what they are, and there is an end of it. Nothing is more or less what it is, or to a certain extent possessed of the properties which it possesses. Idealism has produced habits of confusion even in the minds of those who think that they have rejected it. Ever since Kant there has been a tendency in philosophy to confuse knowledge with what is known.

It is thought that there must be some kind of identity between the knower and the known, and hence the knower infers that the known is also muddle-headed. All this identity of knower and known, and all this supposed intimacy of the relation of knowing, seems to me a delusion. Knowing is an occurrence having a certain relation to some other occurrence, or groups of occurrences, or characteristic of a group of occurrences, which constitutes what is said to be known. When knowledge is vague, this does not apply to the knowing as an occurrence; as an occurrence it is incapable of being either vague or precise, just as all other occurrences are. Vagueness in a cognitive occurrence is a characteristic of its relation to that which is known, not a characteristic of the occurrence in itself.

Let us consider the various ways in which common words are vague, and let us being with such a word as "red". It is perfectly obvious, since colours form a continuum, that there are shades of colour concerning which we shall be in doubt whether to call them red or not, not because we are ignorant of the meaning of the word "red", but because it is a word the extent of whose application is essentially doubtful. This, of course, is the answer to the old puzzle about the man who went bald. It is supposed that at first he was not bald, that he lost his hairs one by one, and that in the end he was bald; therefore, it is argued, there must have been one hair the loss of which converted him into a bald man. This, of course, is absurd. Baldness is a vague conception; some men are certainly bald, some are certainly not bald, while between them there are men of whom it is not true to say they must be either be bald or not bald.

The law of excluded middle is true when precise symbols are employed, but it is not true when symbols are vague, as, in fact, all symbols are. All words denoting sensible qualities have the same kind of vagueness which belongs to the word "red". This vagueness exists also, though in a lesser degree, in the quantitative words which science has tried hardest to make precise, such as a meter or a second. I am not going to invoke Einstein for the purpose of making these words vague. The meter, for example, is defined as the distance between two marks on a certain rod in Paris, when that rod is at a certain temperature. Now the marks are not points, but patches of a finite size, so that the distance between them is not a precise conception. Moreover, temperature cannot be measured with more than a certain degree of accuracy, and the temperature of a rod is never quite uniform. For all these reasons the conception of a meter is lacking in precision. The same applies to a second. The second is defined by relation to the rotation of the earth, but the earth is not a rigid body, and two parts of the earth's surface do not take exactly the same time to rotate; moreover all observations have a margin of error. There are some occurrences of which we can say that they take less than a second to happen, and others of which we can say that they take more, but between the two there will be a number of occurrences of which we believe that they do not all last equally long, but of none of which we can say whether they last more or less than a second. Therefore, when we say an occurrence lasts a second, all that it is worth while to mean is that no possible accuracy of observation will show whether it lasts more or less than a second.

Now let us take proper names. I pass by the irrelevant fact that the same proper name often belongs to many people. I once knew a man called Ebenezer Wilkes Smith, and I decline to believe that anybody else ever had this name. You might say, therefore, that here at last we have discovered an unambiguous symbol. This, however, would be a mistake. Mr.. Ebenezer Wilkes Smith was born, and being born is a gradual process. It would seem natural to suppose that the name was not attributable before birth; if so, there was doubt, while birth was taking place, whether the name was attributable or not. If it be said that the name was attributable before birth, the ambiguity is even more obvious, since no one can decide how long before the name became attributable. Death is also a process: even when it is what is called instantaneous, death must occupy a finite time.

If you continue to apply the name to the corpse, there must gradually come a stage in decomposition when the name ceases to be attributable, but no one can say precisely when this stage has been reached. The fact is that all words are attributable without doubt over a certain area, but become questionable within a penumbra, outside which they are again certainly not attributable. Someone might seek to obtain precision in the use of words by saying that no word is to be applied in the penumbra, but unfortunately the penumbra is itself not accurately definable, and all the vagueness which apply to the primary use of words apply also when we try to fix a limit to their indubitable applicability. This has a reason in our physiological constitution. Stimuli which for various reasons we believe to be different produce in us indistinguishable sensations.

It is not clear whether the sensations themselves are sometimes identical in relevant respects even when the stimuli differ in relevant respects. This is a kind of question which the theory of quanta at some much later stage in its development may be able to answer, but for the present it may be left in doubt. For our purpose it is not the vital question. What is clear is that the knowledge that we can obtain through our sensations is not as fine-grained as the stimuli to those sensations. We cannot see with the naked eye the difference between two glasses of water of which one is wholesome while the other is full of typhoid bacilli. In this case a microscope enables us to see the difference, but in the absence of a microscope the difference is only inferred from the differing effects of things which are sensibly indistinguishable. It is this fact that things which our senses do not distinguish produce different effects — as, for example, one glass of water gives you typhoid while the other does not — that has led us to regard the knowledge derived from the senses as vague. And the vagueness of the knowledge derived from the senses infects all words in the definition of which there is a sensible element. This includes all words which contain geographical or chronological constituents, such as "Julius Caesar", "the twentieth century", or "the solar system".

There remains a more abstract class of words: first, words which apply to all parts of time and space, such as "matter" or "causality"; secondly, the words of pure logic. I shall leave out of discussion the first class of words, since all of them raise great difficulties, and I can scarcely imagine a human being who would deny that they are all more or less vague. I come therefore to the words of pure logic, words such as "or" and "not". Are these words also vague or have they a precise meaning?

Words such as "or" and "not" might seem, at first sight, to have a perfectly precise meaning: "*p* or *q*" is true when *p* is true, when *q* is true, and false when both are false. But the trouble is that this involves the notions of "true" and "false"; and it will be found, I think, that all the concepts of logic involve these notions, directly or indirectly.

Now "true" and "false" can only have a *precise* meaning when the symbols employed — words, perceptions, images, or what not — are themselves precise. We have seen that, in practice, this is not the case. It follows that every proposition that can be framed in practice has a certain degree of vagueness; that is to say, there is not one definite fact necessary and sufficient for its truth, but a certain region of possible facts, any one of which would make it true. And this region is itself ill-defined: we cannot assign to it a definite boundary. This is the difference between vagueness and generality. A proposition involving a general concept — e.g. "This is a man" — will be verified by a number of facts, such as "This" being Brown or Jones or Robinson. But if "man" were a precise idea, the set of possible facts that would verify "this is a man" would be quite definite. Since, however, the conception "man" is more or less vague, it is possible to discover prehistoric specimens concerning which there is no, even in theory, a definite answer to the question "Is this a man?" As applied to such specimens, the proposition "this is a man" is neither definitely true nor definitely false. Since all non-logical words have this kind of vagueness, it follows that the conceptions of truth and falsehood, as applied to propositions composed of or containing non-logical words, are themselves more or less vague. Since propositions containing non-logical words are the substructure on which logical propositions are built, it follows that logical propositions also, so far as we can know them, become vague through the vagueness of "truth" and "falsehood".

We can see an ideal of precision, to which we can approximate indefinitely; but we cannot attain this ideal. Logical words, like the rest, when used by human beings, share the vagueness of all other words. There is, however, less vagueness about logical words than about the words of daily life, because logical words apply essentially to symbols, and may be conceived as applying rather to possible than to actual symbols. We are capable of imagining what a precise symbolism would be, though we cannot actually construct such a symbolism.

Hence we are able to *imagine* a precise meaning for such words as "or" and "not". We can, in fact, see precisely what they would mean if our symbolism were precise. All traditional logic habitually assumes that precise symbols are being employed. It is therefore not applicable to this terrestrial life, but only to an imagined celestial existence. Where, however, this celestial existence would differ from ours, so far as logic is concerned, would be not in the nature of what is known, but only in the accuracy of our knowledge. Therefore, if the hypothesis of a precise symbolism enables us to draw any inferences as to what is symbolized, there is no reason to distrust such inferences merely on the ground that our actual symbolism is not precise. We are able to conceive precision;

indeed, if we could not do so, we could not conceive vagueness, which is merely the contrary of precision. This is one reason why logic takes us nearer to heaven than most other studies. On this point I agree with Plato. But those who dislike logic will, I fear, find my heaven disappointing.

It is now time to tackle the definition of vagueness. Vagueness, though it applies primarily to what is cognitive, is a conception applicable to every kind of representation — for example, a photograph, or a barograph. But before defining vagueness it is necessary to define accuracy. One of the most easily intelligible definitions of accuracy is as follows: One structure is an accurate representation of another when the words describing the one will also describe the other by being given new meanings. For example, "Brutus killed Caesar" has the same structure as "Plato loved Socrates", because both can be represented by the symbol "xRy", by giving suitable meanings to x and R and y. But this definition, though easy to understand, does not give the essence of the matter, since the introduction of words describing the two systems is irrelevant.

The exact definition is as follows: One system of terms related in various ways is an accurate representation of another system of terms related in various other ways if there is a one-one relation of the terms of the one to the terms of the other, and likewise a one-one relation of the relations of the one to the relations of the other, such that, when two or more terms in the one system have a relation belonging to that system, the corresponding terms of the other system have the corresponding relation belonging to the other system. Maps, charts, photographs, catalogues, etc. all come within this definition in so far as they are accurate.

Per contra, a representation is *vague* when the relation of the representing system to the represented system is not one-one, but one-many. For example, a photograph which is so smudged that it might equally represent Brown or Jones or Robinson is vague. A small-scale map is usually vaguer than a large-scale map, because it does not show all the turns and twists of the roads, rivers, etc. so that various slightly different courses are compatible with the representation that it gives.

Vagueness, clearly, is a matter of degree, depending upon the extent of the possible differences between different systems represented by the same representation. Accuracy, on the contrary, is an ideal limit.

Passing from representation in general to the kinds of representation that are specially interesting to the logician, the representing system will consist of words, perceptions, thoughts, or something of the kind, and the would-be one-one relation between the representing system and the represented system will be *meaning*. In an accurate language, meaning would be a one-one relation; no word would have two meanings, and no two words would have the same meaning. In actual languages, as we have seen, meaning is one-many. (It happens often that two words have the same meaning, but this is easily avoided, and can be assumed not to happen without injuring the argument.) That is to say, there is not only one object that a word means, and not only one possible fact that will verify a proposition.

The fact that meaning is a one-many relation is the precise statement of the fact that all language is more or less vague. There is, however, a complication about language as a method of representing a system, namely that words which mean relations are not themselves relations, but just as substantial or unsubstantial as other words. In this respect a map, for instance, is superior to language, since the fact that one place is to the west of another is represented by the fact that the corresponding place on the map is to the left of the other; that is to say, a relation is represented by a relation. But in language this is not the case.

Certain relations of higher order are represented by relations, in accordance with the rules of syntax. For example, "*A* precedes *B*" and "*B* precedes *A*" have different meanings, because the order of the words is an essential part of the meaning of the sentence. But this does not hold of elementary relations; the word "precedes", though it means a relation, is not a relation. I believe that this simple fact is at the bottom of the hopeless muddle which has prevailed in *all* schools of philosophy as to the nature of relations. It would, however, take me too far from my present theme to pursue this line of thought.

It may be said: How do you know that all knowledge is vague, and what does it matter if it is? The case which I took before, of two glasses of water, one of which is wholesome while the other gives you typhoid, will illustrate both points. Without calling in the microscope, it is obvious that you cannot distinguish the wholesome glass of water from the one that will give you typhoid, just as, without calling in the telescope, it is obvious that what you see of a man who is 200 yards away is vague compared to what you see of a man who is 2 feet away; that is to say, many men who look quite different when see close at hand look indistinguishable at a distance, while men who look different at a distance never look indistinguishable when seen close at hand.

Therefore, according to the definition, there is less vagueness in the near appearance than in the distant one. There is still less vagueness about the appearance under the microscope. It is perfectly ordinary facts of this kind that prove the vagueness of most of our knowledge, and lead us to infer the vagueness of all of it.

It would be a great mistake to suppose that vague knowledge must be false. On the contrary, a vague belief has a much better chance of being true than a precise one, because there are more possible facts that would verify it. If I believe that so-and-so is tall, I am more likely to be right than if I believe that his height is between 6 ft. 2 in. and 6 ft. 3 in. In regard to beliefs and propositions, though not in regard to single words, we can distinguish between accuracy and precision.

A belief is *precise* when only one fact would verify it; it is *accurate* when it is both precise and true. Precision diminishes the likelihood of truth, but often increases the pragmatic value of a belief if it is true — for example, in the case of the water that contained the typhoid bacilli. Science is perpetually trying to substitute more precise beliefs for vague ones; this makes it harder for a scientific proposition to be true than for the vague beliefs of uneducated persons to be true, but it makes scientific truth better worth having if it can be obtained. Vagueness in our knowledge is, I believe, merely a particular case of a general law of physics, namely that law that what may be called the appearances of a thing at different places are less and less differentiated as we get further away from the thing. When I speak of "appearances" I am speaking of something purely physical — the sort of thing, in fact, that, if it is visual, can be photographed. From a close-up photograph it is possible to infer a photograph of the same object at a distance, while the contrary inference is much more precarious. That is to say, there is a one-many relation between distant and close-up appearances.

Therefore the distance appearance, regarded as a representation of the close-up appearance, is vague according to our definition. I think all vagueness in language and thought is essentially analogous to this vagueness which may exist in a photograph. My own belief is that most of the problems of epistemology, in so far as they are genuine, are really problems of physics and physiology; moreover, I believe that physiology is only a complicated branch of physics. The habit of treating knowledge as something mysterious and wonderful seems to me unfortunate. People do not say that a barometer "knows" when it is going to rain; but I doubt if there is any essential difference in this respect between the barometer and the meteorologist who observes it.

There is only one philosophical theory, which seems to me in a position to ignore physics, and this is solipsism. If you are willing to believe that nothing exists except what you directly experience, no other person can prove that you are wrong, and probably no valid arguments exist against your view. But if you are going to allow any inferences from what you directly experience to other entities, then physics supplies the safest form of such inferences. And I believe that (apart from illegitimate problems derived from misunderstood symbolism) physics, in its modern forms, supplies materials for answers to all philosophical problems that are capable of being answered, except the one problem raised by solipsism, namely: Is there any valid inference ever from an entity experienced to one inferred? On this problem, I see no refutation of the skeptical position. But the skeptical philosophy is so short as to be uninteresting; therefore it is natural for a person who has learnt to philosophize to work out other alternatives, even if there is no very good ground for regarding them as preferable.

The Metaphysician's Nightmare

My poor friend Andrei Bumblowski, formerly Professor of Philosophy in a now extinct university of Central Europe, appeared to me to suffer from a harmless kind of lunacy. I am myself a person of robust common sense; I hold that the intellect must not be taken as a guide in life, but only as affording pleasant argumentative games and ways of annoying less agile opponents.

Bumblowski, however, did not take this view; he allowed his intellect to lead him whither it would, and the results were odd. He seldom argued, and to most of his friends the grounds of his opinions remained obscure. What was known was that he consistently avoided the word 'not' and all its synonyms. He would not say 'this egg is not fresh', but 'chemical changes have occurred in this egg since it was laid'. He would not say 'I cannot find that book', but 'the books I have found are other than that book'. He would not say 'thou shalt not kill', but 'thou shalt cherish life'. His life was unpractical, but innocent, and I felt for him a considerable affection. It was doubtless this affection which at last unlocked his lips, and led him to relate to me the following very remarkable experience, which I give in his own words:

I had at one time a very bad fever of which I almost died. In my fever I had a long consistent delirium. I dreamt that I was in Hell, and that Hell is a place full of all those happenings that are improbable but not impossible. The effects of this are curious. Some of the damned, when they first arrive below, imagine that they will beguile the tedium of eternity by games of cards. But they find this impossible, because, whenever a pack is shuffled, it comes out in perfect order, beginning with the Ace of Spades and ending with the King of Hearts. There is a special department of Hell for students of probability. In this department there are many typewriters and many monkeys. Every time that a monkey walks on a typewriter, it types by chance one of Shakespeare's sonnets.

There is another place of torment for physicists. In this there are kettles and fires, but when the kettles are put on the fires, the water in them freezes. There are also stuffy rooms. But experience has taught the physicists never to open a window because, when they do, all the air rushes out and leaves the room a vacuum. There is another region for gourmets. These men are allowed the most exquisite materials and the most skilful chefs. But when a beefsteak is served up to them, and they take a confident mouthful, they find that it tastes like a rotten egg; whereas, when they try to eat an egg, it tastes like a bad potato.

There is a peculiarly painful chamber inhabited solely by philosophers who have refuted Hume. These philosophers, though in Hell, have not learned wisdom. They continue to be governed by their animal propensity towards induction. But every time that they have made an induction, the next instance falsifies it. This, however, happens only during the first hundred years of their damnation. After that, they learn to expect that an induction will be falsified, and therefore it is not falsified until another century of logical torment has altered their expectation. Throughout all eternity surprise continues, but each time at a higher logical level.

Then there is the Inferno of the orators who have been accustomed while they lived to sway great multitudes by their eloquence. Their eloquence is undimmed and the multitudes are provided, but strange winds blow the sounds about so that the sounds heard by the multitudes, instead of being those uttered by the orators, are only dull and heavy platitudes.

At the very centre of the infernal kingdom is Satan, to whose presence only the more distinguished among the damned are admitted. The improbabilities become greater and greater as Satan is approached, and He Himself is the most complete improbability imaginable. He is pure Nothing, total non-existence, and yet continually changing.

I, because of my philosophical eminence, was early given audience with the Prince of Darkness. I had read of Satan as *der Geist der stets verneint,* the Spirit of Negation. But on entering the Presence I realized with a shock that Satan has a negative body as well as a negative mind. Satan's body is, in fact, a pure and complete vacuum, empty not only of particles of matter but also of particles of light. His prolonged emptiness is secured by a climax of improbability: whenever a particle approaches His outer surface, it happens by chance to collide with another particle which stops it from penetrating the empty region.

The empty region, since no light ever penetrates it, is absolutely black-not more or less black, like the things to which we loosely ascribe this word, but utterly, completely and infinitely black. It has a shape, and the shape is that which we are accustomed to ascribe to Satan: horns, hooves, tail and all. All the rest of Hell is filled with murky flame, and against this background Satan stands out in awful majesty. He is not immobile. On the contrary, the emptiness of which He is constituted is in perpetual motion. When anything annoys him, He swings the horror of His folded tail like an angry cat. Sometimes He goes forth to conquer new realms. Before going forth, He clothes Himself in shining white armour, which completely conceals the nothingness within. Only His eyes remain unclothed, and from His eyes piercing rays of nothingness shoot forth seeking what they may conquer. Wherever they find negation, wherever they find prohibition, wherever they find a cult of not-doing, there they enter into the inmost substance of those who are prepared to receive Him.

Every negation emanates from Him and returns with a harvest of captured frustrations. The captured frustrations become part of Him, and swell His bulk until He threatens to fill all space. Every moralist whose morality consists of 'don'ts', every timid man who 'lets I dare not wait upon I would', every tyrant who compels his subjects to live in fear, becomes in time a part of Satan.

He is surrounded by a chorus of sycophantic philosophers

who have substituted pandiabolism for pantheism. These men maintain that existence is only apparent; non-existence is the only true reality. They hope in time to make the non-existence of appearance appear, for in that moment what we now take to be existence will be seen to be in truth only an outlying portion of the diabolic essence. Although these metaphysicians showed much subtlety, I could not agree with them. I had been accustomed while on earth to oppose tyrannous authority, and this habit remained with me in Hell. I began to argue with the metaphysical sycophants:

'What you say is absurd,' I expostulated. 'You proclaim that nonexistence is the only reality. You pretend that this black hole which you worship exists. You are trying to persuade me that the non-existent exists. But this is a contradiction: and, however hot the flames of Hell rpay become, I will never so degrade my logical being as to accept a contradiction.'

At this point the President of the sycophants took up the argument: 'You go too fast, my friend,' he said. 'You deny that the non-existent exists? But what is this to which you deny existence? If the non-existent is nothing, any statement about it is nonsense. And so is your statement that it does not exist. I am afraid you have paid too little attention to the logical analysis of sentences, which ought to have been taught you when you were a boy. Do you not know that every sentence has a subject, and that, if the subject were nothing, the sentence would be nonsense? So, when you proclaim, with virtuous heat, that Satan-who is the nonexistent-does not exist, you are plainly contradicting yourself.'

'You', I replied, 'have no doubt been here for some time and continue to embrace somewhat antiquated doctrines. You prate of sentences having subjects, but all that sort of talk is out of date. When I say that Satan, who is the non-existent, does not exist, I mention neither Satan nor the non-existent, but only the word "Satan" and the word "non-existent". Your fallacies have revealed to me a great truth. The great truth is that the word "not" is superfluous. Henceforth I will not use the word "not". At this all the assembled metaphysicians burst into a shout of laughter. 'Hark how the fellow contradicts himself,' they said when the paroxysm,of merriment had subsided. 'Hark at his great commandment which is to avoid negation. He will NOT use the word "not", forsooth!'

Though I was nettled, I kept my temper. I had in my pocket a dictionary. I scratched out all the words expressing negation and said: 'My speech shall be composed entirely of the words that remain in this dictionary. By the help of these words that remain, I shall be able to describe every thing in the universe. My descriptions will be many, but they will all be of things other than Satan. Satan has reigned too long in this infernal realm. His shining armour was real and inspired terror, but underneath the armour there was only a bad linguistic habit. Avoid the word "not", and His empire is at an end.'

Satan, as the argument proceeded, lashed His tail with ever-increasing fury, and savage rays of darkness shot from His cavernous eyes. But at the last, when I denounced Him as a bad linguistic habit, there was a vast explosion, the air rushed in from all sides, and the horrid shape vanished. The murky air of Hell, which had been due to incipated rays of nothingness, cleared as if by magic. What had seemed to be monkeys at the typewriters w ere suddenly seen to be literary critics. The kettles boiled, the cards were jumbled, a fresh breeze blew in at the windows, and the beefsteaks tasted like beefsteaks. With a sense of exquisite liberation, I awoke. I saw that there had been wisdom in my dream, however it might have worn the guise of delirium. From that moment the fever abated, but the delirium-as you may think it-has remained.

What Desires are Politically Important?

I have chosen this subject for my lecture tonight because I think that most current discussions of politics and political theory take insufficient account of psychology. Economic facts, population statistics, constitutional organization, and so on, are set forth minutely. There is no difficulty in finding out how many South Koreans and how many North Koreans there were when the Korean War began. If you will look into the right books you will be able to ascertain what was their average income per head, and what were the sizes of their respective armies. But if you want to know what sort of person a Korean is, and whether there is any appreciable difference between a North Korean and a South Korean; if you wish to know what they respectively want out of life, what are their discontents, what their hopes and what their fears; in a word, what it is that, as they say, «makes them tick», you will look through the reference books in vain. And so you cannot tell whether the South Koreans are enthusiastic about UNO, or would prefer union with their cousins in the North.

Nor can you guess whether they are willing to forgo land reform for the privilege of voting for some politician they have never heard of. It is neglect of such questions by the eminent men who sit in remote capitals that so frequently causes disappointment. If politics is to become scientific, and if the event is not to be constantly surprising, it is imperative that our political thinking should penetrate more deeply into the springs of human action. What is the influence of hunger upon slogans? How does their effectiveness fluctuate with the number of calories in your diet? If one man offers you democracy and another offers you a bag of grain, at what stage of starvation will you prefer the grain to the vote? Such questions are far too little considered. However, let us, for the present, forget the Koreans, and consider the human race.

All human activity is prompted by desire. There is a wholly fallacious theory advanced by some earnest moralists to the effect that it is possible to resist desire in the interests of duty and moral principle. I say this is fallacious, not because no man ever acts from a sense of duty, but because duty has no hold on him unless he desires to be dutiful. If you wish to know what men will do, you must know not only, or principally, their material circumstances, but rather the whole system of their desires with their relative strengths.

There are some desires which, though very powerful, have not, as a rule, any great political importance. Most men at some period of their lives desire to marry, but as a rule they can satisfy this desire without having to take any political action. There are, of course, exceptions; the rape of the Sabine women is a case in point. And the development of northern Australia is seriously impeded by the fact that the vigorous young men who ought to do the work dislike being wholly deprived of female society. But such cases are unusual, and in general the interest that men and women take in each other has little influence upon politics.

The desires that are politically important may be divided into a primary and a secondary group. In the primary group come the necessities of life: food and shelter and clothing. When these things become very scarce, there is no limit to the efforts that men will make, or to the violence that they will display, in the hope of securing them. It is said by students of the earliest history that, on four separate occasions, drought in Arabia caused the population of that country to overflow into surrounding regions, with immense effects, political, cultural, and religious. The last of these four occasions was the rise of Islam. The gradual spread of Germanic tribes from southern Russia to England, and thence to San Francisco, had similar motives. Undoubtedly the desire for food has been, and still is, one of the main causes of great political events.

But man differs from other animals in one very important respect, and that is that he has some desires which are, so to speak, infinite, which can never be fully gratified, and which would keep him restless even in Paradise. The boa constrictor, when he has had an adequate meal, goes to sleep, and does not wake until he needs another meal. Human beings, for the most part, are not like this. When the Arabs, who had been used to living sparingly on a few dates, acquired the riches of the Eastern Roman Empire, and dwelt in palaces of almost unbelievable luxury, they did not, on that account, become inactive. Hunger could no longer be a motive, for Greek slaves supplied them with exquisite viands at the slightest nod. But other desires kept them active: four in particular, which we can label acquisitiveness, rivalry, vanity, and love of power. Acquisitiveness - the wish to possess as much as possible of goods, or the title to goods - is a motive which, I suppose, has its origin in a combination of fear with the desire for necessaries.

I once befriended two little girls from Estonia, who had narrowly escaped death from starvation in a famine. They lived in my family, and of course had plenty to eat. But they spent all their leisure visiting neighbouring farms and stealing potatoes, which they hoarded. Rockefeller, who in his infancy had experienced great poverty, spent his adult life in a similar manner. Similarly the Arab chieftains on their silken Byzantine divans could not forget the desert, and hoarded riches far beyond any possible physical need. But whatever may be the psychoanalysis of acquisitiveness, no one can deny that it is one of the great motives - especially among the more powerful, for, as I said before, it is one of the infinite motives. However much you may acquire, you will always wish to acquire more; satiety is a dream which will always elude you.

But acquisitiveness, although it is the mainspring of the capitalist system, is by no means the most powerful of the motives that survive the conquest of hunger. Rivalry is a much stronger motive. Over and over again in Mohammedan history, dynasties have come to grief because the sons of a sultan by different mothers could not agree, and in the resulting civil war universal ruin resulted.

The same sort of thing happens in modern Europe. When the British Government very unwisely allowed the Kaiser to be present at a naval review at Spithead, the thought which arose in his mind was not the one which we had intended. What he thought was, «I must have a Navy as good as Grandmamma's. And from this thought have sprung all our subsequent troubles. The world would be a happier place than it is if acquisitiveness were always stronger than rivalry. But in fact, a great many men will cheerfully face impoverishment if they can thereby secure complete ruin for their rivals. Hence the present level of taxation.

Vanity is a motive of immense potency. Anyone who has much to do with children knows how they are constantly performing some antic, and saying «Look at me». «Look at me» is one of the most fundamental desires of the human heart. It can take innumerable forms, from buffoonery to the pursuit of posthumous fame. There was a Renaissance Italian princeling who was asked by the priest on his deathbed if he had anything to repent of. «Yes», he said, «there is one thing. On one occasion I had a visit from the Emperor and the Pope simultaneously.

I took them to the top of my tower to see the view, and I neglected the opportunity to throw them both down, which would have given me immortal fame». History does not relate whether the priest gave him absolution. One of the troubles about vanity is that it grows with what it feeds on. The more you are talked about, the more you will wish to be talked about. The condemned murderer who is allowed to see the account of his trial in the press is indignant if he finds a newspaper which has reported it inadequately. And the more he finds about himself in other newspapers, the more indignant he will be with the one whose reports are meagre. Politicians and literary men are in the same case. And the more famous they become, the more difficult the press-cutting agency finds it to satisfy them. It is scarcely possible to exaggerate the influence of vanity throughout the range of human life, from the child of three to the potentate at whose frown the world trembles. Mankind have even committed the impiety of attributing similar desires to the Deity, whom they imagine avid for continual praise.

But great as is the influence of the motives we have been considering, there is one which outweighs them all. I mean the love of power. Love of power is closely akin to vanity, but it is not by any means the same thing. What vanity needs for its satisfaction is glory, and it is easy to have glory without power. The people who enjoy the greatest glory in the United States are film stars, but they can be put in their place by the Committee for Un-American Activities, which enjoys no glory whatever. In England, the King has more glory than the Prime Minister, but the Prime Minister has more power than the King. Many people prefer glory to power, but on the whole these people have less effect upon the course of events than those who prefer power to glory. When Blücher, in 1814, saw Napoleon's palaces, he said, «Wasn't he a fool to have all this and to go running after Moscow.» Napoleon, who certainly was not destitute of vanity, preferred power when he had to choose.

To Blücher, this choice seemed foolish. Power, like vanity, is insatiable. Nothing short of omnipotence could satisfy it completely. And as it is especially the vice of energetic men, the causal efficacy of love of power is out of all proportion to its frequency. It is, indeed, by far the strongest motive in the lives of important men.

Love of power is greatly increased by the experience of power, and this applies to petty power as well as to that of potentates. In the happy days before 1914, when well-to-do ladies could acquire a host of servants, their pleasure in exercising power over the domestics steadily increased with age. Similarly, in any autocratic regime, the holders of power become increasingly tyrannical with experience of the delights that power can afford. Since power over human beings is shown in making them do what they would rather not do, the man who is actuated by love of power is more apt to inflict pain than to permit pleasure.

If you ask your boss for leave of absence from the office on some legitimate occasion, his love of power will derive more satisfaction from a refusal than from a consent. If you require a building permit, the petty official concerned will obviously get more pleasure from saying «No» than from saying «Yes». It is this sort of thing which makes the love of power such a dangerous motive.

But it has other sides which are more desirable. The pursuit of knowledge is, I think, mainly actuated by love of power. And so are all advances in scientific technique. In politics, also, a reformer may have just as strong a love of power as a despot. It would be a complete mistake to decry love of power altogether as a motive. Whether you will be led by this motive to actions which are useful, or to actions which are pernicious, depends upon the social system, and upon your capacities. If your capacities are theoretical or technical, you will contribute to knowledge or technique, and, as a rule, your activity will be useful. If you are a politician you may be actuated by love of power, but as a rule this motive will join itself on to the desire to see some state of affairs realized which, for some reason, you prefer to the status quo.

A great general may, like Alcibiades, be quite indifferent as to which side he fights on, but most generals have preferred to fight for their own country, and have, therefore, had other motives besides love of power. The politician may change sides so frequently as to find himself always in the majority, but most politicians have a preference for one party to the other, and subordinate their love of power to this preference. Love of power as nearly pure as possible is to be seen in various different types of men. One type is the soldier of fortune, of whom Napoleon is the supreme example.

Napoleon had, I think, no ideological preference for France over Corsica, but if he had become Emperor of Corsica he would not have been so great a man as he became by pretending to be a Frenchman. Such men, however, are not quite pure examples, since they also derive immense satisfaction from vanity. The purest type is that of the *eminence grise* - the power behind the throne that never appears in public, and merely hugs itself with the secret thought: «How little these puppets know who is pulling the strings.» Baron Holstein, who controlled the foreign policy of the German Empire from 1890 to 1906, illustrates this type to perfection.

He lived in a slum; he never appeared in society; he avoided meeting the Emperor, except on one single occasion when the Emperor's importunity could not be resisted; he refused all invitations to Court functions, on the ground that he possessed no court dress. He had acquired secrets which enabled him to blackmail the Chancellor and many of the Kaiser's intimates. He used the power of blackmail, not to acquire wealth, or fame, or any other obvious advantage, but merely to compel the adoption of the foreign policy he preferred. In the East, similar characters were not very uncommon among eunuchs. I come now to other motives which, though in a sense less fundamental than those we have been considering, are still of considerable importance. The first of these is love of excitement. Human beings show their superiority to the brutes by their capacity for boredom, though

I have sometimes thought, in examining the apes at the zoo, that they, perhaps, have the rudiments of this tiresome emotion. However that may be, experience shows that escape from boredom is one of the really powerful desires of almost all human beings. When white men first effect contact with some unspoilt race of savages, they offer them all kinds of benefits, from the light of the gospel to pumpkin pie.

These, however, much as we may regret it, most savages receive with indifference. What they really value among the gifts that we bring to them is intoxicating liquor which enables them, for the first time in their lives, to have the illusion for a few brief moments that it is better to be alive than dead. Red Indians, while they were still unaffected by white men, would smoke their pipes, not calmly as we do, but orgiastically, inhaling so deeply that they sank into a faint. And when excitement by means of nicotine failed, a patriotic orator would stir them up to attack a neighbouring tribe, which would give them all the enjoyment that we (according to our temperament) derive from a horse race or a General Election. The pleasure of gambling consists almost entirely in excitement.

Monsieur Huc describes Chinese traders at the Great Wall in winter, gambling until they have lost all their cash, then proceeding to lose all their merchandise, and at last gambling away their clothes and going out naked to die of cold. With civilized men, as with primitive Red Indian tribes, it is, I think, chiefly love of excitement which makes the populace applauds when war breaks out; the emotion is exactly the same as at a football match, although the results are sometimes somewhat more serious.

It is not altogether easy to decide what is the root cause of the love of excitement. I incline to think that our mental make-up is adapted to the stage when men lived by hunting. When a man spent a long day with very primitive weapons in stalking a deer with the hope of dinner, and when, at the end of the day, he dragged the carcass triumphantly to his cave, he sank down in contented weariness, while his wife dressed and cooked the meat. He was sleepy, and his bones ached, and the smell of cooking filled every nook and cranny of his consciousness. At last, after eating, he sank into deep sleep. In such a life there was neither time nor energy for boredom. But when he took to agriculture, and made his wife do all the heavy work in the fields, he had time to reflect upon the vanity of human life, to invent mythologies and systems of philosophy, and to dream of the life hereafter in which he would perpetually hunt the wild boar of Valhalla. Our mental make-up is suited to a life of very severe physical labour. I used, when I was younger, to take my holidays walking. I would cover twenty-five miles a day, and when the evening came I had no need of anything to keep me from boredom, since the delight of sitting amply sufficed. But modern life cannot be conducted on these physically strenuous principles..

A great deal of work is sedentary, and most manual work exercises only a few specialized muscles. When crowds assemble in Trafalgar Square to cheer to the echo an announcement that the government has decided to have them killed, they would not do so if they had all walked twenty-five miles that day. This cure for bellicosity is, however, impracticable, and if the human race is to survive - a thing which is, perhaps, undesirable - other means must be found for securing an innocent outlet for the unused physical energy that produces love of excitement.

This is a matter which has been too little considered, both by moralists and by social reformers. The social reformers are of the opinion that they have more serious things to consider. The moralists, on the other hand, are immensely impressed with the seriousness of all the permitted outlets of the love of excitement; the seriousness, however, in their minds, is that of Sin. Dance halls, cinemas, this age of jazz, are all, if we may believe our ears, gateways to Hell, and we should be better employed sitting at home contemplating our sins. I find myself unable to be in entire agreement with the grave men who utter these warnings.

The devil has many forms, some designed to deceive the young, some designed to deceive the old and serious. If it is the devil that tempts the young to enjoy themselves, is it not, perhaps, the same personage that persuades the old to condemn their enjoyment? And is not condemnation perhaps merely a form of excitement appropriate to old age? And is it not, perhaps, a drug which - like opium - has to be taken in continually stronger doses to produce the desired effect? Is it not to be feared that, beginning with the wickedness of the cinema, we should be led step by step to condemn the opposite political party, dagoes, wops, Asiatics, and, in short, everybody except the fellow members of our club? And it is from just such condemnations, when widespread, that wars proceed: I have never heard of a war that proceeded from dance halls.

What is serious about excitement is that so many of its forms are destructive. It is destructive in those who cannot resist excess in alcohol or gambling. It is destructive when it takes the form of mob violence. And above all it is destructive when it leads to war. It is so deep a need that it will find harmful outlets of this kind unless innocent outlets are at hand. There are such innocent outlets at present in sport, and in politics so long as it is kept within constitutional bounds. But these are not sufficient, especially as the kind of politics that is most exciting is also the kind that does most harm.

Civilized life has grown altogether too tame, and, if it is to be stable, it must provide harmless outlets for the impulses which our remote ancestors satisfied in hunting. In Australia, where people are few and rabbits are many, I watched a whole populace satisfying the primitive impulse in the primitive manner by the skillful slaughter of many thousands of rabbits. But in London or New York some other means must be found to gratify primitive impulse. I think every big town should contain artificial waterfalls that people could descend in very fragile canoes, and they should contain bathing pools full of mechanical sharks. Any person found advocating a preventive war should be condemned to two hours a day with these ingenious monsters. More seriously, pains should be taken to provide constructive outlets for the love of excitement. Nothing in the world is more exciting than a moment of sudden discovery or invention, and many more people are capable of experiencing such moments than is sometimes thought.

Interwoven with many other political motives are two closely related passions to which human beings are regrettably prone: I mean fear and hate. It is normal to hate what we fear, and it happens frequently, though not always, that we fear what we hate. I think it may be taken as the rule among primitive men, that they both fear and hate whatever is unfamiliar. They have their own herd, originally a very small one. And within one herd, all are friends, unless there is some special ground of enmity. Other herds are potential or actual enemies; a single member of one of them who strays by accident will be killed. An alien herd as a whole will be avoided or fought according to circumstances.

It is this primitive mechanism which still controls our instinctive reaction to foreign nations. The completely untravelled person will view all foreigners as the savage regards a member of another herd. But the man who has travelled, or who has studied international politics, will have discovered that, if his herd is to prosper, it must, to some degree, become amalgamated with other herds.

If you are English and someone says to you, The French are your brothers», your first instinctive feeling will be, Nonsense. They shrug their shoulders, and talk French. And I am even told that they eat frogs. If he explains to you that we may have to fight the Russians, that, if so, it will be desirable to defend the line of the Rhine, and that, if the line of the Rhine is to be defended, the help of the French is essential, you will begin to see what he means when he says that the French are your brothers. But if some fellow-traveller were to go on to say that the Russians also are your brothers, he would be unable to persuade you, unless he could show that we are in danger from the Martians. We love those who hate our enemies, and if we had no enemies there would be very few people whom we should love. All this, however, is only true so long as we are concerned solely with attitudes towards other human beings. You might regard the soil as your enemy because it yields reluctantly a niggardly subsistence.

You might regard Mother Nature in general as your enemy, and envisage human life as a struggle to get the better of Mother Nature. If men viewed life in this way, cooperation of the whole human race would become easy. And men could easily be brought to view life in this way if schools, newspapers, and politicians devoted themselves to this end. But schools are out to teach patriotism; newspapers are out to stir up excitement; and politicians are out to get re-elected. None of the three, therefore, can do anything towards saving the human race from reciprocal suicide.

There are two ways of coping with fear: one is to diminish the external danger, and the other is to cultivate Stoic endurance. The latter can be reinforced, except where immediate action is necessary, by turning our thoughts away from the cause of fear.

The conquest of fear is of very great importance. Fear is in itself degrading; it easily becomes an obsession; it produces hate of that which is feared, and it leads headlong to excesses of cruelty. Nothing has so beneficent an effect on human beings as security. If an international system could be established which would remove the fear of war, the improvement in everyday mentality of everyday people would be enormous and very rapid. Fear, at present, overshadows the world.

The atom bomb and the bacterial bomb, wielded by the wicked communist or the wicked capitalist as the case may be, make Washington and the Kremlin tremble, and drive men further along the road toward the abyss. If matters are to improve, the first and essential step is to find a way of diminishing fear. The world at present is obsessed by the conflict of rival ideologies, and one of the apparent causes of conflict is the desire for the victory of our own ideology and the defeat of the other.

I do not think that the fundamental motive here has much to do with ideologies. I think the ideologies are merely a way of grouping people, and that the passions involved are merely those which always arise between rival groups. There are, of course, various reasons for hating communists. First and foremost, we believe that they wish to take away our property.

But so do burglars, and although we disapprove of burglars our attitude towards them is very different indeed from our attitude towards communists - chiefly because they do not inspire the same degree of fear. Secondly, we hate the communists because they are irreligious. But the Chinese have been irreligious since the eleventh century, and we only began to hate them when they turned out Chiang Kai-shek. Thirdly, we hate the communists because they do not believe in democracy, but we consider this no reason for hating Franco.

Fourthly, we hate them because they do not allow liberty; this we feel so strongly that we have decided to imitate them. It is obvious that none of these is the real ground for our hatred. We hate them because we fear them and they threaten us. If the Russians still adhered to the Greek Orthodox religion, if they had instituted parliamentary government, and if they had a completely free press which daily vituperated us, then - provided they still had armed forces as powerful as they have now - we should still hate them if they gave us ground for thinking them hostile.

There is, of course, the *odium theologicum*, and it can be a cause of enmity. But I think that this is an offshoot of herd feeling: the man who has a different theology feels strange, and whatever is strange must be dangerous. Ideologies, in fact, are one of the methods by which herds are created, and the psychology is much the same however the herd may have been generated.

You may have been feeling that I have allowed only for bad motives, or, at best, such as are ethically neutral. I am afraid they are, as a rule, more powerful than more altruistic motives, but I do not deny that altruistic motives exist, and may, on occasion, be effective.

The agitation against slavery in England in the early nineteenth century was indubitably altruistic, and was thoroughly effective. Its altruism was proved by the fact that in 1833 British taxpayers paid many millions in compensation to Jamaican landowners for the liberation of their slaves, and also by the fact that at the Congress of Vienna the British Government was prepared to make important concessions with a view to inducing other nations to abandon the slave trade. This is an instance from the past, but present-day

America has afforded instances equally remarkable. I will not, however, go into these, as I do not wish to become embarked in current controversies.

I do not think it can be questioned that sympathy is a genuine motive, and that some people at some times are made somewhat uncomfortable by the sufferings of some other people. It is sympathy that has produced the many humanitarian advances of the last hundred years. We are shocked when we hear stories ofthe ill-treatment of lunatics, and there are now quite a number of asylums in which they are not ill-treated.

Prisoners in Western countries are not supposed to be tortured, and when they are, there is an outcry if the facts are discovered. We do not approve of treating orphans as they are treated in *Oliver Twist*. Protestant countries disapprove of cruelty to animals. In all these ways sympathy has been politically effective. If the fear of war were removed, its effectiveness would become much greater. Perhaps the best hope for the future of mankind is that ways will be found of increasing the scope and intensity of sympathy.

The time has come to sum up our discussion. Politics is concerned with herds rather than with individuals, and the passions which are important in politics are, therefore, those in which the various members of a given herd can feel alike. The broad instinctive mechanism upon which political edifices have to be built is one of cooperation within the herd and hostility towards other herds. The co-operation within the herd is never perfect. There are members who do not conform, who are, in the etymological sense, «egregious», that is to say, outside the flock. These members are those who have fallen below, or risen above, the ordinary level. They are: idiots, criminals, prophets, and discoverers. A wise herd will learn to tolerate the eccentricity of those who rise above the average, and to treat with a minimum of ferocity those who fall below it. As regards relations to other herds, modern technique has produced a conflict between self-interest and instinct. In old days, when two tribes went to war, one of them exterminated the other, and annexed its territory. From the point of view of the victor, the whole operation was thoroughly satisfactory. The killing was not at all expensive, and the excitement was agreeable. It is not to be wondered at that, in such circumstances, war persisted. Unfortunately, we still have the emotions appropriate to such primitive warfare, while the actual operations of war have changed completely. Killing an enemy in a modern war is a very expensive operation.

If you consider how many Germans were killed in the late war, and how much the victors are paying in income tax, you can, by a sum in long division, discover the cost of a dead German, and you will find it considerable. In the East, it is true, the enemies of the Germans have secured the ancient advantages of turning out the defeated population and occupying their lands. The Western victors, however, have secured no such advantages. It is obvious that modern war is not good business from a financial point of view. Although we won both the world wars, we should now be much richer if they had not occured.

If men were actuated by self-interest, which they are not - except in the case of a few saints - the whole human race would cooperate. There would be no more wars, no more armies, no more navies, no more atom bombs. There would not be armies of propagandists employed in poisoning the minds of Nation A against Nation B, and reciprocally of Nation B against Nation A.

There would not be armies of officials at frontiers to prevent the entry of foreign books and foreign ideas, however excellent in themselves. There would not be customs barriers to ensure the existence of many small enterprises where one big enterprise would be more economic. All this would happen very quickly if men desired their own happiness as ardently as they desired the misery of their neighbours. But, you will tell me, what is the use of these utopian dreams ? Moralists will see to it that we do not become wholly selfish, and until we do the millenium will be impossible.

I do not wish to seem to end upon a note of cynicism. I do not deny that there are better things than selfishness, and that some people achieve these things. I maintain, however, on the one hand, that there are few occasions upon which large bodies of men, such as politics is concerned with, can rise above selfishness, while, on the other hand, there are a very great many circumstances in which populations will fall below selfishness, if selfishness is interpreted as enlightened self-interest.

And among those occasions on which people fall below self-interest are most of the occasions on which they are convinced that they are acting from idealistic motives. Much that passes as idealism is disguised hatred or disguised love of power. When you see large masses of men swayed by what appear to be noble motives, it is as well to look below the surface and ask yourself what it is that makes these motives effective. It is partly because it is so easy to be taken in by a facade of nobility that a psychological inquiry, such as I have been attempting, is worth making. I would say, in conclusion, that if what I have said is right, the main thing needed to make the world happy is intelligence. And this, after all, is an optimistic conclusion, because intelligence is a thing that can be fostered by known methods of education.

Chapter 4

Greek Philosopher, Poet and Lawmaker

INTRODUCTION

Credited by Bertrand Russell with the invention of "metaphysics based on logic," Parmenides represents a dividing point in the history of Presocratic philosophy. Utilizing the first deductive proofs in Western philosophy, Parmenides and his fellow Eleatics, including Zeno, revealed fundamental flaws in the cosmologies previously believed in, thus setting the Presocratics who followed Parmenides on a different course of reasoning. While Parmenides's writing style is rarely praised, he was a pioneer, credited by Richard D. McKirahan with being "the first to undertake explicit philosophical analyses of the concepts: being and coming to be, change, motion, time, and space."

Parmenides asserted that anything that can be thought of must exist and that anything that does not exist cannot be thought of or talked about. He also believed that what exists is one and that since it is timeless such words as "past" and "future" do not apply. Parmenides insisted that change was impossible, a concept that had great impact on later philosophers.

In his single known work, a hexameter poem sometimes called "On Nature," Parmenides relates in the first person a journey by chariot to the edge of the world where Night and Day meet. There he is welcomed by a goddess who explains that she will tell him of two subjects. The first can be called

The Way of Truth, and the second can be called the Way of Opinion. It is the second way which mortals follow.

Biographical Information

Very little is known concerning Parmenides's life. He was the son of Pyres and a citizen of Elea, a Greek colony in southern Italy founded in 540 B.C. His date of birth is commonly thought to be circa 515-510 B.C. According to Diogenes Laertius, Parmenides was part of a wealthy, distinguished family. Precise dating of anything in his life, including when he wrote his poem, is not possible. Attempts to determine dates in the life of Parmenides usually center around dates of Heraclitus, but the dates of Heraclitus are now highly suspect.

There is also no agreement on whether or not Parmenides is referring to Heraclitus in his poem. It is not possible to determine even which of the two men preceded the other, although it is typically assumed that Parmenides followed Heraclitus. Diogenes wrote that although Parmenides was a pupil of Xenophanes, he did not agree with his teachings. Proclus wrote that Parmenides was a Pythagorean, but evidence in the poem itself indicates that Parmenides turned away from this school of thought. Parmenides founded the so-called Eleatic School, the other representatives of which were Zeno and Melissus.

Plato says that Parmenides visited Athens when he was about sixty-five years old and talked with a very young Socrates, on whom he made a major impression. Because Socrates's birth date is reliably 470 or 469 B.C. and because Plato would not have referred to Socrates as very young unless he was less than twenty-five, it seems that Parmenides was some forty years older than Socrates.

This reasoning yields the approximate birth date given above. Parmenides's effort was the first and second-to-last time a Greek expressed a philosophical system in the meter and epic verse of Homer.

The only other Greek to do so was Empedocles, who used Parmenides as his model. Plutarch credits Parmenides with writing the laws that the people of Elea swore annually to uphold. These laws were reportedly in effect for some five centuries. Parmenides died circa 450 B.C.

Major Works: Parmenides wrote a single dactylic hexameter poem, sometimes called "On Nature," in what is now called ancient Greek. While it is possible that Parmenides wrote other pieces, there is no evidence that he did so. Much of what survives—some 154 lines—was included in a commentary by the Neoplatonist scholar Simplicius. Simplicius had access to the original when he copied portions, and his copy is deemed quite accurate, although with an occasional lacuna. The prologue, often referred to as the proem, survives due mostly to Sextus Empiricus.

The proem consists of thirty-two lines of allegory in which Parmenides travels in a chariot pulled by wise mares. After the figure of Jus tice lets him through a bolted gate where Night and Day meet, Parmenides is addressed by a goddess who promises to teach him all things. Then the goddess tells him of two mutually exclusive ways, the Way of Truth and the Way of Opinion. The Way of Opinion is false and deceitful and is the path followed by mortals. This portion of the poem, considered by scholars to be the least important, is represented by very few remaining fragments; Herman Diels estimates them to include ten percent of what was written in the original. Diels estimates that ninety percent of the Way of Truth survives.

Textual History: It is not known when Parmenides first composed his poem or first recited it. In the sixth century A.D., when Simplicius copied the large portions of Parmenides's poem that exist today, he did so because the work was already scarce in his time. Simplicius wanted his readers to be able to refer to the poem to better understand Simplicius's commentary on Aristotle's *Physics.* It appears that there are occasional gaps in Simplicius's copy, or in the rendition of Simplicius's scribes. These gaps, and what originally filled them, are a source of much disagreement and debate among experts. Arguments abound over the arrangement of particular fragments, whether or not words were left out, and whether or not particular words were copied incorrectly. Some word choices that seem more appropriate to the sense of meaning do not work as well metrically, and vice versa. The standard edition of Parmenides's poem in the original Greek is *Die Fragmente der Vorsokratiker,* edited by Hermann Diels. Since the fifth and all editions following were revised with notes by Walter Kranz, the work is commonly referred to as Diels-Kranz. The Diels-Kranz line numbers are also the accepted standard. One fragment, quoted by Plato and Simplicius, is usually considered a misquotation of another fragment and is not included in Diels-Kranz. This fragment is sometimes called the Cornford fragment after Cornford, of one of its staunch defenders. Even if one were a master of ancient Greek, the difficulties in understanding Parmenides's use of it would still be extreme. It is thus advisable to read several different English translations of Parmenides to gain a clear understanding of the poem.

Critical Reception: Parmenides was widely respected in ancient times. He was enormously influential to the philosophers of his era, causing many to break completely with what was believed before him. But exactly what Parmenides expresses in his poem is the subject of much debate. The earliest Greek author who attempted to explain Parmenides's writing was Plato, but Plato's interpretation is not universally accepted. After earlier descriptions of Parmenides's meaning, Socrates refused to discuss it any further, partly so as not to misinterpret it. This safest of reactions has not been followed by scholars since. Parmenides is extremely difficult to understand and seems self-contradictory to many who study him. Sometimes the contradictions are defended as misrepresentations of what Parmenides said. Leonardo Tarán asserts that Aristotle patently misrepresented some of Parmenides's views and that Plato did not accurately describe them either. Edward Hussey calls Parmenides's verse sometimes "downright clumsy." Michael C. Stokes observes that Parmenides wrote in "riddling fashion," and Jonathan Barnes contends that "Parmenides's Greek is desperately hard to understand" and that aspects of it represent an "almost impenetrable obscurity."

The Love of Liberty and the Impulse to Coercion: Bertrand Russell Revisited

Can a true love of liberty exist alongside a compulsion to use force in order to ensure its perpetuation? I instinctively feel the correct answer, the libertarian answer, is "generally not," but that does not mean that libertarians are necessarily pacifists: I have argued previously that true libertarians are anti-war, but there are a few situations, rare in history, in which libertarians accept the need for force to be used – usually to repel an aggressor or expel a tyrant who is oppressing us in our own back yard.

What we are living with today, unfortunately, is the propaganda variety of liberty, under which the memory of such legitimate uses of force, and the noble ideals and vocabulary of liberation which went with them, have been perverted to serve the ends of crony capitalist empire-building, buttressed by the raw fear engendered in the people through clever use of all the instruments available for triggering mass psychosis and delusion, not least of which is the endless 'war on tear-ism.'

Bertrand Russell (1872–1970) was a master at seeing and cutting through this sort of humbug and hypocrisy, and was a relentless seeker after truth. In his 1962 collection of essays entitled, *Fact and Fiction* he wrote, "It is not by delusion, however exalted, that mankind can prosper, but only by unswerving courage in the pursuit of truth," and in his classic and highly readable *Autobiography* he reproduced what he had originally set out in 1951 as his 'Ten Precepts for Freedom of Thought':

- Do not feel absolutely certain of anything.
- Do not think it is worthwhile to proceed by concealing evidence, for the evidence is sure to come to light.
- Never try to discourage thinking, for you are sure to succeed.
- When you meet with opposition, even if it should be from your partner or your children, endeavour to overcome it by argument and not by authority, for a

victory dependent upon authority is unreal and illusory.

- Have no respect for the authority of others, for there are always contrary authorities to be found.
- Do not use power to suppress opinions you think pernicious, for if you do the opinions will suppress you.
- Do not fear to be eccentric in opinion, for every opinion now accepted was once eccentric.
- Find more pleasure in intelligent dissent than in passive agreement, for, if you value intelligence as you should, the former implies a deeper agreement than the latter.
- Be scrupulously truthful, even if the truth is inconvenient, for it is more inconvenient when you try to conceal it.
- Do not feel envious of the happiness of those who live in a fool's paradise, for only a fool will think that it is happiness.

Russell was educated in the classical English liberal tradition, and he was later an unabashed admirer of the Constitution of the United States. He described his early education in the 1880s thus:

"History, or at least English history, was part of my education, from a very early age. Constitutional history especially was implanted in me before I was ten years old.... I was taught as a matter of course that the Americans were right in the war of independence, and although I was allowed a childish pleasure in the victories of Trafalgar and Waterloo, I was told to deplore the British Empire and abhor the makers of the Afghan and Zulu wars which occurred when I was beginning to be politically conscious."

~ *Fact and Fiction*, part 1, chapter 5:

An Education in History: He viewed the US Constitution as the summit of humanity's achievement in defining a nation-state's rules of government, reconciling better than anything which had gone before the need for human liberty with vital limitations on the exercise and abuse of power.

And yet, frustrated by the manifest savageries and dangerous posturings of nation-states in two world wars in his life-time, he saw the next step up from that Constitution as world government, in the process succumbing to the dangerous fallacy of advocating the use of pre-emptive force to impose ideas or values in whose absolute virtue he believed. He was also partial to the perceived benefits of being able to persuade and influence a world-wide audience through mass communication. This has meant that, while he is revered by many an idealist for his passionate commitment to truth, every bizarre practical suggestion he ever floated still tarnishes his memory.

At the end of World War II, the US had for a short time a world monopoly of nuclear weapons. In 1946 Russell advocated the pre-emptive nuclear bombing of cities of Soviet Union, a collectivist totalitarian society and regime which he abhorred, in order to prevent the realization of what he saw as Joseph Stalin's ambition of world domination. Later in life he would apparently deny that he had ever advocated such a thing.

Change the names of the players around a bit, add "WMD," adjust the quantities, and stir. Contemplate the twisted logic of bombing a people in order to liberate them. Does this recipe not begin to sound familiar in our own time?

The 1946 episode, together with his stated beliefs in world government, population control, and the egalitarian redistribution of global wealth[1], have got Russell into no end of trouble with posterity, managing to offend both the politically correct and the politically incorrect. How could such an acute mind, so aware of the historical importance of liberty to humanity's development, and possessed of a keen ability to identify the hypocrisy of imperialist adventure and the false posturing of the rival states in the Cold War, advocate measures which go in the entirely opposite direction, the direction of coercion? To this day his long life and the paradoxical, even muddled impact of his ideas on social and political issues inspire reactions of vitriolic hatred and contempt, while at the same time many feel in sympathy with him and sincerely admire his writing and his politics. The difference is as between night and day.

On the dark side, he is denounced variously as a "prophet of the New World Order" and a neo-pagan[2], as being possessed by Satan[3], as a particularly nasty (because clever and intellectually influential) member of the ruling Anglo-American oligarchic elite, and lately by Jeffrey Steinberg and Lyndon Larouche[4] as the ideological precursor of the Cheney-Rumsfeld "utopian cabal" which has developed the arguments for pre-emptive self-defense contained in the Project for a New American Century and the National Security Strategy. Now implemented in the US foreign policy of global military omnipresence and perpetual war.

Actually I rather doubt that the ruling post-Trotskyist neocon cabal in the US would want to claim Russell as one of their gurus: the American security establishment in the late 1960s saw him as a crackpot, and the anti-war and campaign for nuclear disarmament activities of his later life as a nuisance, so they allegedly had him 'neutralized' – whatever that may mean. At heart Russell, unlike them, was also quintessentially anti-authoritarian. Nevertheless the fact remains that the zany Strangelovean similarities between them are striking.

Others, however, with no such axe to grind, but perhaps having different, sulkier demons lurking in their psyches, have expressed extreme contempt for the man: Ray Monk[5], professor of Philosophy at Southampton University in England, admitted that his dislike of Russell strongly coloured the second volume of his biography, published in 2001, while eminent Australian conservative Rob Stove, in a review of Monk's book[6], implied that Russell did not actually have much idea about anything. One is even left with the uncomfortable feeling, after reading this review, that perhaps it would have been a humane thing to have had Russell put down long before he actually died in 1970, at the ripe old age of 97. Similar regret at the Russell's unusual longevity is expressed by the anonymous writer[7] who feels that he was a "Satanic Malthusian" and "a master of policy-making for the evil elites of the world."

There is no doubt also that Russell greatly upset the men and women of religion with his atheism, which caused him to be barred from teaching at the City University of New York in the 1940s, and for a time to face not inconsiderable financial hardship.

However, if we move out of the darkness into the light for a moment, at least two distinguished critics[8] are in agreement that Ray Monk should perhaps not have written his biography if he found the subject-matter as distasteful as he evidently did. These and many others feel that the personal failures of a man in life, and even gross errors of judgment, should not be allowed to detract from the value of his work, and they are prepared to give Russell the benefit of the doubt by seeing the positive as well as the negative side.

Thomas Nagel for example, professor of Philosophy and Law at New York University and author of the highly readable essay "Concealment and Exposure," which discusses the destruction of the conventions of privacy which the advent of the intrusive society has brought about, comments that "Monk's relentless censoriousness about Russell's personal troubles seems uncalled for; things can go badly wrong in any family, even that of a tireless social commentator" and that Russell "gave incomparably more to the world than he took from it," while Sylvia Nasar of the Columbia School of Journalism, author of the life of John Nash, *A Beautiful Mind,* concludes in her *New York Times* review of Monk that "unfortunately, Monk's dislike of Russell – which he says is based largely on the fate of Russell's son and granddaughters – and his seeming ignorance of the most basic facts about mental illness, have skewed his judgment badly. Biographers who despise their subjects are evidently just as much at risk of getting the story wrong as those who worship blindly."

So it is that different people find in Russell's life and person those 'express and admirable' qualities side by side with the 'quintessence of dust' which Hamlet sees when contemplating his fellow human beings. Alongside optimistic moods and hope, there are dark episodes of despair and disgust. Loving humanity, he often hated people. Such duality is not far removed from schizophrenia, which indeed ran in his family.

I believe it is possible to understand the light and dark sides of Russell's personality, and the chemistry of people's polarized reactions to him, by examining his genetic inheritance and his upbringing, and placing them in their social and historical context (or, as conventional usage has it, the differential impact of nature and nurture). This is a fascinating task, one which is properly the job of the sympathetic but discriminating biographer. An essay such as this cannot hope to do justice to it, but Russell himself in his huge written legacy, and particularly in his Autobiography, goes a long way to doing what is needed. He writes in the Preface:

'Three passions, simple but overwhelmingly strong, have governed my life: the longing for love, the search for knowledge, and unbearable pity for the suffering of mankind. These passions, like great winds, have blown me hither and thither... over a deep ocean of anguish, reaching to the very verge of despair.'

I also believe the morally right attitude to personal struggles like these is that we should be compassionate in relation to such evidence of human suffering and uncertainty. The fact is that when *any* individual in a position of eminence or power takes the battle with his personal demons into the public arena, any innocent party who is anywhere within range when the firing starts and the bombs start to fall risks getting wiped out in the ensuing conflagration. Similar dualities to those which afflicted Russell are not uncommon in many human beings and, in practice, the two sides are not mutually exclusive.

It is even commonly argued that for creative purposes, the struggle between them is actually necessary: the art of writing, for example, involves coercing words and phrases into a coherent and hopefully rational whole, while the search for truth can lead one into all sorts of chaotic dark alleys of irrationality (and yes, on occasion, even into conspiracy theories).

If the reader does allow him- or herself actually to enjoy the duality, he or she will find that there is no need to accept that what the writer says is *all* true, or that one is necessarily guided into suitable or appropriate action on the issues he is writing about.

Historian-philosopher Theòdore Zeldin, author of the fascinating book *An Intimate History of Humanity,* has said that 'all the greatest books have been self-help books,' and 'a book from which you get nothing is a failure.'[9] While there is a sense with many of Russell's books that they are indeed didactic, and often very effectively so, it is a mistake to think that all readers should necessarily be looking for a prescription to remedy all their ills universally and for all time, even – or perhaps especially from one who is renowned as a philosopher.

Thomas Nagel again: "Though it is popularly and journalistically thought to be central to the job description of a philosopher to discover how we should live, and then to reveal the secret to the rest of us, it is in fact rare for philosophers to set themselves this audacious task. Most of the major philosophers of the past have concentrated their efforts on trying to understand the nature of reality, truth and knowledge. While this includes ethical theory, *that is not the same thing as knowing how to live,* since one cannot live merely by not doing what is wrong".

It is also all too easy to analyze a situation correctly, and then not know what to do about it, or give plainly wrong and counterproductive advice. Nagel concludes Russell was 'fearless, outspoken and eloquent' in his analysis of things, and "while his judgement was sometimes egregiously wrong, for someone who spoke out so continually on so many subjects he had a pretty good record."

A disposition to compassionate understanding does not prevent any one of us from still making his or her own critical judgements about the work of the man, and I for one will readily admit that I do not agree with everything that Russell believed in or wrote. Fascinated by the history and significance of liberty, yet he was certainly no libertarian, having twice stood as a socialist party candidate for Parliament and having had the gall (!) to write this heresy: "In the modern world very few individuals can have much influence except as members of organisations, and therefore the question of freedom for organisations is becoming more important than that of freedom for individuals."

What is Freedom?

Yet it is typical of Russell that in the very next paragraph he pulls himself back, stressing the importance of individual freedom in history, and the harm done by persecution of individuals whose views are unpopular.

Oscar Wilde labelled consistency 'the last refuge of the unimaginative,' and said that diversity of opinion about a work of art indicated that it was 'new, complex and vital.' I venture to say the same of Russell, whom I see as an essentially artistic personality, with all the schizoid flaws which that entails, especially the potential for wild fluctuation between the elation experienced in moments of pure joy and the deep despair when confronted by the failure to vanquish his own demons. In such moments he hates everyone in sight, and, like Hamlet, feels there is no way out of the pit of despair in which he finds himself. Is it any surprise that such a personality should breed inconsistency, yet at the same time have the ability to stimulate the grandest flights of the philosophical imagination in others?

J.M. Keynes remarked that Russell trusted too much in the power of reason to solve the problems of irrationality, and Thomas Nagel comments, "irrationality is not in most cases a failure of understanding, so it will not be put right by patient instruction." In other words, the demons within us often make us carry on doing things even when we know, and others have convinced us rationally, that those things are not good for ourselves or for others. There is no ready solution to this, other than perpetual vigilance, an open mind, and a willingness to learn from mistakes and from others. As Russell himself said, in *Fact and Fiction*, "The ultimate basis of liberty...lies not merely in political institutions, but in the general diffusion of a conviction that all opinions have their rights, and that however convinced you may be it is nevertheless possible that you may be mistaken."

It is more productive, as well as more charitable, for the reader to try to derive positive benefits from the manifest struggle between reason and chaos in Russell's life and work, and to take what is best from it. As a rule he is, like most of us, better at diagnosing and pointing out what is wrong than in his often wayward prescriptions for making the world a better place. The fact that he does this diagnosis so well, forging an incisive analysis out of his passionate search for truth, gives his writing a tantalizing, catalytic and stimulating quality, and this in turn is what has made his written legacy so eminently quotable.

As with so much in life, getting the best out of someone or something can only be done by sympathetic understanding coupled with critical discrimination, all based on coherent ethical principles and a commitment to individual liberty consistent with the recognition of identical rights for others.

No-one ever said it would be easy.

Science, Religion & Russell

Why is it that religion and science always seem to come into conflict? What fundamental differences must exist for them to continually fall onto opposite sides of important issues?

This article will explore not only how religion and religious belief can conflict with science, but indeed how they can conflict with the basic principle of democracy and freedom.

I have been fortunate enough to receive a copy of Thom Weidlich's new book *Appointment Denied: The Inquisition of Bertrand Russell.* Although it is primarily about an infamous episode in the history of Bertrand Russell and American higher education, Weidlich also makes a point of explaining how larger issues are involved not simply the obvious question of academic freedom, but also how and why religion and revealed truth come into conflict with science and critical thinking.

Unfortunately, in this story, religion won and science lost - to the detriment of both freedom and education. However, that doesn't mean that it doesn't have much to teach us. These issues of how much power religion should have over the lives of non-adherents and how much voice religious leaders should have in government policies are still very current.

Bertrand Russell himself pointed out at the time that what was happening to him also happened to other professors much less famous than he - but of course without nearly the publicity and with even more unfortunate outcomes. As I shall describe below, not much has changed in fifty years - professors can still have a lot to fear from capricious administrators and religious dogmatism.

Thom Weidlich does a fantastic job of not only explaining what happened to Bertrand Russell in his attempt to teach at the City College in New York City, but also of shedding light on the varying personalities of the key players in this drama. I will be relying heavily on Weidlich's book here, but I won't go into all of the different facets of the case which he explains much better than I could.

I encourage anyone interested in Bertrand Russell, academic freedom, or the conflict between religion and science to read this book. Quite a lot has been written about Bertrand Russell and he is one of the preeminent philosophers for most atheists, especially considering his insightful critiques of Christianity in his famous work ***Why I Am Not A Christian***. But until now, not a lot has been written concerning this particular episode in his life, and it is really worth learning more about.

Just the Facts: In 1940, Bertrand Russell was widely considered one of the greatest philosophers of the day. At the time he was teaching at UCLA in California, having left his home in Britian to escape the war both for the safety of his family and due to his personal commitment to pacificism. One evening in late February, New York City's Board of Higher Education unanimously voted to give him an appointment to the faculty of the publicly funded City College.

The board certainly knew who Russell was, and their goal was to improve the quality of education at City College, not to mention its prestige. It wasn't every college or university which could boast such a distinguished writer and lecturer which could boast such a distinguished writer and lecturer on its staff, and Russell was probably the most distinguished appointment in the college's nearly one hundred year history.

However, the reaction was quite the opposite of what was expected: it created a firestorm of hostility and protest, mostly fed by local religious leaders. It all started with a letter from the Right Reverend William T. Manning, the head of the Protestant Episcopal Diocese in New York. This letter appeared in the city's major newspapers and attacked Russell's more liberal views regarding human sexuality, marriage, divorce and morality.

Bishop Manning: Manning's basic position was that Russell's appointment had to be revoked, and his argument, as quoted by Thom Weidlich, was as follows:

Can any of us wish our young people to accept these teachings as decent, true or worthy of respect? What is to be said of colleges and universities which hold up before our youth as a reputable teacher of philosophy, and as an example of light and leading, a man who is a recognized propagandist against both religion and morality... The fact that he is intellectually brilliant is certainly no excuse for such action.

As we shall see later on, this basic argument against unpopular ideas being taught or even simply held by professors and teachers hasn't changed at all in the last fifty years.

Bishop Manning didn't stop at letter writing - he worked behind the scenes to get other religious leaders on board with his programme to keep Bertrand Russell from teaching at City College. As Weidlich describes him, Manning was a champion of dogmatic theology, fidelity to tradition and military preparedness. This was quite the opposite of Russell, who was committed to secularism, scientific and critical inquiry, questioning custom and tradition, and pacifism. It is curious that a man who was supposed to be a representative of Christ had stronger military leanings than the atheist philosopher, but Weidlich quotes Manning as asserting that "Jesus Christ does not stand for peace at any price. He stands for righteousness at any cost."

It was thus perhaps inevitable that the two would have come into direct conflict eventually. Indeed, Manning had long hated Russell and had previously dogged his attempts to speak at other universities. The two ably represented two differing and ultimately conflicting ideologies: revealed religion and tradition on the one hand and scientific, critical atheism and secularism on the other. Their discord in New York City may not have been a defining moment in American history, but it is clearly emblematic of so many other conflicts.

Religious Objections: It should be kept firmly in mind that the objections to Russell's appointment were fundamentally religious in nature. Remember that Manning was quoted as critical of Russell as "a man who is a recognized propagandist against both religion and morality." But as Weidlich describes it, they did try to use other arguments:

...He was a foreigner, he was immoral, and - despite what his defenders said - his social beliefs were relevant to his teaching ability because a teacher doesn't impart only facts but morals. Even if he didn't teach his social ideas, just coming to admire him would be bad for the students. Taxes shouldn't go to pay for his odious speech; he could teach in a private but not a public school. Many said that he shouldn't be allowed to teach at City College because his ideas ran counter to the moral principles of New Yorkers, as if the city dwellers were of one mind on such questions...

As Franz Boas, a leading anthropologist observed, people were not specifically not attacking Russell's competency as a teacher or intellectual ability - indeed, they often admitted to both. Instead, they almost exclusively focused on his religious - or anti-religious - views. Boas wrote that he and others were "alarmed by the note of a religious test for appointment which has crept into the public debate."

But there were some interesting differences between Russell's detractors and his supporters. Whereas his detractors attacked his ethical and social views regardless of his professional abilities, his supporters often didn't agree with his ethical and social views. John Dewey, one of Russell's biggest supporters, didn't even like Russell personally.

Despite this, people like Dewey did support the principle of academic freedom. Just as importantly, they knew that Russell approached his views scientifically: he arrived at them via critical thinking and was willing to have them critiqued by others. This is one of fundamental principles not only of science but also of a liberal democracy - a principle not generally shared by religions supposedly based upon divinely revealed truths.

Of course, Weidlich does not hesitate to point out that not all religious groups opposed the appointment of Bertrand Russell. As with today, there was division in the social and political goals of various Christian denominations. So we should be willing to acknowledge that in the conflict between religion and science or between religion and freedom, not all religious people and not all religious groups stand in opposition to science and freedom.

Parallels: There are many parallels in history where similar religious opposition was mounted against those who spread or simply held ideas which were contrary to tradition and religion. Socrates was forced by the people of Athens to drink hemlock as punishment for spreading ideas contrary to tradition and religion - in fact, one of the charges was that he was an atheist.

Giordano Bruno was burned at the stake by church authorities for daring to propose that the universe was other than what they declared. Galileo Galilei was effectively imprisoned for agreeing with Copernicus rather than church teachings. Baruch Spinoza was exiled from Amsterdam by rabbis because of his heretical ideas - he, too, was charged with atheism.

The most immediate parallel - one drawn even by people involved in the case - was with the Scopes trial in Tennessee from 1925. At the time, John Scopes was regarded merely as an employee and could thus be forced not to teach things contrary to popular opinion and religion. Academic freedom really didn't exist at the time for Scopes any more than it ultimately did for Russell.

Even Albert Einstein faced such opposition, and his

experiences were probably a factor in his support of Russell. When Einstein was trying to emigrate from Germany to the United States back in 1932, he encountered vociferous opposition from "patriots" who declared that he was a "Bolshevist" and that his theories of relativity were without "scientific value or purpose." It is not coincidental that at the time of his conflict with religious leaders in New York City, Bertrand Russell was also accused of being a Communist.

Although most Americans imagine that communist witch hunts were largely confined to the 1950s and Senator McCarthy, in fact they occurred all through the 1930s and 1940s as well. Most people don't realized that for America, the 1920s were a time of social rebellion and changes not at all unlike the 1960s - and in the decades immediately following there arose a conservative backlash not unlike what has occurred again starting in the late 1970s with the formation of the Religious Right.

Thus, when Einstein came out in support of Russell, Weidlich quotes one priest as declaring that this

> ...confirmed previous reports that he well-known mathematician was interested in smashing moral laws, as well as physical laws which have been accepted as established.

In this context it is no wonder that Einstein wrote that "Great spirits have always found opposition from mediocrities."

Academic Freedom: Bertrand Russell's problems occurred back in 1940 - almost ancient history for some people. Have matters improved today? Some, but not by as much as most may hope or assume. The first U.S. Supreme Court case to even mention the issue of academic freedom did not occur until 1952. And in *Adler v. Board of Education,* the Court actually reaffirmed the police powers of the state to protect schools from the "pollution of alien or subversive" ideas. The concept of academic freedom, although accepted by many people and hopefully many readers, is still tenuous in this country and given more attention in theory than practice.

Ultimately, there is little that any professor can do if his or her academic freedom is violated. The only group which is supposed to fight on behalf on them is the American Association of University Professors, and that effort is often ineffectual. About the only thing the AAUP can do in the end is put the university on its censure list - and the length of the list demonstrates that many universities aren't too concerned with such consequences. Rarely, if ever, does it affect the all-important bottom line of fund raising and tuition revenues.

And all of this is just the case in the secular institutions - in religious universities and seminaries, the situation can be absolutely atrocious. Bob Jones University is a now-famous example of how a religiously motivated administration can create a hostile atmosphere. Academic freedom is a non-issue at BJU, just like concepts like tenure or faculty governance. Even joining a larger academic association like the AAUP is to "sacrifice God's blessing through disobedience" to the institutions hierarchy.

Academic Freedom vs. Religion: But BJU isn't the only institution which has so suffered. Most by now are aware of how far-right fundamentalist took over the Southern Baptist Convention during the 1980s and early 90s - what many are not aware of is how they also took over respected Baptist seminaries across the South.

These institutions had accepted historical-critical approaches to studying both the Bible and Christianity. They had adopted the principle of not only academic freedom, but also open theological inquiry where no one was expected to hold to a party line on political, social or even theological issues. They allowed for the traditional Baptist doctrine that each believer must be free to interpret the Bible as individuals and follow the calling of their hearts. But all of this changed for the worse starting in the early 1990s. Professors who were otherwise well respected and leaders in their field started to be purged if they refused to adopt positions more in line with the political aspirations of fundamentalists. A particularly hot topic was naturally abortion - any professor who held a pro-choice view or even just felt the matter was debatable was in danger. It didn't matter if these people violated no contractual obligations and transgressed against none of the Baptist confessional commitments. These seminaries were being reshaped into the propaganda arms of fundamentalist forces and there was no room for even mild dissent. As with Scopes and Russell before them, educators were declared to be mere employees who had to adopt the political and religious resolutions set before them or leave.

Particularly frightening was the hostile atmospheres created by the fundamentalists seeking any excuse possible to expel dissenting academics. Student vigilantes were recruited to monitor classes held by dissenters and report back to the administration. Anonymous hate notes were circulated and lies were spread about what professors really believed - not unlike what happened to Bertrand Russell. Nowadays controversial subjects are rarely if ever broached in lectures.

The Case of Singer: Of course, it should not be assumed that only religious schools suffer from such problems. Even prestigious Princeton University has had to endure protests against competent professors due to their unpopular and controversial views. Every year, Princeton appoints respected scholars as members of its tenured faculty. For 1999, they appointed Peter Singer as the DeCamp Professor in the University Center for Human Values. Peter Singer is one of the preeminent scholars in the very contemporary field of bioethics and has served as the president of the International Association of Bioethics and edited their official journal, among many other achievements and accolades. You'd think that, as with the case of Russell, such an appointment would be popular; but as with the case of Russell, it primarily created a firestorm of protest.

To be fair, there are differences - for example, Russell's supporters argued that he wasn't hired to teach ethics and so his private views weren't so important. Singer, on the other hand, was specifically hired to teach and explain his theories about ethics. And unlike Russell, Singer was supported by the university administration and did manage to take his faculty position. But the similarities in both cases are much more significant. With both, detractors tended to spread misinformation and misinterpretations of the positions of

Singer and Russell. Both of the philosophers have promoted unpopular, iconoclastic ideas which oppose traditional views of popular wisdom and revealed religion.

Both philosophers were described by their supporters as "intellectually astute"; both were praised for the high quality of their work. And both were lauded for the fact that their work has been open to engagement and critique. Thus, regardless of whether or not you agree with either Russell or Singer, it is important to remember that they take their work seriously and are open to rational, scientific critiques of their ideas.

This stands in sharp contrast to their religious adversaries - much of Singer's opposition has arisen out of the anti-abortion movement and the religious right. The arguments raised against Singer sound just like those raised against Russell. Echoing Bishop Manning almost 50 years before, Richard Willever has written:

I really don't care what the intellectual arguments are in favor of Dr. Peter Singer's appointment to a prestigious professorship in bioethics at Princeton University. His academic credentials may be excellent and he may indeed stimulate discussion on issues of vital concern to all humanity. Nonetheless, giving a glorified soapbox to reprehnsible ideas is a mistake. Thus, according to the opponents of both Peter Singer and Bertrand Russell, professors should only hold important positions if they advocate safe, comfortable ideas.

Fortunately, as with Russell, even some of those who disagree or dislike Singer support his appointment. Adrienne Asch, a professor from Wellesley College, has debated Peter Singer and vehemently opposes his ideas - but when asked if Princeton should rescind Singer's appointment, she has quickly answered "no."

Conclusions: Unlike Peter Singer, Bertrand Russell never got his appointment to City College. Fortunately, he did get a position with another institution, because at the time he was facing destitution and perhaps an inability to feed his family. But it should be noted that religion won against Russell and science.

Throughout the controversy, the principle opposition

came from religious leaders like Bishop Manning. Behind the scenes others, like the ever politically minded Catholic Archbishop Francis J. Spellman, also worked to keep Russell from teaching in the city. For these people, academic freedom was irrelevant, at least is it commonly understood.

They did believe in a "modified" idea of academic freedom: according to them, real freedom meant the freedom to spread True Ideas. As Spellman said two months after the Russell case was over: Catholic education, believing in the objectivity of truth, challenges the wisdom of subsidizing the dissemination of falsehood under the guise of liberty. Falsehood, whatever its sphere has no more legitimate claim to be freely disseminated than have the germs of disease a right to formal cultivation in the blood stream of the individual.

There you have it - the Wrong Ideas which are contrary to traditional religious wisdom are little more than a disease. It is for this reason that traditional, revealed religion stands in stark opposition not only to science, but also democracy. As Thom Weidlich explains (quoting Karl Popper), an open and free society must treat every supposed source of knowledge and factual claim as open to criticism - none may be immune.

It is not coincidental that this idea was expressed by Karl Popper, a philosopher of science. This position - that claims and ideas cannot be immune from critique - is fundamental not just to a free, open democracy but also to science. Russell explained what he thought the "scientific attitude" was in his earlier book *Religion and Science*:

The scientific temper of mind is cautious, tentative, and piecemeal; it does not imagine that it knows the whole truth, or that even its best knowledge is wholly true. It knows that every doctrine needs emendation sooner or later, and that the necesary emendation requires freedom of investigation and freedom of discussion. Religious revelation and religious claims are not, however, left open to criticism. They are not generally tentative an dpiecemeal. Religious claims, particularly those made by fundamentalists, tend to be an all-or-nothing affair and they do imagine that they are the whole truth. Religionists claim not only to have a unique access to the grounds of truth (i.e., the ultimate reality of their god), but also to particular truths established by those grounds. This position is incompatible with science and it is incompatible with the principles necessary for an open society. This is the conflict which the controversy around Bertrand Russell's appointment to City College played out. That is why this conflict was, in so many ways, one between religion and science even though Bertrand Russell was not strictly speaking a scientist.

Thom Weidlich explores many more issues in his book *Appointment Denied: The Inquisition of Bertrand Russell.* As important as the science/religion conflict is, Russell's case also dealt with important questions as to the role of education in a free society and the nature of truth - none of which I have really had time to explore here. I expected Weidlich's book to be interesting, because I am interested in Bertrand Russell - but I was pleasantly surprised to find that it dealt with so much more. Not only is it a fascinating portrait of the people and the times - reading like a novel rather than dry history - but it is also an intriguing exploration of the meaning of science, academic freedom, education, truth and more in societies such as ours. I can, without reservation, recommend Weidlich's book to anyone interested in any of those issues.

Top Myths About Atheism & Atheists: Answers, Refutations, Responses

Atheism is a Denial of God That Requires Faith:

The most common misunderstanding about atheism is the definition. Many insist that atheism is really the denial of the existence of God, but there are two errors here. First, it pretends that atheism is exclusively about their god, the god common to Christians, Jews, and Muslims. Second, it focuses on a narrow sub-set of atheism and atheists to the exclusion of all others. Standard dictionary definitions list "denial of God or gods" second; first comes "disbelief in god or Gods." Disbelief is not the same as denial, it's either the absence of belief or the presence of skepticism.

Atheism is Not the Denial of God...Atheists Choose to Disbelieve in God:

I frequently hear the claim that atheists choose atheism, usually for some morally blameworthy reason like a desire to avoid taking responsibility for their sins. My response is basically the same every time: You may not believe me, but I didn't choose any such thing, and I can't just 'choose' to start believing. Maybe you can, but I can't. I do not believe in any gods. Evidence would make me believe in some god, but all the playacting in the world isn't going to change that. It's arguable, in fact, that no beliefs are choices that people can simply change their minds about.

Atheism is Not a Choice or Act of Will...

What is a "Real" Atheist? How Do "Real" Atheists Behave?:

One effective means for critiquing a belief system and/or its adherents is to point out significant contradictions between how believers behave and the ideals they espouse. These contradictions can suggest that they don't really believe what they say, that the ideals aren't taken seriously, that the system teaches worse things, etc. Atheists do this with religion frequently, but can religious theists do it with atheism? They try by presuming to say how "real" atheists would or would not behave. These arguments fail because atheism isn't a philosophy that compels any particular behaviour.

Who is a Real Atheist...

More People Have Been Killed in the Name of Atheism & Secularism than Religion: A common criticism raised by atheists against religion is how violent religion and religious believers have been in the past. People have slaughtered each other in large numbers because of differences in religious beliefs or because of other differences which are justified and intensified through religious rhetoric. Either way, religion has a lot of blood on its hands.

Can the same be said for atheists and atheism? Haven't atheists killed more people in the name of atheism than religious theists have killed in the name of their religion? No: atheism isn't a philosophy or ideology. Atheism Hasn't Killed Anyone...

Atheists Haven't Experienced the True God or True Religion

Atheists have constructed many trenchant critiques of both religion and theism over the years. Some of these critiques can be responded to reasonably, but others are much more difficult to address in anything like an adequate manner. Sometimes, it may be easier to simply find a way to dismiss atheists entirely and thus avoid having to address any of their critiques in the first place.

Common ways of doing this are to argue that atheists have never had any of the relevant and necessary experiences to teach them about God and religion. If they did, they would understand and believe.

What Do Atheists Know of God...

Do Atheists Have No Reason to be Moral? Are There No Atheistic Moral Standards?:

For most religious theists, their religion and god provide the basis for their entire understanding of morality and values. Because of this, some find it inconceivable that atheists who don't' believe in any gods and who have no religion could possibly have a basis for morality or even understand what true moral behaviour really is. Many go further and argue that this is a good reason to reject atheism, that it leads to immoral behaviour, that it cannot account for the existence of morality, etc. None cf these arguments hold up because they are based on false premises.

Atheists Can Be Moral...

Atheists Lead Meaningless Lives of Despair Without Love or Beauty:

Some theists who cannot defend theism or criticize atheism through logic or evidence are left attacking the alleged implications of atheism. If they cannot prove that atheism unreasonable, they hope to prove that the consequences of atheism are so abhorrent that no one will want to take the chance. One popular target is to claim that atheism leads to hopelessness and despair, that atheism makes life meaningless, or that atheism eliminates reasons to be moral. None of this is true, but even if it were that wouldn't make their theism or religion more likely to be true.

Atheists Don't Lead Meaningful Lives...

Atheists Worship Satan, Themselves, Money, or Some Other God:

The claim that atheists replace worship of God with worship of something else ranges over man possible objects for worship: Satan, themselves, humanity, etc. In addition to being wrong, these myths share the belief that worship is somehow fundamental to human existence such that it simply isn't possible for a person to live a decent life without worshipping something. This is false, though. No matter how important religion or theism is to someone, this isn't a good reason to conclude that they are also important to everyone else, even those who deny having any god or religion.

Atheism is a Product of Rebellion & Pride:

There are many myths about atheism and atheists which claim that people are atheists due to some sort of rebellion (against god, religion, church, families, fathers, etc.) or pride. These myths come primarily from Christians whose religious mythology gives an important place to rebellion against divine rules as the origin of evil in the world (Satan is depicted as having rebelled against God). At most, these myths might be true of some but not all or even most atheists; even if true, however, none of these myths would have any implications for the truth or reasonableness of atheism itself.

Atheists Want to Impose their Secular Religion on America:'

There is a popular belief with America's Christian Right that secularism is an atheistic conspiracy and an attempt by atheists to impose a secular religion on America. This would undermine Christians' religious liberty and force them to conform to atheists' secular, possibly communist, vision for America. None of this is even remotely correct: most atheists are not religious, secularism by definition cannot be a religion, atheists are not trying to undermine religious liberty, and secularism protects all Americans' religious liberty — including Christians' liberty.

Relativity:Philosophical Consequences.

Of the consequences in philosophy which may be supposed to follow from the theory of relativity, some are fairly certain, while others are open to question. There has been a tendency, not uncommon in the case of a new scientific theory, for every philosopher to interpret the work of Einstein in accordance with his own metaphysical system, and to suggest that the outcome is a great accession of strength to the views which the philosopher in question previously held. This cannot be true in all cases; and it may be hoped that it is true in none. It would be disappointing if so fundamental a change as Einstein has introduced involved no philosophical novelty.

Space-Time.—For philosophy, the most important novelty was present already in the special theory of relativity; that is, the substitution of space-time for space and time. In Newtonian dynamics, two events were separated by two kinds of interval, one being distance in space, the other lapse of time. As soon as it was realised that all motion is relative (which happened long before Einstein), distance in space became ambiguous except in the case of simultaneous events, but it was still thought that there was no ambiguity about simultaneity in different places. The special theory of relativity showed, by experimental arguments which were new, and by logical arguments which could have been discovered any time after it became known that light travels with a finite velocity, that simultaneity is only definite when it applies to events in the same place, and becomes more and more ambiguous as the events are more widely removed from each other in space.

This statement is not quite correct, since it still uses the notion of "space." The correct statement is this: Events have a four-dimensional order, by means of which we can say that an event A is nearer to an event B than to an event C; this is a purely ordinal matter, not involving anything quantitative. But, in addition, there is between neighbouring events a quantitative relation called "interval," which fulfils the functions both of distance in space and of lapse of time in the traditional dynamics, but fulfils them with a difference. If a body can move so as to be present at both events, the interval is time-like. If a ray of light can move so as to be present at both events, the interval is zero. If neither can happen, the interval is space-like. When we speak of a body being present "at" an event, we mean that the event occurs in the same place in space-time as one of the events which make up the history of the body; and when we say that two events occur at the same place in space-time, we mean that there is no event between them in the four-dimensional space-time order. All the events which happen to a man at a given moment (in his own time) are, in this sense, in one place; for example, if we hear a noise and see a colour simultaneously, our two perceptions are both in one place in space-time.

When one body can be present at two events which are not in one place in space-time, the time-order of the two events is not ambiguous, though the magnitude of the time-interval will be different in different systems of measurement. But whenever the interval between two events is space-like, their time-order will be different in different equally legitimate systems of measurement; in this case, therefore, the time-order does not represent a physical fact. It follows that, when two bodies are in relative motion, like the sun and a planet, there is no such physical fact as "the distance between the bodies at a given time"; this alone shows that Newton's law of gravitation is logically faulty. Fortunately, Einstein has not only pointed out the defect, but remedied it. His arguments against Newton, however, would have remained valid even if his own law of gravitation had not proved right.

Time not a Single Cosmic Order.—The fact that time is private to each body, not a single cosmic order, involves changes in the notions of substance and cause, and suggests the substitution of a series of events for a substance with changing states. The controversy about the aether thus becomes rather unreal. Undoubtedly, when light-waves travel, events occur, and it used to be thought that these events must be "in" something; the something in which they were was called the aether. But there seems no reason except a logical prejudice to suppose that the events are "in" anything. Matter, also, may be reduced to a law according to which events succeed each other and spread out from centres; but here we enter upon more speculative considerations.

Physical Laws.—Prof. Eddington has emphasised an aspect of relativity theory which is of great philosophical importance, but difficult to make clear without somewhat abstruse mathematics. The aspect in question is the reduction of what used to be regarded as physical laws to the status of truisms or definitions. Prof. Eddington, in a profoundly interesting essay on "The Domain of Physical Science," states the matter as follows:—

In the present stage of science the laws of physics appear to be divisible into three classes—the identical, the statistical and the transcendental. The "identical laws" include the great field-laws which are commonly quoted as typical instances of natural law—the law of gravitation, the law of conservation of mass and energy, the laws of electric and magnetic force and the conservation of electric charge. These are seen to be identities, when we refer to the cycle so as to understand the constitution of the entities obeying them; and unless we have misunderstood this constitution, violation of these laws is inconceivable.

They do not in any way limit the actual basal structure of the world, and are not laws of governance. It is these identical laws that form the subject-matter of relativity theory; the other laws of physics, the statistical and transcendental, lie outside its scope. Thus the net result of relativity theory is to show that the traditional laws of physics, rightly understood, tell us almost nothing about the course of nature, being rather of the nature of logical truisms.

This surprising result is an outcome of increased mathematical skill. As the same author says elsewhere:

In one sense deductive theory is the enemy of experimental physics. The latter is always striving to settle by crucial tests the nature of the fundamental things; the former strives to minimise the successes obtained by showing how wide a nature of things is compatible with all experimental results.

The suggestion is that, in almost any conceivable world, something will be conserved; mathematics gives us the means of constructing a variety of mathematical expressions having this property of conservation. It is natural to suppose that it is useful to have senses which notice these conserved entities; hence mass, energy, and so on seem to have a basis in our experience, but are in fact merely certain quantities which are conserved and which we are adapted for noticing. If this view is correct, physics tells us much less about the real world than was formerly supposed.

Force and Gravitation.—An important aspect of relativity is the elimination of "force." This is not new in idea; indeed, it was already accepted in rational dynamics. But there remained the outstanding difficulty of gravitation, which Einstein has overcome. The sun is, so to speak, at the summit of a hill, and the planets are on the slopes. They move as they do because of the slope where they are, not because of some mysterious influence emanating from the summit. Bodies move as they do because that is the easiest possible movement in the region of space-time in which they find themselves, not because "forces" operate upon them. The apparent need of forces to account for observed motions arises from mistaken insistence upon Euclidean geometry; when once we have overcome this prejudice, we find that observed motions, instead of showing the presence of forces, show the nature of the geometry applicable to the region concerned. Bodies thus become far more independent of each other than they were in Newtonian physics: there is an increase of individualism and a diminution of central government, if one may be permitted such metaphorical language. This may, in time, considerably modify the ordinary educated man's picture of the universe, possibly with far-reaching results.

Realism in Relativity.—It is a mistake to suppose that relativity adopts an idealistic picture of the world—using "idealism" in the technical sense, in which it implies that there can be nothing which is not experience. The "observer" who is often mentioned in expositions of relativity need not be a mind, but may be a photographic plate or any kind of recording instrument. The fundamental assumption of relativity is realistic, namely, that those respects in which all observers agree when they record a given phenomenon may be regarded as objective, and not as contributed by the observers. This assumption is made by common sense. The apparent sizes and shapes of objects differ according to the point of view, but common sense discounts these differences. Relativity theory merely extends this process. By taking into account not only human observers, who all share the motion of the earth, but also possible "observers" in very rapid motion relatively to the earth, it is found that much more depends upon the point of view of the observer than was formerly thought. But there is found to be a residue which is not so dependent; this is the part which can be expressed by the method of "tensors." The importance of this method can hardly be exaggerated; it is, however, quite impossible to explain it in non-mathematical terms.

Relativity Physics.—Relativity physics is, of course, concerned only with the quantitative aspects of the world. The picture which it suggests is somewhat as follows:—In the four-dimensional space-time frame there are events everywhere, usually many events in a single place in space-time. The abstract mathematical relations of these events proceed according to the laws of physics, but the intrinsic nature of the events is wholly and inevitably unknown except when they occur in a region where there is the sort of structure we call a brain. Then they become the familiar sights and sounds and so on of our daily life. We know what it is like to see a star, but we do not know the nature of the events which constitute the ray of light that travels from the star to our eye. And the space-time frame itself is known only in its abstract mathematical properties; there is no reason to suppose it similar in intrinsic character to the spatial and temporal relations of our perceptions as known in experience. There does not seem any possible way of overcoming this ignorance, since the very nature of physical reasoning allows only the most abstract inferences, and only the most abstract properties of our perceptions can be regarded as having objective validity. Whether any other science than physics can tell us more, does not fall within the scope of the present article.

Meanwhile, it is a curious fact that this meagre kind of knowledge is sufficient for the practical uses of physics. From a practical point of view, the physical world only matters in so far as it affects us, and the intrinsic nature of what goes on in our absence is irrelevant, provided we can predict the effects upon ourselves. This we can do, just as a person can use a telephone without understanding electricity. Only the most abstract knowledge is required for practical manipulation of matter. But there is a grave danger when this habit of manipulation based upon mathematical laws is carried over into our dealings with human beings, since they, unlike the telephone wire, are capable of happiness and misery, desire and aversion. It would therefore be unfortunate if the habits of mind which are appropriate and right in dealing with material mechanisms were allowed to dominate the administrator's attempts at social constructiveness.

Theory Of Knowledge

When we have asked ourselves seriously whether we really know anything at all, we are naturally led into an examination of knowing, in the hope of being able to distinguish trustworthy beliefs from such as are untrustworthy. Thus Kant, the founder of modern theory of knowledge, represents a natural reaction against Hume's scepticism. Few philosophers nowadays would assign to this subject quite such a fundamental importance as it had in Kant's "critical" system; nevertheless it remains an essential part of philosophy. It is perhaps unwise to begin with a definition of the subject, since, as elsewhere in philosophical discussions, definitions are controversial, and will necessarily differ for different schools; but we may at least say that the subject is concerned with the general conditions of knowledge, in so far as they throw light upon truth and falsehood.

It will be convenient to divide our discussion into three stages, concerning respectively (1) the definition of knowledge, (2) data, (3) methods of inference. It should be said, however, that in distinguishing between data and inferences we are already taking sides on a debatable question, since some philosophers hold that this distinction is illusory, all knowledge being (according to them) partly immediate and partly derivative.

The Definition of Knowledge

The question how knowledge should be defined is perhaps the most important and difficult of the three with which we shall deal. This may seem surprising: at first sight it might be thought that knowledge might be defined as belief which is in agreement with the facts. The trouble is that no one knows what a belief is, no one knows what a fact is, and no one knows what sort of agreement between them would make a belief true. Let us begin with belief.

Belief: Traditionally, a "belief" is a state of mind of a certain sort. But the behaviourists deny that there are states of mind, or at least that they can be known; they therefore avoid the word "belief", and, if they used it, would mean by it a characteristic of bodily behaviour. There are cases in which this usage would be quite in accordance with common sense. Suppose you set out to visit a friend whom you have often visited before, but on arriving at your destination you find that he has moved, you would say "I thought he was still living at his old house." Yet it is highly probable that you did not think about it at all, but merely pursued the usual route from habit. A "thought" or "belief" may, therefore, in the view of common sense, be shown by behaviour, without any corresponding "mental" occurrence. And even if you use a form of words such as is supposed to express belief, you are still engaged in bodily behaviour, provided you pronounce the words out loud or to yourself. Shall we say, in such cases, that you have a belief? Or is something further required?

It must be admitted that behaviour is practically the same whether you have an explicit belief or not. People who are out of doors when a shower of rain comes on put up their umbrellas, if they have them; some say to themselves "it has begun to rain", others act without explicit thought, but the result is exactly the same in both cases. In very hot weather, both human beings and animals go out of the sun into the shade, if they can; human beings may have an explicit "belief " that the shade is pleasanter, but animals equally seek the shade. It would seem, therefore, that belief, if it is not a mere characteristic of behaviour, is causally unimportant. And the distinction of truth and error exists where there is behaviour without explicit belief, just as much as where explicit belief is present; this is shown by the illustration of going to where your friend used to live. Therefore, if theory of knowledge is to be concerned with distinguishing truth from error, we shall have to include the cases in which there is no explicit belief, and say that a belief may be merely implicit in behaviour. When old Mother Hubbard went to the cupboard, she "believed" that there was a bone there, even if she had no state of mind which could be called cognitive in the sense of introspective psychology.

Words: In order to bring this view into harmony with the facts of human behaviour, it is of course necessary to take account of the influence of words. The beast that desires shade on a hot day is attracted by the sight of darkness; the man can pronounce the word "shade", and ask where it is to be found. According to the behaviourists, it is the use of words and their efficacy in producing conditional responses that constitutes "thinking&". I It is unnecessary for our purposes to inquire whether this view gives the whole truth about the matter. What it is important to realise is that verbal behaviour has the characteristics which lead us to regard it as pre-eminently a mark of "belief", even when the words are repeated as a mere bodily habit.

Just as the habit of going to a certain house when you wish to see your friend may be said to show that you "believe" he lives in that house, so the habit of saying "two and two are four", even when merely verbal, must be held to constitute "belief " in this arithmetical proposition. Verbal habits are, of course, not infallible evidences of belief. We may say every Sunday that we are miserable sinners, while really thinking very well of ourselves. Nevertheless, speaking broadly, verbal habits crystallise our beliefs, and afford the most convenient way of making them explicit. To say more for words is to fall into that superstitious reverence for them which has been the bane of philosophy throughout its history.

Belief and Behaviour: We are thus driven to the view that, if a belief is to be something causally important, it must be defined as a characteristic of behaviour. This view is also forced upon us by the consideration of truth and falsehood, for behaviour may be mistaken in just the way attributable to a false belief, even when no explicit belief is present-for example, when a man continues to hold up his umbrella after the rain has stopped without definitely entertaining the opinion that it is still raining. Belief in this wider sense may be attributed to animals-for example, to a dog who runs to the dining-room when he hears the gong. And when an animal behaves to a reflection in a looking-glass as if it were "real", we should naturally say that he "believes" there is another animal there; this form of words is permitted by our definition.

It remains, however, to say what characteristics of behaviour can be described as beliefs. Both human beings and animals act so as to achieve certain results, e.g. getting food. Sometimes they succeed, sometimes they fail-, when they succeed, their relevant beliefs are "true", but when they fail, at least one is false.

There will usually be several beliefs involved in a given piece of behaviour, and variations of environment will be necessary to disentangle the causal characteristics which constitute the various beliefs. This analysis is effected by language, but would be very difficult if applied to dumb animals. A sentence may be taken as a law of behaviour in any environment containing certain characteristics; it will be "true" if the behaviour leads to results satisfactory to the person concerned, and otherwise it will be "false&". Such, at least, is the pragmatist definition of truth and falsehood.

Truth in Logic: There is also, however, a more logical method of discussing this question. In logic, we take for granted that a word has a "meaning"; what we signify by this can, I think, only be explained in behaviouristic terms, but when once we have acquired a vocabulary of words which have "meaning", we can proceed in a formal manner without needing to remember what "meaning" is. Given the laws of syntax in the language we are using, we can construct propositions by putting together the words of the language, and these propositions have meanings which result from those of the separate words and are no longer arbitrary. If we know that certain of these propositions are true, we can infer that certain others are true, and that vet others are false; sometimes this can be inferred with certainty, sometimes with greater or less probability. In all this logical manipulation, it is unnecessary to remember what constitutes meaning and what constitutes truth or falsehood.

It is in this formal region that most philosophy has lived-and within this region a great deal can be said that is both true and important, without the need of' any fundamental doctrine about meaning. It even seems possible to define "truth" in terms of "meaning" and "fact", as opposed to the pragmatic definition which we gave a moment ago. If so, there will be two valid definitions of "truth", though of course both will apply to the same propositions. The purely formal definition of "truth" may be illustrated by a simple case. The word "Plato" means a certain man; the word "Socrates" means a certain other man; the word "love" means a certain relation. This being given, the meaning of the complex symbol "Plato loves Socrates" is fixed; we say that this complex symbol is "true" if there is a certain fact in the world, namely the fact that Plato loves Socrates, and in the contrary case the complex symbol is false. I do not think this account is false, but, like everything purely formal, it does not probe very deep.

Uncertainty and Vagueness: In defining knowledge, there are two further matters to be taken into consideration, namely the degree of certainty and the degree of precision. All knowledge is more or less uncertain and more or less vague. These are, in a sense, opposing characters: vague knowledge has more likelihood of truth than precise knowledge, but is less useful. One of the aims of science is to increase precision without diminishing certainty. But we cannot confine the word "knowledge" to what has the highest degree of both these qualities; we must include some propositions that are rather vague and some that are only rather probable. It Is important, however, to indicate vagueness and uncertainty where they are present, and, if possible, to estimate their degree. Where this can be done precisely, it becomes "probable error" and "probability". But in most cases precision in this respect is impossible.

The Data

In advanced scientific knowledge, the distinction between what is a datum and what is inferred is clear in fact, though sometimes difficult in theory. In astronomy, for instance, the data are mainly certain black and white patterns on photographic plates. These are called photographs of this or that part of the heavens, but of course much inference is involved in using them to give knowledge about stars or planets. Broadly speaking, quite different methods and a quite different type of skill are required for the observations which provide the data in a quantitative science, and for the deductions by which the data are shown to support this or that theory. There would be no reason to expect Einstein to be particularly good at photographing the stars near the sun during an eclipse. But although the distinction is practically obvious in such cases, It is far less so when we come to less exact knowledge. It may be said that the separation into data and inferences belongs to a well-developed stage of knowledge, and is absent in its beginnings.

Animal Inference: But just as we found it necessary to admit that knowledge may be only a characteristic of behaviour, so we shall have to say about inference. What a logician recognises as inference is a refined operation, belonging to a high degree of intellectual development; but there is another kind of inference which is practised even by animals. We must consider this primitive form of inference before we can become clear as to what we mean by "data".

When a dog hears the gong and immediately goes into the dining-room, he is obviously, in a sense, practising inference. That is to say, his response is appropriate, not to the noise of the gong in itself, but to that of which the noise is a sign: his reaction is essentially similar to our reactions to words. An animal has the characteristic that, when two stimuli have been experienced together, one tends to call out the response which only the other could formerly call out. If the stimuli (or one of them) are emotionally powerful, one joint experience may be enough-, if not, many joint experiences may be required. This characteristic is totally absent in machines. Suppose, for instance, that you went every day for a year to a certain automatic machine, and lit a match in front of it at the same moment at which you inserted a penny-, it would not, at the end, have any tendency to give up its chocolate on the mere sight of a burning match. That is to say, machines do not display inference even in the form in which it is a mere characteristic of behaviour. Explicit inference, such as human beings practise, is a rationalising of the behaviour which we share with the animals. Having experienced *A* and *B* together frequently, we now react to *A* as we originally reacted to B. To make this seem rational, we say that *A* is a "sign" of *B*, and that *B* must really be present though out of sight. This is the principle of induction, upon which almost all science is based. And a great deal of philosophy is an attempt to make the principle seem reasonable.

Whenever, owing to past experience, we react to *A* in the manner in which we originally reacted to *B*, we may say that *A* is a "datum" and *B* is "Inferred". In this sense, animals practise inference. It is clear, also, that much inference of this sort is fallacious: the conjunction of *A* and *B* in past experience may have been accidental. What is less clear is that there is any way of refining this type of inference which will make it valid. That, however, is a question which we shall consider later. What I want consider now is the nature of those elements in our experiences which, to a reflective analysis, appear as "data" in the above-defined sense.

Mental and Physical Data: Traditionally, there are two sorts of data, one physical, derived from the senses, the other mental, derived from introspection. It seems highly questionable whether this distinction can be validly made among data; it seems rather to belong to what is inferred from them. Suppose, for the sake of definiteness, that you are looking at a white triangle drawn on a black-board. You can make the two judgments: "There is a triangle there", and "I see a triangle." These are different propositions, but neither expresses a bare datum; the bare datum seems to be the same in both propositions. To illustrate the difference of the propositions: you might say "There is a triangle there", if you had seen it a moment ago but now had your eyes shut, and in this case you would not say "I see a triangle"; on the other hand, you might see a black dot which you knew to be due to indigestion or fatigue, and in this case you would not say "There is a black dot there." In the first of these cases, you have a clear case of inference, not of a datum.

In the second case, you refuse to infer a public object, open to the observation of others. This shows that "I see a triangle" comes nearer to being a datum than "There is a triangle there." But the words "I" and "see" both involve inferences, and cannot be included in any form of words which aims at expressing a bare datum.

The word "I" derives its meaning, partly, from memory and expectation, since I do not exist only at one moment. And the word "see" is a causal word, suggesting dependence upon the eyes; this involves experience, since a new-born baby does not know that what it sees depends upon its eyes. However, we can eliminate this dependence upon experience, since obviously all seen objects have a common quality, not belonging to auditory or tactual or any other objects. Let us call this quality that of being "visual&". Then we can say:

"There is a visual triangle." This is about as near as we can get in words to the datum for *both* propositions: "There is a triangle there", and "I see a triangle." The difference between the propositions results from different inferences: in the first, to the public world of physics, involving perceptions of others; in the second, to the whole of my experience, in which the visual triangle is an element. The difference between the physical and the mental, therefore, would seem to belong to inferences and constructions, not to data. It would thus seem that data, in the sense in which we are using the word, consist of brief events, rousing in us various reactions, some of which may be called "inferences", or may at least be said to show the presence of inference. The two-fold organisation of these events, on the one hand as constituents of the public world of physics, on the other hand as parts of a personal experience, belongs to what is inferred, not to what is given. For theory of knowledge, the question of the validity of inference is vital. Unfortunately, nothing very satisfactory can be said about it, and the most careful discussions have been the most sceptical. However, let us examine the matter without prejudice.

Methods of Inference

It is customary to distinguish two kinds of inference, Deduction and Induction. Deduction is obviously of great *practical* importance, since it embraces the whole of mathematics. But it may be questioned whether it is, in any strict sense, a form of inference at all. A pure deduction consists merely of saying the same thing in another way. Application to a particular case may have importance, because we bring in the experience that there is such a case-for example, when we infer that Socrates is mortal because all men are mortal. But in this case we have brought in a new piece of experience, not involved in the abstract deductive schema. In pure deduction, we deal with x and y not with empirically given objects such as Socrates and Plato. However this may be, pure deduction does not raise the problems which are of most importance for theory of knowledge, and we may therefore pass it by.

Induction: The important forms of inference for theory of knowledge are those in which we infer the existence of something having certain characteristics from the existence of something having certain other characteristics. For example: you read in the newspaper that a certain eminent man is dead, and you infer that he is dead. Sometimes, of course, the inference is mistaken. I have read accounts of my own death in newspapers, but I abstained from inferring that I was a ghost. In general, however, such inferences are essential to the conduct of life. Imagine the life of a sceptic who doubted the accuracy of the telephone book, or, when he received a letter, considered seriously the possibility that the black marks might have been made accidentally by an inky fly crawling over the paper. We have to accept merely probable knowledge in daily life, and theory of knowledge must help us to decide when it really is probable, and not mere animal prejudice.

Probability: So superior is his work to that of his predecessors that it renders consideration of them unnecessary. Mr. Keynes considers induction and analogy together, and regards the latter as the basis of the former. The bare essence of an inference by analogy is as follows: We have found a number of instances in which two characteristics are combined, and no instances in which they are not combined; we find a new instance in which we know that one of the characteristics is present, but do not know whether the other is present or absent; we argue by analogy that *probably* the other characteristic is also present. The degree of probability which we infer will vary according to various circumstances. It is undeniable that we do make such inferences, and that neither science nor daily life would be possible without them. The question for the logician is as to their validity. Are they valid always, never or sometimes? And in the last case, can we decide when they are valid?

Limitation of Variety: Mr. Keynes considers that mere increase in the number of instances in which two qualities are found together does not do much to strengthen the probability of their being found together in other instances. The important point, according to him, is that in the known cases the instances should have as few other qualities in common as possible. But even then a further assumption is required, which is called the principle of limitation of variety. This assumption is stated as follows: "That the objects in the field, over which our generalisations extend, do not have an infinite number of independent qualities; that, in other words, their characteristics, however numerous, cohere together in groups of invariable connection, which are finite in number." It is not necessary to regard this assumption as *certain;* it is enough if there is some finite probability in its favour.

It is not easy to find any arguments for or against an *a priori* finite probability in favour of the limitation of variety. It should be observed, however, that a "finite" probability, in Mr. Keynes's terminology, means a probability greater than some numerically measurable probability, e.g. the probability of a penny coming "heads" a million times running. When this is realised, the assumption certainly seems plausible. The strongest argument on the side of scepticism is that both men and animals are constantly led to beliefs (in the behaviouristic sense), which are caused by what may be called invalid inductions; this happens whenever some accidental collocation has produced an association not in accordance with any objective law. Dr. Watson caused an infant to be terrified of white rats by beating a gong behind its head at the moment of showing it a white *rat (Behaviourism*). On the whole, however, accidental collocations will usually tend to be different for different people, and therefore the inductions in which men are agreed have a good chance of being valid. Scientific inductive or analogical inferences may, in the best cases, be assumed to have a high degree of probability, if the above principle of limitation of variety is true or finitely probable. This result is not so definite as we could wish, but it is at least preferable to Hume's complete scepticism. And it is not obtained, like Kant's answer to Hume, by a philosophy *ad hoc;* it proceeds on the ordinary lines of scientific method.

Grades of Certainty: Theory of knowledge, as we have seen, is a subject which is partly logical, partly psychological; the connection between these parts is not very close. The logical part may, perhaps, come to be mainly an organisation of what passes for knowledge according to differing grades of certainty: some portions of our beliefs involve more dubious assumptions than are involved in other parts. Logic and mathematics on the one hand, and the facts of perception on the other, have the highest grade of certainty; where memory comes in, the certainty is lessened; where unobserved matter comes in, the certainty is further lessened; beyond all these stages comes what a cautious man of science would admit to be doubtful. The attempt to increase scientific certainty by means of some special philosophy seems hopeless, since, in view of the disagreement of philosophers, philosophical propositions must count as among the most doubtful of those to which serious students give an unqualified assent. For this reason, we have confined ourselves to discussions which do not assume any definite position on philosophical as opposed to scientific questions.

Bibliography

Broad, C.D. (1973) "*Bertrand Russell, as Philosopher,*" Bulletin of the London Mathematical Society, 5, 328-341.

Carnap, Rudolf (1931) "*The Logicist Foundations of Mathematics,*" Erkenntnis, 2, 91-105. Repr. in Benacerraf, Paul, and Hilary Putnam (eds), Philosophy of Mathematics, 2nd ed., Cambridge: Cambridge University Press, 1983, 41-52; in Klemke, E.D. (ed.), Essays on Bertrand Russell, Urbana: University of Illinois Press, 1970, 341-354; and in Pears, David F. (ed.), Bertrand Russell: A Collection of Critical Essays, Garden City, New York: Anchor Books, 1972, 175-191.

Church, Alonzo (1976) "*Comparison of Russell's Resolution of the Semantical Antinomies with That of Tarski,*" Journal of Symbolic Logic, 41, 747-760. Repr. in A.D. Irvine, Bertrand Russell: Critical Assessments, vol. 2, New York and London: Routledge, 1999, 96-112.

Church, Alonzo (1974) "*Russellian Simple Type Theory,*" Proceedings and Addresses of the American Philosophical Association, 47, 21-33.

Gandy, R.O. (1973) "*Bertrand Russell, as Mathematician,*" Bulletin of the London Mathematical Society, 5, 342-348.

Gödel, Kurt (1944) "*Russell's Mathematical Logic,*" in Schilpp, Paul Arthur (ed.), The Philosophy of Bertrand Russell, 3rd ed., New York: Tudor, 1951, 123-153. Repr. in Benacerraf, Paul, and Hilary Putnam (eds), Philosophy of Mathematics, 2nd ed., Cambridge: Cambridge University Press, 1983, 447-469; and in Pears, David F. (ed.) (1972) Bertrand Russell: A Collection of Critical Essays, Garden City, New York: Anchor Books, 192-226.

Hylton, Peter W. (1990)